Practical Java Programming: Concepts and Its Applications

Anshuman Mishra

AWADHESH KUMAR

Published by Anshuman Mishra, 2025.

ABOUT THE BOOK

PRACTICAL JAVA PROGRAMMING : CONCEPTS AND ITS APPLICATIONS IS A COMPREHENSIVE GUIDE TAILORED FOR SOFTWARE PROFESSIONALS AND STUDENTS AIMING TO EXCEL IN JAVA PROGRAMMING AND ACE TECHNICAL INTERVIEWS. THE BOOK PROVIDES AN IN-DEPTH EXPLORATION OF JAVA FUNDAMENTALS, OBJECT-ORIENTED CONCEPTS, ADVANCED FEATURES, AND PRACTICAL PROBLEM-SOLVING APPROACHES, ENSURING A STRONG FOUNDATION FOR CODING EXCELLENCE.

THE FIRST CHAPTER DELVES INTO JAVA'S ARCHITECTURE, SYNTAX, AND KEY DIFFERENCES WITH C++, FOLLOWED BY A HANDS-ON APPROACH TO COMPILING, EXECUTING PROGRAMS, AND UNDERSTANDING CORE CONSTRUCTS LIKE VARIABLES, DATA TYPES, OPERATORS, AND LOOPS. SUBSEQUENT CHAPTERS BUILD UPON THIS BY COVERING ARRAYS, STRINGS, OBJECT-ORIENTED PROGRAMMING, INHERITANCE, INTERFACES, EXCEPTION HANDLING, MULTI-THREADING, NETWORKING, AND DATABASE CONNECTIVITY.

PRACTICAL EXAMPLES, STEP-BY-STEP EXPLANATIONS, AND INTERVIEW-SPECIFIC SCENARIOS MAKE THIS BOOK A VALUABLE RESOURCE FOR BOTH BEGINNERS AND EXPERIENCED DEVELOPERS. CONCLUDING WITH APPLETS, EVENT HANDLING, AND GUI DESIGN, THIS BOOK ENSURES YOU'RE WELL-PREPARED FOR CHALLENGES IN TOP SOFTWARE COMPANIES.

"Java Programming code should be written for developers to comprehend, and only incidentally for the compiler to execute."

— **Anshuman Mishra**

Copyright Page

Title: **PRACTICAL JAVA PROGRAMMING : CONCEPTS AND ITS APPLICATIONS**

Topics

ABOUT THE AUTHORS

ANSHUMAN KUMAR MISHRA

ANSHUMAN KUMAR MISHRA IS AN ACCOMPLISHED ACADEMIC WITH A STRONG BACKGROUND IN COMPUTER SCIENCE. HE COMPLETED HIS MTECH IN COMPUTER SCIENCE FROM BIT MESRA, ONE OF THE PRESTIGIOUS INSTITUTES IN INDIA. WITH OVER 18 YEARS OF TEACHING EXPERIENCE, ANSHUMAN HAS HONED HIS EXPERTISE IN VARIOUS ASPECTS OF COMPUTER SCIENCE EDUCATION. CURRENTLY, HE SERVES AS AN ASSISTANT PROFESSOR AT DORANDA COLLEGE, RANCHI, WHERE HE SHARES HIS VAST KNOWLEDGE WITH UNDERGRADUATE AND POSTGRADUATE STUDENTS. ANSHUMAN'S TEACHING PHILOSOPHY REVOLVES AROUND FOSTERING CRITICAL THINKING, PROBLEM-SOLVING SKILLS, AND A DEEP UNDERSTANDING OF CORE COMPUTER SCIENCE CONCEPTS.

THROUGHOUT HIS CAREER, HE HAS CONTRIBUTED TO THE ACADEMIC COMMUNITY BY CREATING ENGAGING AND INFORMATIVE CONTENT FOR STUDENTS AND BY WORKING ON VARIOUS CURRICULUM DEVELOPMENT PROJECTS. HIS PASSION FOR TEACHING AND CONTINUOUS LEARNING HAS MADE HIM A RESPECTED FIGURE AMONG HIS COLLEAGUES AND STUDENTS.

AWADHESH KUMAR

AWADHESH KUMAR IS AN EXPERIENCED ASSISTANT PROFESSOR AT DORANDA COLLEGE, RANCHI, WITH OVER 5 YEARS OF TEACHING EXPERIENCE. HE COMPLETED HIS MCA AND HAS SINCE BEEN DEDICATED TO IMPARTING KNOWLEDGE IN THE FIELD OF COMPUTER APPLICATIONS. HIS TEACHING STYLE FOCUSES ON CLARITY, PRACTICALITY, AND ENCOURAGING STUDENTS TO APPLY THEIR THEORETICAL KNOWLEDGE TO REAL-WORLD SCENARIOS.

AWADHESH'S EXPERTISE LIES IN VARIOUS AREAS OF COMPUTER SCIENCE AND INFORMATION TECHNOLOGY. HIS DEDICATION TO EDUCATION AND HIS ABILITY TO EXPLAIN COMPLEX CONCEPTS IN AN EASY-TO-UNDERSTAND MANNER HAS MADE HIM A FAVORITE AMONG STUDENTS. AWADHESH'S ENTHUSIASM FOR TEACHING AND HIS COMMITMENT TO STAYING UPDATED WITH THE LATEST TECHNOLOGICAL ADVANCEMENTS CONTRIBUTE SIGNIFICANTLY TO THE ACADEMIC GROWTH OF HIS STUDENTS.

TOGETHER, ANSHUMAN KUMAR MISHRA AND AWADHESH KUMAR HAVE COLLABORATED ON CREATING THIS BOOK, BRINGING THEIR COMBINED YEARS OF EXPERIENCE AND EXPERTISE TO PROVIDE AN INSIGHTFUL AND PRACTICAL GUIDE FOR JAVA PROGRAMMING. THEIR JOINT EFFORTS AIM TO HELP STUDENTS AND PROFESSIONALS ENHANCE THEIR PROGRAMMING SKILLS AND DEEPEN THEIR UNDERSTANDING OF JAVA CONCEPTS AND APPLICATIONS.

CHAPTER 1: INTRODUCTION TO JAVA

1.1 Java Architecture and Features

- The Java Virtual Machine (JVM): Execution Process
- The Java Runtime Environment (JRE)
- The Java Development Kit (JDK): Tools and Utilities
- Key Features of Java:
  o Platform Independence (Write Once, Run Anywhere - WORA)
  o Object-Oriented Programming
  o Automatic Memory Management and Garbage Collection
  o Robust and Secure Programming Features
  o Multithreading and Concurrency
  o Dynamic Linking and Extensibility
  o High Performance with Just-In-Time (JIT) Compiler

The Java Virtual Machine (JVM): Execution Process

The Java Virtual Machine (JVM) is an integral part of the Java Runtime Environment (JRE) that provides the runtime environment to execute Java bytecode. It acts as an abstraction layer between Java programs and the underlying operating system. The execution process in the JVM involves several steps:

1. **Loading**: The ClassLoader subsystem loads the required class files into memory. These files are verified for integrity and compatibility.
2. **Linking**: Linking includes verification, preparation, and (optionally) resolution of symbolic references to memory addresses.
3. **Initialization**: Static blocks and static variables of the class are initialized.
4. **Execution**: The execution engine interprets or compiles the bytecode into machine code using an interpreter or a Just-In-Time (JIT) compiler for execution on the host machine.

The JVM also manages memory via heap and stack areas and employs garbage collection to automatically free up unused objects.

The Java Runtime Environment (JRE)

The Java Runtime Environment (JRE) is a software layer that provides all the necessary libraries and components required to run Java applications. It includes the JVM, core libraries, and other supporting files but does not contain development tools like compilers or debuggers.

- **Key Components**:

- **JVM**: Executes the Java bytecode.
- **Core Libraries**: Provide essential APIs for input/output, networking, and data structures.
- **Deployment Technologies**: Includes tools for deploying Java applications like Java Web Start and Java Plug-in.

JRE is essential for running Java applications but is not suitable for writing or compiling Java code.

The Java Development Kit (JDK): Tools and Utilities

The Java Development Kit (JDK) is a complete development environment for building Java applications. It contains the JRE along with tools and utilities for development.

- **Key Tools and Utilities**:
- **javac**: Java compiler to convert source code (.java) to bytecode (.class).
- **java**: JVM launcher to run Java applications.
- **javadoc**: Tool to generate API documentation from Java source code.
- **jar**: Utility to package Java classes and resources into a JAR file.
- **jdb**: Debugger for Java programs.

The JDK is necessary for developers to write, compile, and debug Java applications.

Key Features of Java

1. Platform Independence (Write Once, Run Anywhere - WORA) Java programs are compiled into platform-independent bytecode, which can be executed on any device with a JVM. This feature ensures that Java applications are portable and can run across various operating systems without modification.

2. Object-Oriented Programming (OOP) Java follows OOP principles such as inheritance, encapsulation, polymorphism, and abstraction. These principles allow developers to create modular, reusable, and scalable code by treating data and behavior as a single entity (objects).

3. Automatic Memory Management and Garbage Collection Java provides automatic memory management, relieving developers of manual memory allocation and deallocation tasks. The JVM's garbage collector identifies and removes unused objects, preventing memory leaks and enhancing application stability.

4. Robust and Secure Programming Features Java offers several features to create reliable and secure applications:

- **Exception Handling**: Manages runtime errors effectively.
- **Type Checking**: Detects errors during compilation.
- **Security Manager**: Restricts unauthorized access to resources.
- **Bytecode Verification**: Ensures code integrity and prevents malicious activities.

5. Multithreading and Concurrency Java supports multithreading, allowing multiple threads to run concurrently. This feature enables efficient utilization of CPU resources and the creation of responsive applications like games, multimedia apps, and web servers.

6. Dynamic Linking and Extensibility Java applications dynamically link classes at runtime, making it easy to add or update functionality without recompiling the entire application. Java's dynamic class loading ensures flexibility and adaptability.

7. High Performance with Just-In-Time (JIT) Compiler The JIT compiler in the JVM translates frequently used bytecode into native machine code during runtime, significantly improving execution speed. It optimizes code paths and ensures high performance for Java applications.

These features collectively make Java a versatile and powerful language for developing a wide range of applications, from desktop software to enterprise-level systems and web applications.

1.2 Semantic and Syntax Differences Between C++ and Java

- Memory Management: Manual in C++ vs Automatic in Java
- Multiple Inheritance in C++ vs Single Inheritance in Java
- Pointers and References: Present in C++ but not exposed in Java
- Use of `#include` in C++ vs Importing Packages in Java
- Exception Handling Mechanisms
- Explicit vs Implicit Casting
- Operator Overloading in C++ vs No Overloading in Java
- Destructors in C++ vs Garbage Collection in Java

1.2 Semantic and Syntax Differences Between C++ and Java

Memory Management: Manual in C++ vs Automatic in Java

- In C++, memory management is manual. Developers must explicitly allocate memory using `new` and deallocate it using `delete`. Improper memory handling can lead to memory leaks or dangling pointers.

- In Java, memory management is automatic. The JVM uses a Garbage Collector to automatically reclaim memory occupied by objects that are no longer in use, reducing the likelihood of memory leaks.

Multiple Inheritance in C++ vs Single Inheritance in Java

- C++ supports multiple inheritance, allowing a class to inherit from multiple base classes. This can lead to complexity, such as the diamond problem, which C++ addresses with virtual inheritance.
- Java does not support multiple inheritance with classes to avoid such complications. Instead, Java uses interfaces to achieve a form of multiple inheritance. A class can implement multiple interfaces but inherit from only one superclass.

Pointers and References: Present in C++ but Not Exposed in Java

- C++ provides pointers and references, allowing direct memory access and manipulation. This feature is powerful but can be risky, leading to errors such as buffer overflows or segmentation faults.
- Java abstracts away pointers for security and simplicity. Developers use references to objects, but direct memory access is not allowed, ensuring safer and more secure code.

Use of #include in C++ vs Importing Packages in Java

- In C++, `#include` is used to include header files, which define declarations and functions. The preprocessor processes these inclusions before compilation.
- Java uses the `import` keyword to include packages and classes. Unlike C++, this is managed at runtime and does not involve a separate preprocessor step.

Exception Handling Mechanisms

- C++ uses exception handling through `try`, `catch`, and `throw` blocks. However, not all errors need to be exceptions, and handling is not as strongly enforced.
- Java also uses `try`, `catch`, `throw`, `throws`, and `finally`. Java enforces exception handling for checked exceptions, making the code more robust by ensuring that critical errors are handled.

Explicit vs Implicit Casting

- C++ supports both explicit casting (e.g., `(int)value`) and implicit casting (automatic type conversion). However, improper implicit conversions can lead to unexpected behaviors.
- Java enforces stricter casting rules. Implicit casting is allowed only for widening conversions (e.g., `int` to `long`), while narrowing conversions (e.g., `long` to `int`) require explicit casting to avoid data loss.

Operator Overloading in C++ vs No Overloading in Java

- C++ supports operator overloading, allowing developers to define custom behaviors for operators like +, -, or * for user-defined types. This can make code concise but also harder to understand if misused.
- Java does not support operator overloading (except for string concatenation with +) to maintain simplicity and readability.

Destructors in C++ vs Garbage Collection in Java

- C++ uses destructors to clean up resources when an object goes out of scope. Destructors are user-defined and must be implemented to ensure proper resource management.
- Java does not have destructors. Instead, it relies on garbage collection to automatically manage memory. Developers can use the `finalize()` method for cleanup, but it is rarely needed and not guaranteed to be called.

These differences highlight how C++ and Java cater to different programming paradigms and priorities, with C++ focusing on control and performance, and Java emphasizing safety, simplicity, and platform independence.

1.3 Compiling and Executing a Java Program

- Writing Your First Java Program: "Hello, World!"
- Compiling Java Code: The Role of `javac`
- Understanding the Bytecode and `.class` Files
- Running Java Code with the `java` Command
- Working with IDEs (Integrated Development Environments): Eclipse, IntelliJ IDEA, and NetBeans

Writing Your First Java Program: "Hello, World!"

Writing a "Hello, World!" program is the traditional first step in learning a new programming language. In Java, the process involves the following steps:

1. **Create a Source File**:
   - Open a text editor and write the following code:

```
public class HelloWorld {
    public static void main(String[] args) {
        System.out.println("Hello, World!");
    }
}
```

   - Save the file as `HelloWorld.java`. The file name must match the class name.
2. **Code Explanation**:
   - `public class HelloWorld`: Declares a public class named `HelloWorld`.
   - `public static void main(String[] args)`: Defines the entry point of the program where execution begins.
   - `System.out.println("Hello, World!");`: Prints "Hello, World!" to the console.

Compiling Java Code: The Role of `javac`

Java code must be compiled into bytecode before it can be executed by the JVM. The `javac` (Java Compiler) command performs this task:

1. **Compilation Process**:
   - Open a terminal or command prompt.
   - Navigate to the directory where `HelloWorld.java` is saved.
   - Run the command:

```
javac HelloWorld.java
```

2. **Output**:
   - If there are no errors, the compiler generates a file named `HelloWorld.class` in the same directory.

Understanding the Bytecode and `.class` Files

- The `.class` file contains bytecode, an intermediate representation of the Java source code.
- Bytecode is platform-independent and can be executed on any system with a compatible JVM.
- Bytecode improves portability as the same `.class` file can run on various platforms without modification.

Running Java Code with the `java` Command

After compiling the program, you can execute it using the `java` command:

1. **Execution Process**:
   o In the terminal or command prompt, run:

   ```
   java HelloWorld
   ```

2. **Output**:
   o The program outputs:

   ```
   Hello, World!
   ```

3. **Important Notes**:
   o Do not include the `.class` extension when running the program.
   o Ensure that the `HelloWorld.class` file is in the same directory as the terminal's current working directory.

Working with IDEs (Integrated Development Environments): Eclipse, IntelliJ IDEA, and NetBeans

IDEs streamline the process of writing, compiling, and debugging Java code. Popular Java IDEs include Eclipse, IntelliJ IDEA, and NetBeans.

1. **Eclipse**:
   o **Features**: Code auto-completion, debugging tools, and plugin support.
   o **Usage**: Create a new Java project, add a class file, write the program, and run it using the built-in run button.
2. **IntelliJ IDEA**:
   o **Features**: Intelligent code suggestions, version control integration, and robust debugging.
   o **Usage**: Create a new project, configure the JDK, write the code, and execute it using the IDE's interface.
3. **NetBeans**:
   o **Features**: Simple interface, support for multiple languages, and built-in GUI builder.
   o **Usage**: Start a new project, add Java files, write the code, and use the run option.

Advantages of IDEs:

- Simplified project management.
- Highlighting syntax errors in real-time.
- Integrated debugging and testing tools.

Choosing an IDE depends on personal preference and project requirements. For beginners, IDEs like Eclipse and IntelliJ IDEA offer user-friendly interfaces to ease the learning curve.

These foundational steps and tools are essential for anyone starting with Java programming.

1.4 Variables, Constants, Keywords, and Data Types

- Declaring and Initializing Variables
- Constants in Java: `final` Keyword
- Java Keywords: Reserved Words and Their Purpose
- Primitive Data Types: `int`, `float`, `char`, `boolean`, etc.
- Non-Primitive Data Types: Classes, Arrays, and Strings
- Scope of Variables: Local, Instance, and Static Variables

Declaring and Initializing Variables in Java

In Java, variables need to be declared before they can be used. A variable declaration specifies the type and the name of the variable. Initialization is the process of assigning an initial value to a variable after it is declared.

Syntax:

```
<datatype> <variable_name> = <value>;
```

For example:

```
int age = 25;  // Declaration and initialization of an integer variable
String name = "John";  // Declaration and initialization of a String variable
```

Variables can also be declared without initialization, but they must be initialized before they are used.

```
int age; // Declaring a variable without initializing
age = 30; // Initializing the variable later
```

Constants in Java: `final` Keyword

In Java, constants are variables whose values cannot be changed once assigned. The `final` keyword is used to declare constants.

Syntax:

```
final <datatype> <variable_name> = <value>;
```

Example:

```
final int MAX_AGE = 100; // Declaring a constant MAX_AGE with a value of
100
```

Once a variable is declared as `final`, its value cannot be modified. Attempting to change the value of a final variable will result in a compilation error.

Java Keywords: Reserved Words and Their Purpose

Java keywords are reserved words that have special meanings in Java programming. These words are predefined in the Java language and cannot be used as identifiers (variable names, class names, etc.).

Common Java keywords include:

- `int`, `boolean`, `char`, `float`, `double`: Used to define primitive data types.
- `class`, `interface`, `extends`, `implements`: Used for defining classes and interfaces.
- `public`, `private`, `protected`: Access modifiers.
- `static`, `final`: Modifiers that change the behavior of methods, variables, and classes.
- `void`: Specifies that a method does not return a value.
- `if`, `else`, `while`, `for`, `switch`: Control flow statements.
- `try`, `catch`, `finally`: Exception handling.

Example:

```
public class Example {
    public static void main(String[] args) {
        int age = 30; // 'int' is a keyword for the data type
    }
}
```

Primitive Data Types: `int`, `float`, `char`, `boolean`, etc.

Primitive data types are the most basic types in Java. They represent simple values like numbers and characters.

1. **int**: Used to store integer values (whole numbers).
   Example: `int num = 10;`
2. **float**: Used to store floating-point numbers (decimal numbers).
   Example: `float price = 19.99f;` (Note the `f` suffix)
3. **double**: Used for double-precision floating-point numbers. It has more precision than `float`.
   Example: `double salary = 99999.99;`

4. **char**: Used to store a single character.
   Example: `char letter = 'A';`
5. **boolean**: Used to store `true` or `false` values.
   Example: `boolean isJavaFun = true;`
6. **byte**, **short**, **long**: Integer types with different ranges of values.
   o `byte` (8-bit): `byte b = 100;`
   o `short` (16-bit): `short s = 30000;`
   o `long` (64-bit): `long l = 100000L;` (Note the `L` suffix)

Non-Primitive Data Types: Classes, Arrays, and Strings

Non-primitive data types, also called reference types, are more complex types that refer to objects and arrays.

1. **Classes**: A class is a blueprint for creating objects. It can contain fields (variables) and methods (functions).
   Example:

```
class Person {
    String name;
    int age;

    void greet() {
        System.out.println("Hello, my name is " + name);
    }
}
```

2. **Arrays**: An array is a collection of elements of the same type. Arrays are objects in Java.
   Example:

```
int[] numbers = {1, 2, 3, 4, 5};   // Array of integers
String[] names = {"John", "Jane", "Doe"};   // Array of Strings
```

3. **Strings**: A String is a sequence of characters. In Java, Strings are objects, even though they behave similarly to primitive types.
   Example:

```
String greeting = "Hello, world!";
```

Scope of Variables: Local, Instance, and Static Variables

The **scope** of a variable refers to the region of the program where the variable can be accessed.

1. **Local Variables**: These are declared within a method, constructor, or block and can only be used within that scope. They are created when the method is called and destroyed when the method finishes.

Example:

```java
public void myMethod() {
    int localVariable = 10; // Local variable
    System.out.println(localVariable);
}
```

2. **Instance Variables**: These are declared inside a class but outside any method, constructor, or block. They are tied to a specific instance (object) of the class. Each object has its own copy of instance variables.

Example:

```java
class Person {
    String name;  // Instance variable
    int age;      // Instance variable
}
```

3. **Static Variables**: These are declared using the `static` keyword and are shared by all instances of the class. There is only one copy of the static variable, no matter how many objects of the class are created.

Example:

```java
class Counter {
    static int count = 0;  // Static variable
}
```

In conclusion:

- **Local variables** are limited to the method where they are declared.
- **Instance variables** belong to objects and each object has its own copy.
- **Static variables** belong to the class itself and are shared by all objects of that class.

1. Declaring and Initializing Variables

Program:

```java
public class VariableExample {
    public static void main(String[] args) {
        // Declaring and initializing variables
        int age = 25;
        double salary = 55000.50;
        char grade = 'A';
        boolean isEmployed = true;

        // Printing variables
        System.out.println("Age: " + age);
```

```
        System.out.println("Salary: " + salary);
        System.out.println("Grade: " + grade);
        System.out.println("Employed: " + isEmployed);
    }}
```

Output:

```
Age: 25
Salary: 55000.5
Grade: A
Employed: true
```

2. Constants in Java: `final` Keyword

Program:

```java
public class FinalKeywordExample {
    public static void main(String[] args) {
        final double PI = 3.14159; // Declaring a constant
        double radius = 5.0;
        double area = PI * radius * radius; // Using the constant

        System.out.println("Radius: " + radius);
        System.out.println("Area of Circle: " + area);

        // Uncommenting the next line will cause a compilation error
        // PI = 3.14; // Cannot reassign a final variable
    }}
```

Output:

```
Radius: 5.0
Area of Circle: 78.53975
```

3. Java Keywords: Reserved Words and Their Purpose

Program:

```java
public class KeywordExample {
    public static void main(String[] args) {
        int number = 10; // 'int' is a keyword for declaring an integer
variable
        if (number > 0) { // 'if' is a keyword for decision-making
            System.out.println("The number is positive.");
        } else {
            System.out.println("The number is not positive.");
        }
    }
```

```
}
```

Output:

```
The number is positive.
```

Explanation:
Keywords like `int`, `if`, `else` are reserved in Java and have specific purposes such as data type declaration and conditional logic.

---

4. Primitive Data Types: `int, float, char, boolean`

Program:

```java
public class PrimitiveTypesExample {
    public static void main(String[] args) {
        int age = 30;
        float height = 5.9f;
        char initial = 'J';
        boolean isStudent = false;

        System.out.println("Age: " + age);
        System.out.println("Height: " + height);
        System.out.println("Initial: " + initial);
        System.out.println("Is Student: " + isStudent);
    }}
```

Output:

```
Age: 30
Height: 5.9
Initial: J Is Student: false
```

---

5. Scope of Variables: Local, Instance, and Static Variables

Program:

```java
class VariableScope {
    static int staticVar = 100; // Static variable
    int instanceVar = 50;       // Instance variable

    public void displayVariables() {
        int localVar = 25;       // Local variable
        System.out.println("Local Variable: " + localVar);
        System.out.println("Instance Variable: " + instanceVar);
        System.out.println("Static Variable: " + staticVar);
    }
```

```
public static void main(String[] args) {
    VariableScope obj = new VariableScope();
    obj.displayVariables();
}
}
```

Output:

```
Local Variable: 25
Instance Variable: 50
Static Variable: 100
```

Explanation:

- Local Variable: Declared inside a method and accessible only within that method.
- Instance Variable: Declared in the class but outside any method, belongs to an instance of the class.
- Static Variable: Declared with the `static` keyword, shared across all instances of the class.

1.5 Operators: Arithmetic, Logical, and Bitwise

- Arithmetic Operators: +, -, *, /, %
- Logical Operators: &&, ||, !
- Bitwise Operators: &, |, ^, ~, <<, >>
- Relational Operators: ==, !=, <, >, <=, >=
- Assignment Operators and Compound Assignments
- Operator Precedence and Associativity

Arithmetic Operators: +, -, *, /, %

Arithmetic operators are used to perform basic mathematical operations.

1. **Addition (+)**: Adds two operands.
   Example:

   ```
   int sum = 5 + 3;   // sum = 8
   ```

2. **Subtraction (-)**: Subtracts the right operand from the left operand.
   Example:

   ```
   int difference = 5 - 3;   // difference = 2
   ```

3. **Multiplication (*)**: Multiplies two operands.
   Example:

```
int product = 5 * 3;   // product = 15
```

4. **Division (/)**: Divides the left operand by the right operand. For integer division, the result will be an integer.
Example:

```
int quotient = 5 / 2;   // quotient = 2 (integer division)
```

5. **Modulo (%)**: Returns the remainder when the left operand is divided by the right operand.
Example:

```
int remainder = 5 % 2;   // remainder = 1
```

Logical Operators: &&, ||, !

Logical operators are used to perform logical operations on boolean values.

1. **Logical AND (&&)**: Returns true if both operands are true.
Example:

```
boolean result = true && false;   // result = false
```

2. **Logical OR (||)**: Returns true if at least one of the operands is true.
Example:

```
boolean result = true || false;   // result = true
```

3. **Logical NOT (!)**: Reverses the logical state of its operand. If the operand is true, it returns false, and vice versa.
Example:

```
boolean result = !true;   // result = false
```

Bitwise Operators: &, |, ^, ~, <<, >>

Bitwise operators perform bit-level operations on integers.

1. **Bitwise AND (&)**: Performs a bitwise AND operation on two operands.
Example:

```
int result = 5 & 3;   // 5 = 0101, 3 = 0011, result = 0001 = 1
```

2. **Bitwise OR (|)**: Performs a bitwise OR operation on two operands.
Example:

```
int result = 5 | 3;   // 5 = 0101, 3 = 0011, result = 0111 = 7
```

3. **Bitwise XOR (^):** Performs a bitwise XOR operation on two operands. The result is 1 if the corresponding bits are different, 0 if they are the same.
Example:

```
int result = 5 ^ 3;   // 5 = 0101, 3 = 0011, result = 0110 = 6
```

4. **Bitwise NOT (~):** Flips the bits of its operand. Inverts each bit (1 becomes 0 and 0 becomes 1).
Example:

```
int result = ~5;   // 5 = 0101, result = 1010 = -6 (in two's complement)
```

5. **Left Shift (<<):** Shifts the bits of the left operand to the left by the number of positions specified by the right operand. This is equivalent to multiplying the number by 2^n, where n is the number of positions shifted.
Example:

```
int result = 5 << 2;   // 5 = 0101, result = 10100 = 20
```

6. **Right Shift (>>):** Shifts the bits of the left operand to the right by the number of positions specified by the right operand. This is equivalent to dividing the number by 2^n, where n is the number of positions shifted.
Example:

```
int result = 5 >> 1;   // 5 = 0101, result = 0010 = 2
```

Relational Operators: ==, !=, <, >, <=, >=

Relational operators are used to compare two values.

1. **Equality (==):** Returns true if both operands are equal.
Example:

```
boolean result = 5 == 3;   // result = false
```

2. **Not Equal (!=):** Returns true if both operands are not equal.
Example:

```
boolean result = 5 != 3;   // result = true
```

3. **Less Than (<):** Returns true if the left operand is less than the right operand.
Example:

```
boolean result = 5 < 3;   // result = false
```

4. **Greater Than (>):** Returns true if the left operand is greater than the right operand.
Example:

```
boolean result = 5 > 3;  // result = true
```

5. **Less Than or Equal To (<=)**: Returns `true` if the left operand is less than or equal to the right operand.
   Example:

```
boolean result = 5 <= 3;  // result = false
```

6. **Greater Than or Equal To (>=)**: Returns `true` if the left operand is greater than or equal to the right operand.
   Example:

```
boolean result = 5 >= 3;  // result = true
```

Assignment Operators and Compound Assignments

Assignment operators are used to assign values to variables.

1. **Simple Assignment (=)**: Assigns the right operand's value to the left operand.
   Example:

```
int a = 5;  // Assigns 5 to variable 'a'
```

2. **Compound Assignment**: Combines an arithmetic operation with assignment.
   o **Add and Assign (+=)**: Adds the right operand to the left operand and assigns the result to the left operand.
   Example:

```
int a = 5;
a += 3;  // a = a + 3, so a = 8
```

   o **Subtract and Assign (-=)**: Subtracts the right operand from the left operand and assigns the result to the left operand.
   Example:

```
int a = 5;
a -= 3;  // a = a - 3, so a = 2
```

   o **Multiply and Assign (*=)**: Multiplies the left operand by the right operand and assigns the result to the left operand.
   Example:

```
int a = 5;
a *= 3;  // a = a * 3, so a = 15
```

   o **Divide and Assign (/=)**: Divides the left operand by the right operand and assigns the result to the left operand.
   Example:

```
int a = 6;
a /= 3;   // a = a / 3, so a = 2
```

o   **Modulo and Assign (%=)**: Finds the remainder of the division of the left operand by the right operand and assigns the result to the left operand.
Example:

```
int a = 5;
a %= 3;   // a = a % 3, so a = 2
```

Operator Precedence and Associativity

Operator Precedence determines the order in which operators are evaluated in an expression.

1. Operators with higher precedence are evaluated first.
2. For example, * and / have higher precedence than + and –.

Precedence Example:

```
int result = 5 + 3 * 2;   // result = 5 + (3 * 2) = 5 + 6 = 11
```

Associativity determines the direction in which operators are evaluated when they have the same precedence.

- **Left-to-right**: Most operators like +, –, *, and / are evaluated left to right.
- **Right-to-left**: Assignment operators (=, +=, –=) and the conditional operator (?:) are evaluated right to left.

Example of Associativity:

```
int a = 5;
int b = 3;
a = b = 10;   // Right-to-left associativity, a = 10, b = 10
```

Example 1: Arithmetic Operators

Problem: Perform basic arithmetic operations: addition, subtraction, multiplication, division, and modulus.

```
public class ArithmeticOperators {
    public static void main(String[] args) {
        int a = 15, b = 4;
        System.out.println("Addition: " + (a + b));
        System.out.println("Subtraction: " + (a - b));
```

```
        System.out.println("Multiplication: " + (a * b));
        System.out.println("Division: " + (a / b)); // Integer division
        System.out.println("Modulus: " + (a % b));
    }
}
```

Output:

```
Addition: 19
Subtraction: 11
Multiplication: 60
Division: 3
Modulus: 3
```

Example 2: Logical Operators

Problem: Demonstrate the use of logical AND (&&), OR (||), and NOT (!).

```
public class LogicalOperators {
    public static void main(String[] args) {
        boolean x = true, y = false;
        System.out.println("x && y: " + (x && y)); // Logical AND
        System.out.println("x || y: " + (x || y)); // Logical OR
        System.out.println("!x: " + (!x));          // Logical NOT
    } }
```

Output:

```
x && y: false
x || y: true
!x: false
```

Example 3: Bitwise Operators

Problem: Perform bitwise operations: AND (&), OR (|), XOR (^), NOT (~), left shift (<<), and right shift (>>).

```
public class BitwiseOperators {
    public static void main(String[] args) {
        int a = 5;  // Binary: 0101
```

```
        int b = 3;   // Binary: 0011
        System.out.println("a & b: " + (a & b)); // AND
        System.out.println("a | b: " + (a | b)); // OR
        System.out.println("a ^ b: " + (a ^ b)); // XOR
        System.out.println("~a: " + (~a));        // NOT
        System.out.println("a << 1: " + (a << 1)); // Left Shift
        System.out.println("a >> 1: " + (a >> 1)); // Right Shift
    }
}
```

Output:

```
a & b: 1
a | b: 7
a ^ b: 6
~a: -6
a << 1: 10
a >> 1: 2
```

Example 4: Relational Operators

Problem: Compare two numbers using relational operators: ==, !=, <, >, <=, >=.

```
public class RelationalOperators {
    public static void main(String[] args) {
        int x = 10, y = 20;
        System.out.println("x == y: " + (x == y)); // Equal
        System.out.println("x != y: " + (x != y)); // Not equal
        System.out.println("x < y: " + (x < y));   // Less than
        System.out.println("x > y: " + (x > y));   // Greater than
        System.out.println("x <= y: " + (x <= y)); // Less than or equal
        System.out.println("x >= y: " + (x >= y)); // Greater than or
equal
    }}
```

Output:

```
x == y: false
x != y: true
x < y: true
x > y: false
x <= y: true
x >= y: false
```

Example 5: Operator Precedence and Associativity

Problem: Evaluate an expression considering operator precedence and associativity.

```
public class OperatorPrecedence {
    public static void main(String[] args) {
```

```
int a = 5, b = 10, c = 15;
int result = a + b * c / a - c % b;
// Precedence:
// 1. b * c = 150
// 2. 150 / a = 30
// 3. c % b = 5
// 4. a + 30 = 35
// 5. 35 - 5 = 30
System.out.println("Result: " + result);
} }
```

Output:

```
Result: 30
```

1.6 Expressions and Comments

- Understanding Expressions and Their Evaluation
- Java Commenting Style:
o Single-line Comments (//)
o Multi-line Comments (/* */)
o Documentation Comments (/** */)
- Best Practices for Writing Comments in Code

1.6 Expressions and Comments

Understanding Expressions and Their Evaluation

An **expression** in Java is a combination of variables, operators, and values that evaluates to a single result. Expressions are fundamental building blocks of Java programs and can be as simple as a single value or as complex as a combination of variables and operators.

Types of Expressions:

1. **Arithmetic Expressions**: These perform mathematical operations.
o Example:
o `int sum = 5 + 3;   // sum is 8`
2. **Relational Expressions**: These compare two values.
o Example:

```
boolean result = 5 > 3;   // result is true
```

3. **Logical Expressions**: These evaluate to `true` or `false`.
o Example:

```
boolean isTrue = (5 > 3) && (3 < 4);   // isTrue is true
```

4. **Assignment Expressions**: These assign values to variables.
   o Example:

```
int x = 5;   // x is 5
```

5. **Increment and Decrement Expressions**: These modify a variable by increasing or decreasing its value by one.
   o Example:

```
int i = 5;
i++;   // i becomes 6
```

Evaluation of Expressions: When an expression is evaluated, Java applies operator precedence and associativity rules to determine the order of evaluation. Expressions are evaluated from left to right unless specified otherwise by parentheses or operator precedence.

- **Operator Precedence**: Determines the order in which operators are applied (e.g., * and / have higher precedence than + and -).
- **Parentheses**: You can override operator precedence using parentheses to ensure expressions are evaluated in the desired order.

Example:

```
int result = (5 + 3) * 2;   // result is 16, parentheses ensure addition
happens first
```

Java Commenting Style

Comments are used in code to provide explanations, clarify complex sections, or temporarily disable code without deleting it. Java supports three types of comments:

1. **Single-line Comments (//)**:
   o These comments are used for short explanations or notes that fit on one line. They begin with // and extend to the end of the line.
   o Example:

```
int sum = 5 + 3;   // This calculates the sum of 5 and 3
```

2. **Multi-line Comments (/* */)**:
   o These comments can span multiple lines and are enclosed within /* and */. They are useful for longer explanations or when commenting out larger sections of code.
   o Example:

```
/*
 * This block of code calculates the sum of two numbers,
 * stores the result, and prints it to the console.
 */
int sum = 5 + 3;
System.out.println(sum);
```

3. Documentation Comments (/** */):

o   Documentation comments are used to generate API documentation and are placed before class, method, or field declarations. These comments begin with /** and end with */.

o   Example:

```
/**
 * This method calculates the sum of two integers.
 * @param a the first integer
 * @param b the second integer
 * @return the sum of a and b
 */
public int add(int a, int b) {
    return a + b;
}
```

Best Practices for Writing Comments in Code

1. Use Comments to Explain "Why", Not "What":

o   Comments should explain the reasoning behind a decision or logic that may not be immediately obvious. Don't use comments to explain what the code does (this should be clear from the code itself).

o   Example:

```
// Bad: Explains what the code does
int sum = 5 + 3;   // Adds 5 and 3

// Good: Explains why the code is doing something
// We add 5 and 3 because these are the initial values given by the user.
int sum = 5 + 3;
```

2. Avoid Overuse of Comments:

o   Too many comments clutter the code and make it harder to read. Instead of commenting every line, focus on explaining the complex parts of the code.

3. Update Comments with Code Changes:

o   If the code changes, ensure that comments are updated accordingly. Outdated comments can mislead other developers.

4. Use Proper Formatting for Documentation Comments:

o   When documenting methods, classes, or fields, use proper tags like @param, @return, and @throws to make your documentation clear and generate useful API docs.

Example:

```
/**
 * This method checks if a number is positive.
 * @param number the number to check
 * @return true if the number is positive, false otherwise
 */
public boolean isPositive(int number) {
    return number > 0;
```

```
}
```

5. **Comment Temporarily Disabled Code**:
o If you need to comment out code for debugging or testing purposes, clearly indicate why it is being commented out.
o Example:

```
// TODO: Revisit this logic when we have the new requirement
// int sum = 5 + 3;
```

6. **Avoid Obvious Comments**:
o Don't comment on things that are self-explanatory or already well-known.
o Example:

```
// Bad: This is obvious
int x = 10;   // Assigning 10 to x

// Good: Just the code, no comment needed
int x = 10;
```

In summary, comments should be used strategically to make your code easier to understand and maintain. Proper commenting is an essential skill for writing clean, maintainable code, especially when working on larger projects with other developers.

1.7 Basic Program Output

- Using `System.out.println()` and `System.out.print()`
- Printing Variables and Expressions
- String Concatenation in Output Statements
- Formatting Output with `printf()` and `String.format()`

1.7 Basic Program Output

In Java, producing output to the console or terminal is an essential part of interacting with the user or debugging a program. Java provides several methods to output data, with `System.out.println()`, `System.out.print()`, `printf()`, and `String.format()` being some of the most commonly used.

Using `System.out.println()` and `System.out.print()`

1. `System.out.println()`:
o This method is used to print data to the console followed by a new line. After printing the output, it automatically moves the cursor to the next line.
o Commonly used when you want each output to appear on a new line.

o   Example:

```
System.out.println("Hello, World!");
System.out.println(5 + 3);
```

Output:

```
Hello, World!
8
```

2. `System.out.print()`:
o   This method is similar to `println()`, but it does not add a newline after printing the output. The cursor remains on the same line.
o   Useful when you want to print multiple outputs on the same line.
o   Example:

```
System.out.print("Hello, ");
System.out.print("World!");
```

Output:

```
Hello, World!
```

In summary:

- `println()` is used when you want to move to the next line after printing.
- `print()` is used when you want to continue printing on the same line.

Printing Variables and Expressions

In Java, you can print variables or the result of expressions using `System.out.println()` or `System.out.print()`.

1. **Printing Variables**:
o   You can print the value of variables directly.
o   Example:

```
int x = 5;
System.out.println(x);   // Output: 5
```

2. **Printing Expressions**:
o   Java allows you to print the result of expressions (arithmetic, logical, etc.) directly.
o   Example:

```
int a = 10, b = 5;
System.out.println(a + b);   // Output: 15
```

3. **Combining Text and Variables/Expressions**:

o You can mix text and variables/expressions in a single output statement.
o Example:

```
int a = 10, b = 5;
System.out.println("The sum of a and b is: " + (a + b));   // Output: The
sum of a and b is: 15
```

String Concatenation in Output Statements

String concatenation allows you to combine strings with other data types (e.g., numbers, variables) into a single output statement.

- **Concatenating Strings and Other Data Types**:
o You can use the + operator to concatenate (combine) strings and other data types (integers, floats, etc.).
o Example:

```
String name = "Alice";
int age = 25;
System.out.println(name + " is " + age + " years old.");
```

Output:

```
Alice is 25 years old.
```

- **Automatic Type Conversion**:
o When concatenating non-string data types (like integers or floats) with strings, Java automatically converts those data types to their string representation.
o Example:

```
double price = 19.99;
System.out.println("The price is: " + price);
```

Output:

```
The price is: 19.99
```

Formatting Output with `printf()` and `String.format()`

Java provides `printf()` and `String.format()` methods for formatted output. These methods allow you to control the formatting of data in a more structured way.

1. **Using `printf()`:**

○ The `printf()` method is similar to C's `printf()`. It allows you to specify format specifiers to control the appearance of the output (e.g., setting the width of numbers, precision of floating-point values).

○ The format string contains placeholders for the variables or expressions to be printed.

○ Example:

```
double pi = 3.14159;
System.out.printf("Value of pi: %.2f\n", pi);  // Output: Value of pi:
3.14
```

Explanation: `%.2f` formats the `pi` variable as a floating-point number with 2 decimal places.

2. Common Format Specifiers in `printf()`:

○ `%d`: For integers (decimal format).

○ `%f`: For floating-point numbers.

○ `%s`: For strings.

○ `%c`: For characters.

○ `%x`: For hexadecimal integers.

○ Example:

```
int x = 123;
System.out.printf("x = %d\n", x);  // Output: x = 123
```

3. Using `String.format()`:

○ `String.format()` works similarly to `printf()`, but it returns the formatted string instead of printing it directly to the console. You can assign the result to a variable or use it later.

○ Example:

```
double price = 19.99;
String formattedPrice = String.format("The price is: %.2f", price);
System.out.println(formattedPrice);  // Output: The price is: 19.99
```

Formatting Numbers with Width and Precision:

○ You can specify the width (minimum number of characters) and precision (number of digits after the decimal) for numeric values.

○ Example:

```
double number = 3.14159;
System.out.printf("Formatted value: |%10.2f|\n", number);  // Output:
Formatted value: |      3.14|
```

Explanation: The `10` specifies the width of the number, and `.2` specifies 2 decimal places.

Summary of Output Methods

- **`System.out.println()`**: Prints output with a newline.
- **`System.out.print()`**: Prints output without a newline.
- **String Concatenation**: Combines strings and other types using the + operator.

- `printf()`: Provides more control over output formatting (e.g., decimals, padding).
- `String.format()`: Similar to `printf()`, but returns a formatted string.

1.8 Decision-Making Constructs: Conditional Statements and Loops

- `if`, `if-else`, and `if-else-if` Ladder
- `switch` Statements and Cases
- Syntax and Examples of Loops:
- `for` Loop
- `while` Loop
- `do-while` Loop
- Using Break and Continue Statements

1.8 Decision-Making Constructs: Conditional Statements and Loops

Decision-making constructs are essential in programming to control the flow of execution based on specific conditions. Java provides **conditional statements** (like `if`, `else`, and `switch`) and **looping constructs** (like `for`, `while`, and `do-while`) to implement logic that allows your program to make decisions and repeat actions.

1. Conditional Statements

1. **`if` Statement**:
   - The `if` statement is used to execute a block of code only if the condition provided evaluates to `true`.
   - **Syntax**:

```
if (condition) {
    // code block to be executed if the condition is true
}
```

   - **Example**:

```
int age = 20;
if (age >= 18) {
    System.out.println("You are an adult.");
}
// Output: You are an adult.
```

2. **`if-else` Statement**:
   - The `if-else` statement allows you to execute one block of code if the condition is `true` and a different block of code if the condition is `false`.

o **Syntax**:

```
if (condition) {
    // code block if the condition is true
} else {
    // code block if the condition is false
}
```

o **Example**:

```
int age = 16;
if (age >= 18) {
    System.out.println("You are an adult.");
} else {
    System.out.println("You are a minor.");
}
// Output: You are a minor.
```

3. `if-else-if` **Ladder**:
   o The `if-else-if` ladder is used when you have multiple conditions to check, and you want to execute different blocks of code for each condition. This construct tests multiple conditions in sequence.
   o **Syntax**:

```
if (condition1) {
    // code block if condition1 is true
} else if (condition2) {
    // code block if condition2 is true
} else {
    // code block if no conditions are true
}
```

o **Example**:

```
int score = 75;
if (score >= 90) {
    System.out.println("Grade A");
} else if (score >= 75) {
    System.out.println("Grade B");
} else if (score >= 50) {
    System.out.println("Grade C");
} else {
    System.out.println("Fail");
}
// Output: Grade B
```

4. `switch` **Statement**:
   o The `switch` statement is used to simplify multiple `if-else-if` statements. It allows you to check a variable or expression against a series of `case` values, and execute a block of code when a match is found.

○ **Syntax**:

```
switch (expression) {
    case value1:
        // code block if expression equals value1
        break;
    case value2:
        // code block if expression equals value2
        break;
    default:
        // code block if no cases match
}
```

○ **Example**:

```
int day = 3;
switch (day) {
    case 1:
        System.out.println("Monday");
        break;
    case 2:
        System.out.println("Tuesday");
        break;
    case 3:
        System.out.println("Wednesday");
        break;
    case 4:
        System.out.println("Thursday");
        break;
    case 5:
        System.out.println("Friday");
        break;
    case 6:
        System.out.println("Saturday");
        break;
    case 7:
        System.out.println("Sunday");
        break;
    default:
        System.out.println("Invalid day");
}
// Output: Wednesday
```

○ **Explanation**: The switch statement evaluates the expression (day in this case), and matches it with one of the case values. The break statement exits the switch block once the corresponding case is executed.

___

2. Loops in Java

Loops are used to repeat a block of code multiple times until a condition is met. Java provides three types of loops:

1. **for Loop**:
   o The `for` loop is used when the number of iterations is known beforehand. It has three parts: initialization, condition, and increment/decrement.
   o **Syntax**:

```
for (initialization; condition; increment/decrement) {
    // code block to be executed
}
```

   o **Example**:

```
for (int i = 1; i <= 5; i++) {
    System.out.println(i);
}
// Output: 1 2 3 4 5
```

2. **while Loop**:
   o The `while` loop is used when the number of iterations is not known, and the loop continues to execute as long as the condition is `true`.
   o **Syntax**:

```
while (condition) {
    // code block to be executed
}
```

   o **Example**:

```
int i = 1;
while (i <= 5) {
    System.out.println(i);
    i++;
}
// Output: 1 2 3 4 5
```

3. **do-while Loop**:
   o The `do-while` loop is similar to the `while` loop, but it guarantees that the code block will be executed at least once, because the condition is checked after the execution of the loop.
   o **Syntax**:

```
do {
    // code block to be executed
} while (condition);
```

   o **Example**:

```
int i = 1;
do {
    System.out.println(i);
    i++;
} while (i <= 5);
// Output: 1 2 3 4 5
```

3. Using break and continue Statements

1. **break Statement**:
o   The break statement is used to exit from the loop or switch statement prematurely.
o   It can be used in any loop (like for, while, do-while) or switch block to stop further iterations or cases.
o   **Example**:

```java
for (int i = 1; i <= 5; i++) {
    if (i == 3) {
        break;  // Exits the loop when i is 3
    }
    System.out.println(i);
}
// Output: 1 2
```

2. **continue Statement**:
o   The continue statement is used to skip the current iteration of the loop and continue with the next iteration.
o   It can be used in any loop to skip the remaining code in the current iteration.
o   **Example**:

```java
for (int i = 1; i <= 5; i++) {
    if (i == 3) {
        continue;  // Skips the rest of the code for i = 3
    }
    System.out.println(i);
}
// Output: 1 2 4 5
```

Summary

- **Conditional Statements** (if, else, switch) control the flow of the program based on conditions, allowing different actions to be performed depending on the logic.
- **Loops** (for, while, do-while) repeat a block of code multiple times based on certain conditions, helping avoid redundancy.
- **break** and **continue** help manage flow within loops and switch statements by either exiting or skipping iterations as needed.

1. `if` Statement

Program:

```java
Copy code
public class IfExample {
    public static void main(String[] args) {
        int number = 10;
        if (number > 0) {
            System.out.println("The number is positive.");
        }   }}
```

Output:

```
The number is positive.
```

2. `if-else` Statement

Program:

```java
public class IfElseExample {
    public static void main(String[] args) {
        int number = -5;
        if (number > 0) {
            System.out.println("The number is positive.");
        } else {
            System.out.println("The number is not positive.");
        }
    }}
```

Output:

```
The number is not positive.
```

3. `if-else-if` Ladder

Program:

```java
public class IfElseIfExample {
    public static void main(String[] args) {
        int marks = 85;
        if (marks >= 90) {
            System.out.println("Grade: A+");
        } else if (marks >= 75) {
            System.out.println("Grade: A");
```

```
        } else if (marks >= 50) {
            System.out.println("Grade: B");
        } else {
            System.out.println("Grade: F");
        }
    }
}
```

Output:

```
Grade: A
```

4. switch Statement

Program:

```
public class SwitchExample {
    public static void main(String[] args) {
        int day = 3;
        switch (day) {
            case 1:
                System.out.println("Monday");
                break;
            case 2:
                System.out.println("Tuesday");
                break;
            case 3:
                System.out.println("Wednesday");
                break;
            default:
                System.out.println("Invalid day");
        }   }}
```

Output:

```
Wednesday
```

5. for Loop

Program:

```
public class ForLoopExample {
    public static void main(String[] args) {
        for (int i = 1; i <= 5; i++) {
            System.out.println("Iteration: " + i);
        }
    }
}
```

Output:

```
Iteration: 1
Iteration: 2
Iteration: 3
Iteration: 4
Iteration: 5
```

6. while Loop

Program:

```java
public class WhileLoopExample {
    public static void main(String[] args) {
        int i = 1;
        while (i <= 5) {
            System.out.println("Count: " + i);
            i++;
        }
    }
}
```

Output:

```
makefile
Copy code
Count: 1
Count: 2
Count: 3
Count: 4
Count: 5
```

7. do-while Loop

Program:

```java
java
Copy code
public class DoWhileExample {
    public static void main(String[] args) {
        int i = 1;
        do {
            System.out.println("Count: " + i);
```

```
            i++;
        } while (i <= 5);
    }
}
```

Output:

```
Count: 1
Count: 2
Count: 3
Count: 4
Count: 5
```

8. Nested `for` Loops

Program:

```java
public class NestedForLoop {
    public static void main(String[] args) {
        for (int i = 1; i <= 3; i++) {
            for (int j = 1; j <= 2; j++) {
                System.out.println("i: " + i + ", j: " + j);
            }
        }
    }
}
```

Output:

```
i: 1, j: 1
i: 1, j: 2
i: 2, j: 1
i: 2, j: 2
i: 3, j: 1
i: 3, j: 2
```

9. Using `break` in Loops

Program:

```java
public class BreakExample {
    public static void main(String[] args) {
        for (int i = 1; i <= 5; i++) {
            if (i == 3) {
                break;
            }
            System.out.println("Iteration: " + i);
        }
```

```
        }
}
```

Output:

```
Iteration: 1
Iteration: 2
```

10. Using `continue` in Loops

Program:

```java
public class ContinueExample {
    public static void main(String[] args) {
        for (int i = 1; i <= 5; i++) {
            if (i == 3) {
                continue;
            }
            System.out.println("Iteration: " + i);
        }
    }}
```

Output:

```
Iteration: 1
Iteration: 2
Iteration: 4
Iteration: 5
```

11. `while` Loop to Calculate Factorial

Program:

```java
public class FactorialWhile {
    public static void main(String[] args) {
        int num = 5, fact = 1, i = 1;
        while (i <= num) {
            fact *= i;
            i++;
        }
        System.out.println("Factorial: " + fact);
    }
}
```

Output:

```
Factorial: 120
```

12. `do-while` Loop for Sum of Digits

Program:

```
public class SumDigits {
    public static void main(String[] args) {
        int num = 123, sum = 0;
        do {
            sum += num % 10;
            num /= 10;
        } while (num > 0);
        System.out.println("Sum of digits: " + sum);
    }
}
```

Output:

```
Sum of digits: 6
```

13. Prime Number Check Using `for` Loop

Program:

```
public class PrimeCheck {
    public static void main(String[] args) {
        int num = 7;
        boolean isPrime = true;
        for (int i = 2; i <= num / 2; i++) {
            if (num % i == 0) {
                isPrime = false;
                break;
            }
        }
        System.out.println("Is Prime: " + isPrime);
    }}
```

Output: Is `Prime:` true

14. Pattern Printing Using Nested Loops

Program:

```
public class PatternPrinting {
    public static void main(String[] args) {
        for (int i = 1; i <= 5; i++) {
            for (int j = 1; j <= i; j++) {
                System.out.print("* ");
            }
```

```
            System.out.println();
        }
    }
}
```

Output:

```
*
* *
* * *
* * * *
* * * * *
```

15. Fibonacci Series Using `while` Loop

Program:

```java
public class FibonacciSeries {
    public static void main(String[] args) {
        int n = 10, a = 0, b = 1, i = 0;
        System.out.print("Fibonacci Series: ");
        while (i < n) {
            System.out.print(a + " ");
            int next = a + b;
            a = b;
            b = next;
            i++;
        }
    }
}
```

Output:

```
Fibonacci Series: 0 1 1 2 3 5 8 13 21 34
```

16. Leap Year Check Using `if-else`

Program:

```java
public class LeapYearCheck {
    public static void main(String[] args) {
        int year = 2024;
        if (year % 4 == 0) {
            if (year % 100 == 0) {
                if (year % 400 == 0) {
                    System.out.println(year + " is a leap year.");
                } else {
```

```
                    System.out.println(year + " is not a leap year.");
                }
            } else {
                System.out.println(year + " is a leap year.");
            }
        } else {
            System.out.println(year + " is not a leap year.");
        }
    }
}
```

Output:

```
2024 is a leap year.
```

17. Multiplication Table Using `for` Loop

Program:

```java
public class MultiplicationTable {
    public static void main(String[] args) {
        int num = 7;
        for (int i = 1; i <= 10; i++) {
            System.out.println(num + " x " + i + " = " + (num * i));
        }
    }
}
```

Output:

```
7 x 1 = 7
7 x 2 = 14
7 x 3 = 21
...
7 x 10 = 70
```

18. Sum of Numbers Using `while` Loop

Program:

```java
public class SumUsingWhile {
    public static void main(String[] args) {
        int n = 5, sum = 0, i = 1;
        while (i <= n) {
            sum += i;
            i++;
        }
        System.out.println("Sum of first " + n + " numbers: " + sum);
```

```
        }
}
```

Output:

```
Sum of first 5 numbers: 15
```

---

19. Factorial Using `for` Loop

Program:

```java
public class FactorialForLoop {
    public static void main(String[] args) {
        int num = 6, fact = 1;
        for (int i = 1; i <= num; i++) {
            fact *= i;
        }
        System.out.println("Factorial of " + num + " is: " + fact);
    }
}
```

Output:

```
Factorial of 6 is: 720
```

---

20. Reverse a Number Using `do-while` Loop

Program:

```java
public class ReverseNumber {
    public static void main(String[] args) {
        int num = 1234, reversed = 0;
        do {
            int digit = num % 10;
            reversed = reversed * 10 + digit;
            num /= 10;
        } while (num != 0);
```

```
        System.out.println("Reversed number: " + reversed);
    }
}
```

Output:

```
Reversed number: 4321
```

1.9 Nesting of Loops

- Definition and Use Cases of Nested Loops
- Syntax and Examples of Nested `for`, `while`, and `do-while` Loops
- Common Applications: Multiplication Tables, Patterns, and Complex Iterations
- Performance Considerations of Nested Loops

1.9 Nesting of Loops

Nesting of loops refers to placing one loop inside another. The inner loop runs completely for every single iteration of the outer loop. This allows for the creation of more complex operations and patterns. Nested loops are especially useful when you need to perform repeated actions in a matrix-like structure or when handling complex iterations involving multiple variables.

1. Definition and Use Cases of Nested Loops

- **Nested Loops**: A nested loop occurs when one loop is placed inside another loop. The outer loop controls the number of iterations of the inner loop. For each iteration of the outer loop, the inner loop runs to completion.
- **Use Cases**:
- **2D data structures**: Nested loops are commonly used to process 2D arrays or matrices. Each element of the matrix is accessed using two indexes: one for the row and one for the column.
- **Patterns and graphics**: Nested loops help in printing patterns like stars, numbers, or other graphical structures.
- **Complex calculations**: Nested loops are used in scenarios where complex iterations need to be performed, such as in combinatorics, sorting algorithms, or simulations.

2. Syntax and Examples of Nested for, while, and do-while Loops

1. **Nested `for` Loop**: The `for` loop is most commonly used for nesting due to its concise structure (initialization, condition, and increment/decrement are all in one statement).
- **Syntax**:

```
for (initialization; condition; increment) {
    for (initialization; condition; increment) {
        // code block to be executed
    }
```

```
}
```

- o **Example**: Printing a multiplication table using a nested `for` loop:

```
for (int i = 1; i <= 5; i++) {   // Outer loop
    for (int j = 1; j <= 5; j++) {   // Inner loop
        System.out.print(i * j + "\t");   // Print multiplication result
    }
    System.out.println();   // Move to next line after each row
}
// Output:
// 1    2    3    4    5
// 2    4    6    8    10
// 3    6    9    12   15
// 4    8    12   16   20
// 5    10   15   20   25
```

2. **Nested `while` Loop**: The `while` loop can also be nested, but you must handle initialization and increment separately outside the loop.
- o **Syntax**:

```
initialization;
while (condition) {
    initialization;
    while (condition) {
        // code block to be executed
    }
}
```

- o **Example**: Printing a pattern using a nested `while` loop:

```
int i = 1;
while (i <= 5) {   // Outer loop
    int j = 1;
    while (j <= i) {   // Inner loop
        System.out.print("* ");   // Print stars
        j++;
    }
    System.out.println();   // Move to next line
    i++;
}
// Output:
// *
// * *
// * * *
// * * * *
// * * * * *
```

3. **Nested `do-while` Loop**: Similar to the `while` loop, the `do-while` loop guarantees that the inner loop will run at least once.
- o **Syntax**:

```
do {
```

```
    do {
        // code block to be executed
    } while (condition);
} while (condition);
```

o **Example**: Printing a reversed pyramid pattern using a nested `do-while` loop:

```
int i = 5;
do {
    int j = 1;
    do {
        System.out.print("* ");  // Print stars
        j++;
    } while (j <= i);
    System.out.println();  // Move to next line
    i--;
} while (i > 0);
// Output:
// * * * * *
// * * * *
// * * *
// * *
// *
```

3. Common Applications of Nested Loops

1. **Multiplication Tables**: Nested loops are commonly used to generate multiplication tables, where each row is generated by the outer loop and the values in each row are calculated by the inner loop.
2. **Patterns**: Patterns like triangles, pyramids, diamonds, etc., are often created with nested loops. The outer loop handles the number of rows, and the inner loop handles the number of characters to print in each row.
o Example: Print a right-angled triangle of stars.

```
for (int i = 1; i <= 5; i++) {
    for (int j = 1; j <= i; j++) {
        System.out.print("* ");
    }
    System.out.println();
}
// Output:
// *
// * *
// * * *
// * * * *
// * * * * *
```

3. **Complex Iterations**: Nested loops are useful when you need to iterate over a matrix, grid, or any multi-dimensional structure.

o   Example: Summing all elements in a 2D array:

```
int[][] matrix = {{1, 2, 3}, {4, 5, 6}, {7, 8, 9}};
int sum = 0;
for (int i = 0; i < matrix.length; i++) {
    for (int j = 0; j < matrix[i].length; j++) {
        sum += matrix[i][j];  // Summing elements
    }
}
System.out.println("Sum of all elements: " + sum);
// Output: Sum of all elements: 45
```

4. Performance Considerations of Nested Loops

While nested loops are powerful, they can have a significant impact on performance, especially when the number of iterations grows large. Each loop contributes to the total number of iterations, and as a result, the time complexity of nested loops increases rapidly.

- **Time Complexity**:
o   For two nested loops, each running n times, the time complexity is **$O(n^2)$**. For three nested loops, the time complexity becomes **$O(n^3)$**, and so on.
o   The more levels of nesting you add, the higher the time complexity. This can lead to performance issues in algorithms that require large datasets.
- **Example**: A simple nested loop with two loops:

```
for (int i = 0; i < n; i++) {
    for (int j = 0; j < n; j++) {
        // Constant time operation
    }
}
// Time complexity: O(n^2)
```

- **Optimizations**:
o   **Break or Continue**: Use break to exit the loop early if a condition is met or continue to skip unnecessary iterations.
o   **Reduce Loop Nesting**: If possible, reduce the depth of nested loops by using more efficient algorithms or data structures (e.g., flattening a 2D array or using matrix operations).
o   **Efficient Loop Order**: Sometimes switching the order of the loops (i.e., switching the outer and inner loops) can improve cache locality or lead to fewer operations.

Summary

- **Nesting of Loops**: Placing one loop inside another is common in many programming scenarios, especially when dealing with multi-dimensional structures, complex iterations, or patterns.

- **Types of Nested Loops**: You can use `for`, `while`, and `do-while` loops to nest one inside another based on your requirement. Each loop type has its own advantages, especially in handling different loop conditions.
- **Applications**: Common applications of nested loops include multiplication tables, pattern generation, and working with 2D arrays or matrices.
- **Performance Considerations**: Nested loops increase the time complexity of an algorithm. It is important to understand the implications of the loop's depth and optimize accordingly for large data sets.

Example 1: Multiplication Table (Nested `for` Loop)

Problem: Display the multiplication tables from 1 to 5 using nested loops.

```java
public class MultiplicationTable {
    public static void main(String[] args) {
        for (int i = 1; i <= 5; i++) {
            System.out.println("Multiplication Table of " + i);
            for (int j = 1; j <= 10; j++) {
                System.out.println(i + " x " + j + " = " + (i * j));
            }
            System.out.println();
        }    }}
```
Output:
```
Multiplication Table of 1
1 x 1 = 1
1 x 2 = 2
...
1 x 10 = 10

Multiplication Table of 2
2 x 1 = 2
2 x 2 = 4
...
2 x 10 = 20
...
```

Example 2: Pyramid Pattern (`for` Loop)

Problem: Print a pyramid pattern of stars.

```java
public class PyramidPattern {
    public static void main(String[] args) {
        int rows = 5;
        for (int i = 1; i <= rows; i++) {
            for (int j = rows - i; j > 0; j--) {
                System.out.print(" ");
            }
            for (int k = 1; k <= i * 2 - 1; k++) {
                System.out.print("*");
```

```
                }
            System.out.println();
        }
    }
}
```

Output:

```
    *
   ***
  *****
 *******
*********
```

Example 3: Nested `while` Loop for Sum of Elements

Problem: Calculate the sum of elements in a 2D array.

```
public class Sum2DArray {
    public static void main(String[] args) {
        int[][] array = {
            {1, 2, 3},
            {4, 5, 6},
            {7, 8, 9}
        };
        int sum = 0;
        int i = 0;
        while (i < array.length) {
            int j = 0;
            while (j < array[i].length) {
                sum += array[i][j];
                j++;
            }
            i++;
        }
        System.out.println("Sum of all elements: " + sum);
    }
}
```

Output:

```
Sum of all elements: 45
```

Example 4: Displaying Days of a Month (Nested `for` Loop)

Problem: Display the days of each week for 4 weeks in a month.

```
public class WeeklyDays {
    public static void main(String[] args) {
```

```
        String[] days = {"Monday", "Tuesday", "Wednesday", "Thursday",
"Friday", "Saturday", "Sunday"};
        for (int week = 1; week <= 4; week++) {
            System.out.println("Week " + week + ":");
            for (int day = 0; day < days.length; day++) {
                System.out.println(days[day]);
            }
            System.out.println();
        }
    }
}
```

Output:

```
Week 1:
Monday
Tuesday
Wednesday
...
Week 4:
Monday
Tuesday
...
```

Example 5: Checking Prime Numbers in a Range (`for` and `while` Loop)

Problem: Check for prime numbers between 1 and 50 using nested loops.

```
public class PrimeNumbers {
    public static void main(String[] args) {
        for (int num = 2; num <= 50; num++) {
            boolean isPrime = true;
            int divisor = 2;
            while (divisor <= Math.sqrt(num)) {
                if (num % divisor == 0) {
                    isPrime = false;
                    break;
                }
                divisor++;
            }
            if (isPrime) {
                System.out.print(num + " ");
            }
        }
    }
}
```

Output:

```
Copy code
2 3 5 7 11 13 17 19 23 29 31 37 41 43 47
```

1.10 Java Methods: Defining, Scope, Passing, and Returning Arguments

- Defining Methods: Syntax and Structure
- Scope of Methods: Public, Private, Protected, and Default
- Passing Arguments: Call by Value vs Call by Reference
- Returning Values from Methods
- Overloading Methods in Java

1.10 Java Methods: Defining, Scope, Passing, and Returning Arguments

In Java, **methods** are blocks of code that perform a specific task. They help in code reusability and organization. Understanding how to define, scope, pass arguments to, and return values from methods is essential in Java programming. This section covers the fundamentals of methods in Java.

---

1. Defining Methods: Syntax and Structure

A **method** in Java is defined by the following structure:

Syntax:

```
<access modifier> <return type> <method name>(<parameter list>) {
    // Method body
    // Statements or code to execute
    return <value>; // if the method has a return type
}
```

- **Access Modifier**: Determines the visibility of the method. It could be `public`, `private`, `protected`, or package-private (default).
- **Return Type**: Specifies what type of value the method will return. If the method doesn't return any value, use `void`.
- **Method Name**: The name used to call the method. Method names should be descriptive and follow camelCase convention.
- **Parameter List**: The input values passed to the method. It can be empty if no parameters are required.
- **Method Body**: Contains the code that defines what the method will do.

Example:

```
public class Calculator {
```

```
    // Method to add two numbers
    public int add(int a, int b) {
        return a + b;
    }
}
```

In this example:

- The method `add` is defined with `int` as the return type.
- The method takes two `int` parameters (`a` and `b`).
- It returns the sum of `a` and `b`.

---

2. Scope of Methods: Public, Private, Protected, and Default

The **scope** of a method refers to its visibility in the program. The access modifiers control how the method can be accessed by other parts of the program:

1. **Public**:
   o A `public` method is accessible from any other class in the project.
   o It has the broadest scope.

```
public void printMessage() {
    System.out.println("Hello, world!");
}
```

2. **Private**:
   o A `private` method can only be accessed within the same class where it is defined.
   o It cannot be called directly from other classes or objects.

```
private void helperMethod() {
    System.out.println("This is a private method.");
}
```

3. **Protected**:
   o A `protected` method is accessible within the same package and by subclasses (even if they are in a different package).
   o It has more restricted access than `public`, but broader access than `private`.

```
protected void display() {
    System.out.println("This is a protected method.");
}
```

4. **Default (Package-private)**:
   o If no access modifier is specified, the method has **default** or **package-private** access.
   o This means it is accessible only within the same package.

```
void displayMessage() {
```

```
        System.out.println("This is a default access method.");
}
```

3. Passing Arguments: Call by Value vs Call by Reference

When calling a method, arguments can be passed in two ways:

1. **Call by Value**:
   o In **call by value**, a copy of the actual argument is passed to the method. Changes made to the parameter inside the method do not affect the original value.
   o This is how primitive data types (e.g., int, char, boolean, etc.) are passed in Java.

```java
public class Example {
    public void changeValue(int num) {
        num = 10;
    }

    public static void main(String[] args) {
        Example ex = new Example();
        int value = 5;
        ex.changeValue(value);
        System.out.println(value);   // Output: 5 (unchanged)
    }
}
```

2. **Call by Reference**:
   o In **call by reference**, the method gets access to the original memory address of the object. Changes made to the parameter inside the method affect the original object.
   o In Java, **call by reference** applies only to objects, as objects are passed by reference, not their copies.

```java
public class Example {
    public void modifyList(ArrayList<String> list) {
        list.add("New Element");
    }

    public static void main(String[] args) {
        Example ex = new Example();
        ArrayList<String> myList = new ArrayList<>();
        myList.add("First Element");
        ex.modifyList(myList);
        System.out.println(myList);   // Output: [First Element, New
Element]
    }
}
```

4. Returning Values from Methods

Methods in Java can return a value to the calling code. The return type in the method signature indicates what type of value will be returned. If a method does not return anything, the return type should be `void`.

- **Returning a Value**:
o A `return` statement is used to send the result from the method to the calling code.
o The `return` statement must match the return type declared in the method signature.

Example:

```java
public class MathOperations {
    // Method that returns the sum of two numbers
    public int addNumbers(int a, int b) {
        return a + b;
    }

    public static void main(String[] args) {
        MathOperations math = new MathOperations();
        int result = math.addNumbers(3, 5);
        System.out.println("Sum: " + result);  // Output: Sum: 8
    }
}
```

5. Overloading Methods in Java

Method Overloading occurs when multiple methods with the same name are defined in the same class, but they differ in their **parameters** (number, type, or both). Method overloading is resolved at **compile-time**.

- **Key Points**:
o Methods can be overloaded based on different **parameter types** or **number of parameters**.
o The return type is not a factor in overloading.

Example:

```java
public class Calculator {

    // Method to add two integers
    public int add(int a, int b) {
        return a + b;      }

    // Overloaded method to add three integers
    public int add(int a, int b, int c) {
        return a + b + c;
    }

    // Overloaded method to add two doubles
    public double add(double a, double b) {
```

```
        return a + b;
    }

    public static void main(String[] args) {
        Calculator calc = new Calculator();
        System.out.println(calc.add(3, 4));          // Output: 7
        System.out.println(calc.add(3, 4, 5));       // Output: 12
        System.out.println(calc.add(3.5, 4.5));      // Output: 8.0
    }
}
```

In this example:

- The `add` method is overloaded to handle both `int` and `double` types, as well as different numbers of parameters.

Summary:

- **Defining Methods**: Methods are defined using access modifiers, return types, method names, and parameters. They are crucial for code reusability.
- **Scope**: Methods can have different levels of access: `public`, `private`, `protected`, and default (package-private), determining their visibility.
- **Passing Arguments**: Java uses **call by value** for primitive types and **call by reference** for objects.
- **Returning Values**: Methods can return values using the `return` keyword. If no value is returned, use `void`.
- **Overloading Methods**: You can define multiple methods with the same name but different parameter types or numbers, allowing for flexibility in method calls.

1.11 Type Conversion and Type Checking

- Implicit (Widening) Type Conversion
- Explicit (Narrowing) Type Conversion or Type Casting
- Checking Data Types Using `instanceof`
- Avoiding Type Conversion Errors
- Using Wrapper Classes for Type Conversion

1.11 Type Conversion and Type Checking

In Java, **type conversion** refers to the process of converting one data type to another. Java provides two types of type conversion: **implicit (widening)** and **explicit (narrowing)**. Additionally, type checking can be done using the `instanceof` keyword, and Java also offers wrapper classes for type conversion. Understanding these concepts is crucial for avoiding errors and ensuring that data is handled correctly across different types.

1. Implicit (Widening) Type Conversion

Implicit Type Conversion (also known as **widening conversion**) happens automatically when a **smaller** data type is converted to a **larger** data type. In Java, this kind of conversion is performed by the compiler, and it doesn't require any special syntax.

Key Points:

- **Widening conversion** occurs when you convert a primitive data type with a **smaller size** to a **larger size**.
- No **explicit casting** is required, as the conversion is **safe** (no data loss).

Example:

```
public class ImplicitConversion {
    public static void main(String[] args) {
        int num = 100;          // int (4 bytes)
        long longNum = num;     // Implicitly converted from int to long (8
bytes)
        System.out.println(longNum);  // Output: 100
    }
}
```

In this example, the `int` variable `num` is automatically converted to a `long` type. This is a widening conversion because `long` has a larger range than `int`.

2. Explicit (Narrowing) Type Conversion or Type Casting

Explicit Type Conversion (also known as **narrowing conversion** or **type casting**) happens when you convert a **larger** data type to a **smaller** data type. This conversion may result in data loss, so the programmer needs to specify it using **casting**.

Key Points:

- **Narrowing conversion** requires **explicit casting** using parentheses `()`.
- It can result in **loss of data** if the value cannot fit into the smaller data type.
- Java requires the developer to indicate the conversion explicitly to avoid unexpected behavior.

Syntax:

```
<targetType> variable = (<targetType>) sourceVariable;
```

Example:

```
public class ExplicitConversion {
    public static void main(String[] args) {
        double num = 9.78;          // double (8 bytes)
        int intNum = (int) num;     // Explicitly converting double to int
(narrowing)
        System.out.println(intNum);  // Output: 9 (decimal part is
truncated)
    }
}
```

In this case, num is a double and is explicitly cast to an int. The fractional part is discarded during the conversion, which is why the output is 9.

3. Checking Data Types Using `instanceof`

In Java, the `instanceof` keyword is used to **check** whether an object is an instance of a particular class or subclass. This is commonly used in type checking, especially when working with inheritance, to determine the runtime type of an object.

Syntax:

```
object instanceof ClassName
```

- It returns `true` if the `object` is an instance of the `ClassName` or its subclass.
- It returns `false` if the `object` is not an instance of the `ClassName`.

Example:

```
public class InstanceofExample {
    public static void main(String[] args) {
        String str = "Hello, World!";

        // Checking if str is an instance of String class
        if (str instanceof String) {
            System.out.println("str is an instance of String");
        }
    }
}
```

In this example:

- `str instanceof String` evaluates to `true` because `str` is an instance of the `String` class.
- `instanceof` is useful in scenarios like checking the type of objects in polymorphic code or handling different types in a method.

4. Avoiding Type Conversion Errors

While **type conversion** can be useful, improper or careless conversion can lead to errors, especially in **narrowing conversions**. Here are a few best practices to avoid such errors:

1. **Use Implicit Conversion Where Possible**: If Java can convert a smaller data type to a larger one automatically (widening), it's safe to rely on implicit conversion.
2. **Check for Potential Data Loss in Narrowing Conversion**: Before performing a narrowing conversion (e.g., `double` to `int`), ensure that the value will fit into the smaller type without loss. Otherwise, you might need to round the value or handle exceptions.
3. **Use the `instanceof` Operator for Type Checking**: In object-oriented programming, use `instanceof` to check if an object can be safely cast to a specific type.

Example:

```
public class AvoidConversionError {
    public static void main(String[] args) {
        double num = 12345.6789;  // A large decimal number
        int intNum = (int) num;   // Explicit cast that may lose precision

        // Check if the casting would cause loss of data
        if (num > Integer.MAX_VALUE || num < Integer.MIN_VALUE) {
            System.out.println("Data loss will occur during casting");
        } else {
            intNum = (int) num;
            System.out.println(intNum);  // Output may not be the expected
value
        }
    }
}
```

In this case, we check whether the value exceeds the bounds of the `int` type, thus avoiding potential data loss when casting.

5. Using Wrapper Classes for Type Conversion

Java provides **wrapper classes** for each of the **primitive data types**. These classes allow you to convert between primitive types and their corresponding object types, as well as provide utility methods for type conversion.

The common **wrapper classes** are:

- `Integer` for `int`
- `Double` for `double`
- `Character` for `char`

- `Boolean` **for** `boolean`
- `Float` **for** `float`
- `Long` **for** `long`
- `Short` **for** `short`
- `Byte` **for** `byte`

These wrapper classes have methods that allow for **conversions** and **parsing** strings into primitive types.

Examples:

- **Converting from String to primitive**:

```
String str = "123";
int num = Integer.parseInt(str);  // Converting String to int
System.out.println(num);  // Output: 123
```

- **Converting from primitive to Wrapper Object**:

```
int num = 10;
Integer obj = Integer.valueOf(num);  // Boxing: primitive to object
System.out.println(obj);  // Output: 10
```

- **Converting Wrapper Object to primitive**:

```
Integer obj = 20;
int num = obj.intValue();  // Unboxing: object to primitive
System.out.println(num);  // Output: 20
```

- **Using Wrapper Classes for Type Conversion**:

```
double num = 10.5;
String str = Double.toString(num);  // Convert double to String
System.out.println(str);  // Output: "10.5"
```

Wrapper classes also offer methods like `parseInt()`, `parseDouble()`, `parseBoolean()`, and so on, for **parsing** primitive values from Strings.

Summary:

- **Implicit Type Conversion** (widening) automatically converts smaller data types to larger ones without losing data.
- **Explicit Type Conversion** (narrowing) requires manual casting and can cause data loss if not handled properly.
- Use the `instanceof` operator for checking the type of an object at runtime.
- To avoid errors during type conversion, ensure that conversions are safe, especially narrowing conversions.
- **Wrapper classes** provide an easy way to convert between primitive types and objects and offer utility methods for type conversion.

1

1.12 Built-in Java Class Methods

- Methods from the `Math` Class:
o `abs()`, `pow()`, `sqrt()`, `random()`, etc.
- Methods from the `String` Class:
o `charAt()`, `substring()`, `length()`, `equals()`, etc.
- Using the `Scanner` Class for Input
- Methods from the `System` Class
- Utility Methods from the `Arrays` Class

Example 1: Methods from the `Math` Class

Problem: Demonstrate the use of `abs()`, `pow()`, `sqrt()`, and `random()` methods from the `Math` class.

```
public class MathClassMethods {
    public static void main(String[] args) {
        int num = -10;
        double base = 2, exponent = 3;

        System.out.println("Absolute value of -10: " + Math.abs(num));
        System.out.println("2 raised to the power of 3: " + Math.pow(base,
exponent));
        System.out.println("Square root of 16: " + Math.sqrt(16));
        System.out.println("Random number (0 to 1): " + Math.random());
    }
}
```

Output:

```
Absolute value of -10: 10
2 raised to the power of 3: 8.0
Square root of 16: 4.0
```

```
Random number (0 to 1): 0.5432 (varies with each execution)
```

Example 2: Methods from the `String` Class

Problem: Demonstrate the use of `charAt()`, `substring()`, `length()`, and `equals()` methods from the `String` class.

```
public class StringClassMethods {
    public static void main(String[] args) {
        String str = "Hello World";

        System.out.println("Character at index 4: " + str.charAt(4));
        System.out.println("Substring from index 6: " + str.substring(6));
        System.out.println("Length of the string: " + str.length());
        System.out.println("Is string equal to 'Hello': " +
str.equals("Hello"));
    }
}
```

Output:

```
Character at index 4: o
Substring from index 6: World
Length of the string: 11
Is string equal to 'Hello': false
```

Example 3: Using the `Scanner` Class for Input

Problem: Use the `Scanner` class to take user input and perform operations.

```
import java.util.Scanner;

public class ScannerExample {
    public static void main(String[] args) {
        Scanner scanner = new Scanner(System.in);

        System.out.print("Enter your name: ");
        String name = scanner.nextLine();

        System.out.print("Enter your age: ");
        int age = scanner.nextInt();

        System.out.println("Hello, " + name + "! You are " + age + " years
old.");
    }
}
```

Output:

```
Enter your name: John
Enter your age: 25
Hello, John! You are 25 years old.
```

Example 4: Methods from the System Class

Problem: Demonstrate the use of System.currentTimeMillis(), System.nanoTime(), and System.getProperty() methods.

```java
public class SystemClassMethods {
    public static void main(String[] args) {
        System.out.println("Current Time in Milliseconds: " +
System.currentTimeMillis());
        System.out.println("Current Time in Nanoseconds: " +
System.nanoTime());
        System.out.println("Java Version: " +
System.getProperty("java.version"));
    }
}
```

Output:

```
Current Time in Milliseconds: 1702389655321
Current Time in Nanoseconds: 2934567890123
Java Version: 17.0.2 (varies with the installed version)
```

Example 5: Utility Methods from the Arrays Class

Problem: Demonstrate the use of Arrays.sort(), Arrays.toString(), and Arrays.binarySearch().

```java
import java.util.Arrays;

public class ArraysClassMethods {
    public static void main(String[] args) {
        int[] numbers = {5, 1, 8, 3, 2};

        Arrays.sort(numbers); // Sort the array
        System.out.println("Sorted Array: " + Arrays.toString(numbers));

        int key = 3;
        int index = Arrays.binarySearch(numbers, key); // Search for key
        System.out.println("Index of 3 in the array: " + index);
    }
}
```

Output:

```
Sorted Array: [1, 2, 3, 5, 8]
Index of 3 in the array: 2
```

50 MCQ ON THESE TOPICS

1.1 Java Architecture and Features

1. Which component of Java architecture translates bytecode into machine code?
   a) JVM
   b) JDK
   c) JRE
   d) Bytecode Translator
   Answer: a) JVM
2. What feature of Java ensures platform independence?
   a) Garbage Collection
   b) Bytecode
   c) Multithreading
   d) Dynamic Binding
   Answer: b) Bytecode
3. Java is a _____ programming language.
   a) Procedural
   b) Object-oriented
   c) Functional
   d) None of the above
   Answer: b) Object-oriented
4. Which of these is not a Java feature?
   a) Multithreading
   b) Platform Independence
   c) Explicit Pointers
   d) Automatic Garbage Collection
   Answer: c) Explicit Pointers
5. What is the core of Java's portability?
   a) Syntax similarity with C++
   b) JVM
   c) Dynamic libraries
   d) Built-in methods
   Answer: b) JVM

1.2 Semantic and Syntax Differences Between C++ and Java

6. In Java, which keyword is used to define a constant variable?
   a) const

b) final
c) static
d) immutable
Answer: b) final

7. Which of the following is absent in Java but present in C++?
a) Classes
b) Pointers
c) Interfaces
d) Exception Handling
Answer: b) Pointers

8. In Java, the destructor concept is replaced by _____.
a) finalize() method
b) Garbage Collector
c) Both a and b
d) None of the above
Answer: c) Both a and b

9. Java uses _____ for memory allocation.
a) malloc
b) calloc
c) new
d) memalloc
Answer: c) new

10. Which operator is supported in C++ but not in Java?
a) +
b) &
c) ->
d) >>>
Answer: c) ->

1.3 Compiling and Executing a Java Program

11. What is the default entry point for a Java program?
a) main()
b) Main()
c) main() inside a class
d) public main()
Answer: c) main() inside a class

12. What is the file extension for a compiled Java program?
a) .java
b) .class
c) .exe
d) .bin
Answer: b) .class

13. Which of the following commands compiles a Java program?
    a) java
    b) javac
    c) compile-java
    d) jvm
    Answer: b) javac
14. The output of the compilation of a Java program is stored as _____.
    a) Source code
    b) Executable file
    c) Bytecode
    d) Object file
    Answer: c) Bytecode
15. What tool is used to execute a compiled Java program?
    a) JDK
    b) JVM
    c) javac
    d) jre
    Answer: b) JVM

1.4 Variables, Constants, Keywords, and Data Types

16. Which keyword is used to define a constant variable in Java?
    a) static
    b) final
    c) const
    d) immutable
    Answer: b) final
17. What is the default value of a boolean variable in Java?
    a) true
    b) false
    c) 0
    d) null
    Answer: b) false
18. Which of the following is not a primitive data type in Java?
    a) int
    b) byte
    c) string
    d) char
    Answer: c) string
19. What is the range of byte data type in Java?
    a) -128 to 127
    b) -256 to 255
    c) -32768 to 32767

d) -2147483648 to 2147483647
Answer: a) -128 to 127
20. A variable declared as `final` in Java is _____.
   a) Unchangeable
   b) Mutable
   c) Dynamic
   d) None of the above
   Answer: a) Unchangeable

1.5 Operators: Arithmetic, Logical, and Bitwise

21. Which of the following is a logical operator in Java?
   a) &
   b) &&
   c) ||
   d) Both b and c
   Answer: d) Both b and c
22. What is the result of the expression `10 % 3`?
   a) 1
   b) 3
   c) 10
   d) 0
   Answer: a) 1
23. Which of the following operators is used for bitwise XOR in Java?
   a) ^
   b) &
   c) |
   d) ~
   Answer: a) ^
24. What will be the result of `true || false && true`?
   a) true
   b) false
   c) Error
   d) None of the above
   Answer: a) true
25. Which operator is used to perform division in Java?
   a) /
   b) %
   c) div
   d) None of the above
   Answer: a) /

1.6 Expressions and Comments

26. What is the correct syntax for a single-line comment in Java?
    a) /* */
    b) //
    c) #
    d) $
    Answer: b) //

27. Which of the following is not a valid expression in Java?
    a) 2 + 3
    b) a = b = c = 5;
    c) System.out.println("Hello");
    d) None of the above
    Answer: d) None of the above

1.6 Expressions and Comments

28. Which of the following can contain both multiline and single-line comments in Java?
    a) // and /* /
    b) // and #
    c) // and ###
    d) None of the above
    Answer: a) // and //*

29. What will `System.out.println(2 + "3" + 4);` output?
    a) 234
    b) 9
    c) 23
    d) 7
    Answer: a) 234

1.7 Basic Program Output

30. Which of the following methods is used to print output in Java?
    a) print()
    b) printf()
    c) println()
    d) All of the above
    Answer: d) All of the above

31. What does the `println` method do after printing the output?
    a) Ends the program
    b) Moves to the next line
    c) Stays on the same line
    d) Throws an exception
    Answer: b) Moves to the next line

32. Which of the following is the correct syntax to print "Hello World" in Java?
    a) System.out.println("Hello World");
    b) Print("Hello World");
    c) echo("Hello World");
    d) cout << "Hello World";
    Answer: a) System.out.println("Hello World");

33. What is the result of the following code?

```
System.out.print("Hello ");
System.out.println("World!");
```

    a) Hello World! on the same line
    b) Hello on one line and World! on the next line
    c) Syntax Error
    d) Compilation Error
    Answer: a) Hello World! on the same line

1.8 Decision-Making Constructs: Conditional Statements and Loops

34. Which of these is not a decision-making construct in Java?
    a) if-else
    b) switch
    c) for
    d) while
    Answer: d) while

35. What will the following code output?

```
if (true)
    System.out.println("Hello");
else
    System.out.println("World");
```

    a) Hello
    b) World
    c) Compilation Error
    d) Runtime Error
    Answer: a) Hello

36. What is the correct syntax for a switch statement in Java?
    a) switch(expression) { case value: statements; break; }
    b) switch { case expression: statements; break; }
    c) case switch(expression) { statements; break; }
    d) None of the above
    Answer: a) switch(expression) { case value: statements; break; }

37. How many times will the following loop execute?

```
for (int i = 0; i < 5; i++) {
    System.out.println(i);
}
```

a) 4
b) 5
c) 6
d) Infinite
Answer: b) 5

38. What will the following code snippet do?

```
int x = 5;
while (x < 10) {
    System.out.println(x);
}
```

a) Print numbers from 5 to 9
b) Print 5 infinitely
c) Compilation Error
d) None of the above
Answer: b) Print 5 infinitely

1.9 Nesting of Loops

39. How many times will the inner loop execute in the following code?

```
for (int i = 0; i < 3; i++) {
    for (int j = 0; j < 2; j++) {
        System.out.println(i + " " + j);
    }
}
```

a) 2
b) 3
c) 6
d) 5
Answer: c) 6

40. Which of the following is true about nested loops?
a) They cannot have different loop types (e.g., for and while).
b) The inner loop executes completely for every iteration of the outer loop.
c) Nesting is not allowed in Java.
d) None of the above.
Answer: b) The inner loop executes completely for every iteration of the outer loop.

1.10 Java Methods: Defining, Scope, Passing, and Returning Arguments

41. What is the default return type of a method in Java if not specified?
    a) int
    b) void
    c) None
    d) String
    Answer: b) void

42. Which of these is the correct syntax to define a method in Java?
    a) public void myMethod() {}
    b) public myMethod() {}
    c) void myMethod{}
    d) None of the above
    Answer: a) public void myMethod() {}

43. Which keyword is used to pass arguments by reference in Java?
    a) ref
    b) pointer
    c) Java does not support passing by reference
    d) deref
    Answer: c) Java does not support passing by reference

1.11 Type Conversion and Type Checking

44. Which of the following is an example of implicit type conversion?
    a) int to float
    b) float to int
    c) String to int
    d) None of the above
    Answer: a) int to float

45. Which keyword is used to check the type of an object in Java?
    a) typeOf
    b) instanceof
    c) isType
    d) checkType
    Answer: b) instanceof

1.12 Built-in Java Class Methods

46. Which class is used to work with mathematical operations in Java?
    a) Math
    b) Arithmetic
    c) Operations
    d) Utils
    Answer: a) Math

47. Which method is used to convert a string to an integer in Java?
    a) parseInt()
    b) toInt()
    c) valueOf()
    d) convertToInt()
    Answer: a) parseInt()

48. What does `Math.sqrt(16)` return?
    a) 16
    b) 4
    c) 8
    d) 2
    Answer: b) 4

49. What is the output of `Math.pow(2, 3)`?
    a) 6
    b) 8
    c) 9
    d) 12
    Answer: b) 8

50. Which method is used to find the length of a string in Java?
    a) length()
    b) size()
    c) count()
    d) measure()
    Answer: a) length()

CHAPTER 2: ARRAYS, STRINGS, AND I/O

2.1 Arrays, Strings, and I/O

2.1 Creating and Using Arrays: One-Dimensional and Multi-Dimensional

- **Definition of Arrays**: Memory allocation for one-dimensional and multi-dimensional arrays.
- **Declaring and Initializing Arrays**: Syntax and initialization (static and dynamic).
- Example: `int[] arr = {1, 2, 3};` (1D), `int[][] matrix = new int[3][3];` (2D).
- **Accessing and Modifying Array Elements**: Indexing, iterating with loops.
- **Multi-Dimensional Arrays**: Representation as tables or matrices.
- Example: Manipulating 2D arrays using nested loops.
- **Enhanced `for` Loop with Arrays**: Simplified iteration.
- **Common Array Operations**: Finding length, sorting, searching, etc.

2.1 Creating and Using Arrays: One-Dimensional and Multi-Dimensional

Arrays in Java are fundamental data structures that allow you to store multiple values of the same type in a single variable. Arrays can be **one-dimensional** (1D) or **multi-dimensional** (2D, 3D, etc.), and they are commonly used to handle large amounts of data efficiently. In this section, we'll explore how to declare, initialize, and manipulate both **one-dimensional** and **multi-dimensional arrays**, along with common array operations.

---

1. Definition of Arrays: Memory Allocation for One-Dimensional and Multi-Dimensional Arrays

An array is a container object that holds a fixed number of values of a single type. Arrays in Java are indexed, meaning each element is accessed using an index starting from 0.

- **One-dimensional array**: This is a simple list of elements.
- **Multi-dimensional array**: These arrays consist of multiple arrays within an array, typically represented as rows and columns, or matrices.

Memory Allocation:

- **One-dimensional arrays**: When you create a 1D array, the memory is allocated in a contiguous block.
- **Multi-dimensional arrays**: Java represents multi-dimensional arrays as arrays of arrays. The outer array holds references to the inner arrays, and memory is allocated for each inner array separately.

Example:

```
int[] arr = new int[5];   // 1D array of size 5
int[][] matrix = new int[3][3];   // 2D array (matrix) with 3 rows and 3
columns
```

For the **1D array**, memory is allocated as a single block for the 5 elements. In the **2D array**, memory is allocated for the outer array (3 rows), and each row (inner array) gets its own memory allocation.

2. Declaring and Initializing Arrays: Syntax and Initialization (Static and Dynamic)

- **Declaration**: You declare an array in Java by specifying the type of the array, followed by square brackets, and the array variable name.

Syntax:

```
type[] arrayName;   // Declaring an array
```

- **Initialization**: There are two main ways to initialize arrays:
o **Static initialization**: You define the values directly at the time of array creation.
o **Dynamic initialization**: You create an array and later assign values to its elements.

Static Initialization (1D and 2D):

```
// One-dimensional array
int[] arr = {1, 2, 3, 4, 5};

// Two-dimensional array (2x3 matrix)
int[][] matrix = {{1, 2, 3}, {4, 5, 6}};
```

Dynamic Initialization (1D and 2D):

```
// One-dimensional array
int[] arr = new int[5];   // Array of 5 integers
arr[0] = 10;              // Assigning values to elements
arr[1] = 20;

// Two-dimensional array
int[][] matrix = new int[3][3];   // 3x3 matrix
matrix[0][0] = 1;                 // Assigning value to element
```

For **dynamic initialization**, the size of the array is specified, but the elements are initially set to the default value for their type (0 for numeric types, `null` for objects).

3. Accessing and Modifying Array Elements: Indexing, Iterating with Loops

- **Indexing**: You access array elements using the index. The index starts at 0 for the first element, 1 for the second element, and so on.

Example (Accessing and Modifying Elements):

```
int[] arr = {1, 2, 3, 4, 5};
System.out.println(arr[0]);  // Output: 1 (Access first element)
arr[2] = 10;  // Modifying third element
System.out.println(arr[2]);  // Output: 10 (Modified element)
```

- **Using Loops**: Arrays are often iterated using loops like for, while, and enhanced for loops.

Example (Iterating with a standard for loop):

```
for (int i = 0; i < arr.length; i++) {
    System.out.println(arr[i]);  // Prints each element of the array
}
```

For **multi-dimensional arrays**, nested loops are typically used to access or modify elements.

Example (Iterating through a 2D array):

```
int[][] matrix = {{1, 2}, {3, 4}};
for (int i = 0; i < matrix.length; i++) {
    for (int j = 0; j < matrix[i].length; j++) {
        System.out.println(matrix[i][j]);  // Accessing element at row i,
column j
    }}
```

4. Multi-Dimensional Arrays: Representation as Tables or Matrices

A **multi-dimensional array** is an array of arrays. In a 2D array, you can think of the array as a **matrix** or a **table** with rows and columns. Java allows you to create arrays with more than two dimensions, such as 3D arrays.

Example (2D Array):

```
int[][] matrix = new int[3][3];   // 3x3 matrix
```

```
matrix[0][0] = 1;
matrix[0][1] = 2;
matrix[0][2] = 3;
// The matrix is:
// 1 2 3  // 0 0 0  // 0 0 0
```

In this example, we have a **3x3 matrix**. You can visualize it as having 3 rows and 3 columns.

5. Enhanced for Loop with Arrays: Simplified Iteration

The **enhanced for loop** (also known as the **for-each loop**) is a simplified version of the `for` loop, specifically designed for iterating through arrays. It is especially useful for **read-only** iteration, where you don't need to modify the array elements.

Syntax:

```
for (type var : array) {
    // Use var to access each element
}
```

Example (Using enhanced for loop):

```
int[] arr = {1, 2, 3, 4, 5};
for (int num : arr) {
    System.out.println(num);  // Prints each element in the array
}
```

The **enhanced for loop** makes code simpler and easier to read, especially when you only need to access the elements of the array.

6. Common Array Operations: Finding Length, Sorting, Searching, etc.

- **Finding Length**: The `length` property of an array returns the number of elements in the array.

```
int[] arr = {1, 2, 3, 4, 5};
System.out.println(arr.length);  // Output: 5 (length of the array)
```

- **Sorting**: Java provides the `Arrays.sort()` method to sort arrays.

```
int[] arr = {5, 2, 8, 1};
Arrays.sort(arr);  // Sorts the array in ascending order
System.out.println(Arrays.toString(arr));  // Output: [1, 2, 5, 8]
```

- **Searching**: You can use `Arrays.binarySearch()` to search for an element in a sorted array.

```
int[] arr = {1, 2, 5, 8};
int index = Arrays.binarySearch(arr, 5);  // Returns index of 5 (2)
System.out.println(index);
```

- **Other Operations**:
  - ○ **Array Copying**: `Arrays.copyOf()`, `System.arraycopy()`
  - ○ **Array Equality**: `Arrays.equals()`
  - ○ **Filling Arrays**: `Arrays.fill()`

Summary

- **One-dimensional arrays** are simple lists of elements, and **multi-dimensional arrays** represent tables or matrices.
- Arrays can be **statically initialized** (using `{ }`) or **dynamically initialized** (using `new` keyword).
- **Indexing** is used to access array elements, and loops (including the enhanced for loop) are used for iterating.
- **Multi-dimensional arrays** are useful for representing matrices and are accessed using nested loops.
- Common operations include **finding length**, **sorting**, and **searching** arrays.

Example 1: One-Dimensional Array – Declaration, Initialization, and Access

Problem: Declare a one-dimensional array, initialize it, and access its elements.

```java
public class OneDimensionalArray {
    public static void main(String[] args) {
        // Static Initialization
        int[] arr = {10, 20, 30, 40, 50};

        // Accessing and modifying elements
        System.out.println("Original element at index 2: " + arr[2]);
        arr[2] = 35; // Modify the element
        System.out.println("Modified element at index 2: " + arr[2]);

        // Iterating over the array
        System.out.println("Array Elements:");
        for (int i = 0; i < arr.length; i++) {
            System.out.print(arr[i] + " ");
        }
    }
}
```

Output:

```
Original element at index 2: 30
Modified element at index 2: 35
Array Elements:
10 20 35 40 50
```

Example 2: Multi-Dimensional Array – Representation as a Matrix

Problem: Declare and initialize a two-dimensional array to represent a matrix, then print the matrix.

```java
public class TwoDimensionalArray {
    public static void main(String[] args) {
        // Static initialization
        int[][] matrix = {
            {1, 2, 3},
            {4, 5, 6},
            {7, 8, 9}
        };

        System.out.println("Matrix Representation:");
        for (int i = 0; i < matrix.length; i++) {
            for (int j = 0; j < matrix[i].length; j++) {
                System.out.print(matrix[i][j] + " ");
            }
            System.out.println();
        }
    }
}
```

Output:

```
Matrix Representation:
1 2 3
4 5 6
7 8 9
```

Example 3: Finding Maximum Element in a 1D Array

Problem: Use a one-dimensional array to find the maximum element.

```java
public class ArrayMax {
    public static void main(String[] args) {
        int[] arr = {15, 42, 7, 89, 23};
        int max = arr[0];

        for (int i = 1; i < arr.length; i++) {
            if (arr[i] > max) {
                max = arr[i];
            }        }

        System.out.println("Maximum Element: " + max);
    }}
```

Output:

```
Maximum Element: 89
```

Example 4: Enhanced for Loop with Arrays

Problem: Use an enhanced for loop to iterate over a one-dimensional array and calculate the sum of its elements.

```java
public class EnhancedForLoop {
    public static void main(String[] args) {
        int[] arr = {5, 10, 15, 20, 25};
        int sum = 0;

        for (int num : arr) {
            sum += num;
        }

        System.out.println("Sum of Array Elements: " + sum);
    }
}
```

Output:

```
Sum of Array Elements: 75
```

Example 5: Manipulating a Multi-Dimensional Array

Problem: Create a 3x3 matrix, initialize it dynamically, and calculate the sum of all elements.

```java
public class MatrixSum {
    public static void main(String[] args) {
        int[][] matrix = new int[3][3];
        int value = 1, sum = 0;

        // Dynamically initializing the matrix
        for (int i = 0; i < matrix.length; i++) {
            for (int j = 0; j < matrix[i].length; j++) {
                matrix[i][j] = value++;
                sum += matrix[i][j];
            }
        }

        // Printing the matrix
        System.out.println("Matrix:");
        for (int i = 0; i < matrix.length; i++) {
            for (int j = 0; j < matrix[i].length; j++) {
                System.out.print(matrix[i][j] + " ");
            }
```

```
            System.out.println();
        }

        System.out.println("Sum of Matrix Elements: " + sum);
    }
}
```

Output:

```
Matrix:
1 2 3
4 5 6
7 8 9
Sum of Matrix Elements: 45
```

2.2 Referencing Arrays Dynamically

- **Dynamic Array Allocation**: Allocating arrays at runtime using `new`.
- **Changing Array Size**: Workarounds for resizing (using `Arrays.copyOf`).
- **Ragged Arrays**: Multi-dimensional arrays with varying row lengths.
- Example: `int[][] ragged = new int[3][];`
- **Memory Efficiency**: Advantages of dynamic referencing over fixed-size arrays.

2.2 Referencing Arrays Dynamically

In Java, arrays are fixed in size once created, meaning the size of an array cannot be changed after it is allocated. However, there are techniques and workarounds that allow for more flexible, dynamic array management, such as allocating arrays at runtime, resizing arrays, and using ragged arrays. Let's explore these concepts in detail.

1. Dynamic Array Allocation: Allocating Arrays at Runtime Using `new`

Dynamic array allocation allows you to create arrays during program execution based on runtime conditions. This is particularly useful when the exact size of the array is not known beforehand.

Syntax:

```
type[] arrayName = new type[size];
```

Here, the size of the array is determined at runtime, allowing you to allocate memory dynamically for the array.

Example:

```
int size = 5;
int[] dynamicArray = new int[size];  // Array of integers with size 5,
allocated at runtime
```

In this example, the size of the array is determined during execution (e.g., based on user input or program logic). The new keyword dynamically allocates memory for the array.

You can also dynamically allocate arrays of different data types, including multi-dimensional arrays:

```
String[] stringArray = new String[10];  // Array of 10 strings, allocated
dynamically
```

2. Changing Array Size: Workarounds for Resizing Arrays (Using `Arrays.copyOf`)

Once an array is created in Java, its size is fixed and cannot be changed. However, if you need to resize an array, you can use a workaround by creating a new array and copying the elements of the original array into it. Java provides a built-in utility, Arrays.copyOf(), to simplify this process.

`Arrays.copyOf()` Method:

The Arrays.copyOf() method creates a new array, copies the contents of the original array, and resizes it according to the specified new size.

Syntax:

```
T[] newArray = Arrays.copyOf(originalArray, newSize);
```

- originalArray: The array whose contents you want to copy.
- newSize: The new size of the array.

Example:

```
int[] arr = {1, 2, 3};
int[] newArr = Arrays.copyOf(arr, 5);  // Resizing the array to size 5

System.out.println(Arrays.toString(newArr));  // Output: [1, 2, 3, 0, 0]
```

In this example:

- The original array arr has 3 elements.
- Arrays.copyOf() creates a new array newArr with a size of 5, and the original elements are copied over.

- The new array is filled with the default value 0 (for integer arrays) for the remaining spaces.

This method is efficient for resizing arrays when you don't know the final size in advance.

---

3. Ragged Arrays: Multi-Dimensional Arrays with Varying Row Lengths

A **ragged array** (also called a **jagged array**) is a multi-dimensional array where the length of each row can vary. Unlike regular multi-dimensional arrays where all rows have the same length, a ragged array allows each row to have a different number of elements.

Declaration:

A ragged array is declared similarly to a 2D array, but the second dimension is left undefined, allowing each row to have a different length.

Syntax:

```
type[][] raggedArray = new type[rows][];
```

- `rows`: The number of rows in the array.
- The second dimension is unspecified, allowing different row sizes.

Example:

```
int[][] ragged = new int[3][];  // Declare a ragged array with 3 rows

ragged[0] = new int[2];  // First row has 2 elements
ragged[1] = new int[3];  // Second row has 3 elements
ragged[2] = new int[1];  // Third row has 1 element

// Initialize the elements
ragged[0][0] = 1;
ragged[0][1] = 2;
ragged[1][0] = 3;
ragged[1][1] = 4;
ragged[1][2] = 5;
ragged[2][0] = 6;

System.out.println(Arrays.deepToString(ragged));  // Output: [[1, 2], [3, 4, 5], [6]]
```

In this example:

- The ragged array `ragged` has 3 rows.
- Each row can be initialized to a different size.
- The array can represent a table or matrix where each row has a different number of columns.

Ragged arrays are useful when dealing with data where rows have a variable number of elements, such as storing lists of varying lengths.

---

4. Memory Efficiency: Advantages of Dynamic Referencing Over Fixed-Size Arrays

Dynamic referencing, where arrays are allocated at runtime, offers several advantages over using fixed-size arrays. These advantages help optimize memory usage and program flexibility.

Advantages:

1. **Memory Efficiency**:
   - Fixed-size arrays allocate a predefined block of memory, which might lead to unused memory space if the array is larger than necessary.
   - Dynamic arrays allow memory to be allocated only when needed, potentially saving memory, especially when the size of the data is uncertain.
2. **Flexibility**:
   - With dynamic arrays, the size can be adjusted as the program runs. You can resize arrays when the data size changes or is not known in advance.
   - For example, using `Arrays.copyOf()` allows for dynamic resizing of arrays.
3. **Handling Variable Data**:
   - With ragged arrays, you can handle data where the rows have different lengths. This allows for more efficient use of memory when dealing with irregular data structures.
4. **Adaptability**:
   - Dynamic referencing allows for greater adaptability in situations where the array size needs to change as the program executes, especially when data grows or shrinks unpredictably.

Example:

Consider a scenario where you're reading a list of names from an external file or input. The number of names might not be known initially, so allocating a fixed-size array might be inefficient. Instead, you can dynamically allocate memory and resize the array as needed.

Summary

- **Dynamic Array Allocation**: Java allows arrays to be allocated dynamically at runtime using the `new` keyword, which provides flexibility when the array size is not known in advance.
- **Resizing Arrays**: Since array size in Java is fixed after creation, resizing is typically done by creating a new array and copying the contents of the old array using `Arrays.copyOf()`.
- **Ragged Arrays**: Multi-dimensional arrays in Java can have rows of different lengths, known as ragged arrays. These are useful for representing data with variable row sizes.

- **Memory Efficiency**: Dynamic referencing and resizing arrays at runtime offer advantages over fixed-size arrays, including better memory utilization and more flexibility in handling dynamic data sizes.

2.3 The Java String Class and String Objects

- **String Declaration and Initialization**: `String str = "Hello";` vs `String str = new String("Hello");`.
- **String Pool Concept**: Memory management for immutable strings.
- **Common Methods in the `string` Class**:
o `length()`, `charAt()`, `substring()`, `indexOf()`, `replace()`.
- **String Concatenation**: Using + operator and `concat()` method.

2.3 The Java String Class and String Objects

In Java, strings are objects that represent sequences of characters. The `String` class is one of the most commonly used classes in Java, as it provides essential functionality for string manipulation. Let's dive into some important aspects of the `String` class, including string declaration, memory management, common methods, and string concatenation.

1. String Declaration and Initialization:

In Java, strings can be declared and initialized in two ways: using the string literal syntax or using the `new` keyword.

1.1 String Literal Declaration:

```
String str = "Hello";
```

- **Explanation**: In this case, `"Hello"` is a string literal. When you use a string literal, Java looks for this string in the **String Pool** (a special area of memory where string literals are stored). If the string already exists in the pool, it simply references the existing object. If it doesn't exist, a new string object is created and added to the pool.

1.2 Using the `new` Keyword:

```
String str = new String("Hello");
```

- **Explanation**: Here, the string `"Hello"` is created in the heap memory, rather than being stored in the String Pool. This means that a new string object is created every time this statement is executed, even if the same string already exists in the pool. This approach is less memory efficient than using string literals because it bypasses the string pool.

String Pool Concept:

- **String Pool**: The **String Pool** is a special memory area in Java that stores all string literals. When you use a string literal (e.g., `"Hello"`), Java checks if the string already exists in the pool. If it does, Java simply reuses the reference, reducing memory usage. If the string does not exist, it is added to the pool.
- **Memory Management**: The String class in Java is immutable, meaning once a string object is created, its value cannot be changed. When you modify a string, a new object is created instead of modifying the existing one. This is one of the reasons why string literals are used in Java, as it ensures that memory is efficiently managed and that the same string values can be reused without creating new objects.

2. Common Methods in the String Class:

Java provides many built-in methods in the `String` class to manipulate and work with strings. Here are some of the most commonly used ones:

2.1 `length()`:

- **Description**: Returns the number of characters present in the string.
- **Syntax**:

```
int len = str.length();
```

- **Example**:

```
String str = "Hello";
int len = str.length();  // len will be 5
```

2.2 `charAt()`:

- **Description**: Returns the character at the specified index in the string.
- **Syntax**:

```
char ch = str.charAt(index);
```

- **Example**:

```
String str = "Hello";
char ch = str.charAt(1);  // ch will be 'e'
```

2.3 `substring()`:

- **Description**: Returns a new string that is a substring of the original string, starting from the specified index (or from a range of indices).
- **Syntax**:

```
String subStr = str.substring(startIndex);
String subStr = str.substring(startIndex, endIndex);
```

- **Example**:

```
String str = "Hello, World!";
String subStr = str.substring(7);   // subStr will be "World!"
String subStr2 = str.substring(0, 5);   // subStr2 will be "Hello"
```

2.4 `indexOf()`:

- **Description**: Returns the index of the first occurrence of a specified character or substring.
- **Syntax**:

```
int index = str.indexOf("substring");
int index = str.indexOf(char);
```

- **Example**:

```
String str = "Hello, World!";
int index = str.indexOf("World");   // index will be 7
```

2.5 `replace()`:

- **Description**: Replaces all occurrences of a specified character or substring with another character or substring.
- **Syntax**:

```
String newStr = str.replace(oldChar, newChar);
String newStr = str.replace(oldSubstring, newSubstring);
```

- **Example**:

```
String str = "Hello, World!";
String newStr = str.replace("World", "Java");   // newStr will be "Hello, Java!"
```

3. String Concatenation: Using + Operator and `concat()` Method:

String concatenation is the process of joining two or more strings together. Java provides two main ways to concatenate strings: using the + operator and the `concat()` method.

3.1 Using the + Operator:

- **Description**: The + operator is the simplest way to concatenate strings in Java. It combines two or more strings into a single string.
- **Syntax**:

```
String result = str1 + str2;
```

- **Example**:

```
String str1 = "Hello";
String str2 = " World";
String result = str1 + str2;   // result will be "Hello World"
```

3.2 Using `concat()` Method:

- **Description**: The `concat()` method is another way to concatenate two strings. It appends the specified string to the end of the original string.
- **Syntax**:

```
String result = str1.concat(str2);
```

- **Example**:

```
String str1 = "Hello";
String str2 = " World";
String result = str1.concat(str2);   // result will be "Hello World"
```

Performance Note:

While both the + operator and the `concat()` method are commonly used for string concatenation, the + operator can be less efficient in loops due to the creation of intermediate string objects. The `concat()` method can be slightly more efficient for single concatenations. However, for concatenating multiple strings, using a `StringBuilder` or `StringBuffer` is recommended to improve performance.

Summary:

1. **String Declaration and Initialization**:
   o Use string literals (`"Hello"`) for memory efficiency and reuse via the string pool.

o   Use the `new` keyword (`new String("Hello")`) when you need a new string object each time, but this is less efficient.

2. **String Pool Concept**:
o   Strings in Java are managed in a special memory area called the **String Pool**. Using string literals helps save memory by reusing existing string objects.

3. **Common Methods in the String Class**:
o   Methods like `length()`, `charAt()`, `substring()`, `indexOf()`, and `replace()` are fundamental for string manipulation.

4. **String Concatenation**:
o   Strings can be concatenated using the + operator or the `concat()` method. For better performance when concatenating in loops, consider using `StringBuilder`.

1. String Declaration and Initialization

- **String Literal Initialization**:
o   Syntax: `String str = "Hello";`
o   This method directly creates a string in the **String Pool**, saving memory as identical literals share the same reference.
- **String Object Initialization**:
o   Syntax: `String str = new String("Hello");`
o   Creates a new string object in the heap memory even if an identical string exists in the **String Pool**.
- **Difference**:
o   String literal: Optimized memory usage.
o   String object: Creates a new memory allocation.

2. String Pool Concept

- **Definition**:
o   A special area in the heap memory where Java stores **immutable strings** for reusability.
o   Example:

```
String s1 = "Hello";
String s2 = "Hello";
String s3 = new String("Hello");
```

- `s1 == s2` (true, both refer to the same string in the pool).
- `s1 == s3` (false, different memory locations).
- **Advantages**:
o   Reduces memory usage.

o Enhances performance.

---

3. Common Methods in the String Class

1. `length()`:
o Returns the length of the string.
o Example: `"Hello".length()` returns `5`.
2. `charAt(int index)`:
o Retrieves the character at a specific index.
o Example: `"Hello".charAt(1)` returns `'e'`.
3. `substring(int start, int end)`:
o Extracts a portion of the string from `start` to `end-1`.
o Example: `"HelloWorld".substring(0, 5)` returns `"Hello"`.
4. `indexOf(String str)`:
o Finds the first occurrence of a substring.
o Example: `"HelloWorld".indexOf("World")` returns `5`.
5. `replace(char oldChar, char newChar)`:
o Replaces all occurrences of a character.
o Example: `"banana".replace('a', 'o')` returns `"bonono"`.

---

4. String Concatenation

1. **Using the + Operator**:
o Combines two strings.
o Example:

```
String s1 = "Hello";
String s2 = "World";
String result = s1 + " " + s2; // Output: "Hello World"
```

2. **Using the `concat()` Method**:
o Concatenates two strings.
o Example:

```
String s1 = "Hello";
String s2 = "World";
String result = s1.concat(" ").concat(s2); // Output: "Hello World"
```

Practical Examples with Solutions

Example 1: String Declaration and Initialization

```java
public class StringInitialization {
    public static void main(String[] args) {
        String str1 = "Hello"; // Literal
        String str2 = new String("Hello"); // Object

        System.out.println("Literal String: " + str1);
        System.out.println("Object String: " + str2);
        System.out.println("Comparing References: " + (str1 == str2)); //
false
        System.out.println("Comparing Values: " + str1.equals(str2)); //
true
    }
}
```

Output:

```
Literal String: Hello
Object String: Hello
Comparing References: false
Comparing Values: true
```

Example 2: Demonstrating String Pool Concept

```java
public class StringPoolDemo {
    public static void main(String[] args) {
        String s1 = "Java";
        String s2 = "Java";
        String s3 = new String("Java");
        System.out.println("s1 == s2: " + (s1 == s2)); // true
        System.out.println("s1 == s3: " + (s1 == s3)); // false
        System.out.println("s1 equals s3: " + s1.equals(s3)); // true
    }}
```

Output:

```
s1 == s2: true
s1 == s3: false
s1 equals s3: true
```

Example 3: Using Common String Methods

```java
public class StringMethodsDemo {
    public static void main(String[] args) {
        String str = "Programming";

        System.out.println("Length: " + str.length()); // 11
        System.out.println("Character at index 3: " + str.charAt(3)); // g
        System.out.println("Substring (0, 6): " + str.substring(0, 6)); //
Progra
```

```
        System.out.println("Index of 'gram': " + str.indexOf("gram")); //
3
        System.out.println("Replacing 'm' with 'n': " + str.replace('m',
'n')); // Progranming
    }
}
```

Output:

```
Length: 11
Character at index 3: g
Substring (0, 6): Progra
Index of 'gram': 3
Replacing 'm' with 'n': Progranming
```

Example 4: Concatenating Strings

```
public class StringConcatenation {
    public static void main(String[] args) {
        String str1 = "Hello";
        String str2 = "World";

        // Using +
        String result1 = str1 + " " + str2;
        System.out.println("Using +: " + result1); // Hello World

        // Using concat()
        String result2 = str1.concat(" ").concat(str2);
        System.out.println("Using concat(): " + result2); // Hello World
    }
}
```

Output:

```
Using +: Hello World
Using concat(): Hello World
```

Example 5: Combining String Methods

```
public class CombinedStringMethods {
    public static void main(String[] args) {
        String str = "  Welcome to Java Programming!  ";

        String trimmedStr = str.trim(); // Remove leading/trailing spaces
        System.out.println("Trimmed: " + trimmedStr);

        String upperCaseStr = trimmedStr.toUpperCase(); // Convert to
uppercase
        System.out.println("Uppercase: " + upperCaseStr);

        String replacedStr = upperCaseStr.replace("JAVA", "KOTLIN"); //
Replace substring
```

```
        System.out.println("Replaced: " + replacedStr);
    }
}
```

Output:

```
Trimmed: Welcome to Java Programming!
Uppercase: WELCOME TO JAVA PROGRAMMING!
Replaced: WELCOME TO KOTLIN PROGRAMMING!
```

2.4 Manipulating Strings: Immutability and Equality

- **Immutability of Strings**: Why strings cannot be modified directly.
o Example: Assigning new values creates a new object.
- **String Comparisons**:
o `==` vs `equals()` vs `compareTo()` for equality.
o Examples showcasing case-sensitive and case-insensitive comparison.
- **String Operations**: Splitting, joining, and trimming strings.

1. Immutability of Strings

- **Definition**:
o Strings in Java are **immutable**, meaning their content cannot be changed once created.
o Any operation that seems to modify a string actually creates a **new string object**.
- **Why Strings are Immutable**:
o Security: Used in sensitive areas like keys and URLs.
o Performance: Enables **String Pool** for efficient memory management.
- **Example of Immutability**:

```
String str = "Hello";
str.concat(" World"); // Creates a new string "Hello World" but doesn't
modify `str`
System.out.println(str); // Output: Hello
```

2. String Comparisons

1. **Using ==**:
o Compares references, not content.
o Example:

```
String s1 = "Hello";
String s2 = "Hello";
System.out.println(s1 == s2); // true (same reference in string pool)
```

2. **Using `equals()`**:
o Compares content of strings.

o   Example:

```
String s1 = new String("Hello");
String s2 = new String("Hello");
System.out.println(s1.equals(s2)); // true (compares content)
```

3. **Using `compareTo()`:**
o   Returns:
▪   0 if strings are equal.
▪   Negative if the first string is lexicographically smaller.
▪   Positive if the first string is larger.
o   Example:

```
String s1 = "Apple";
String s2 = "Banana";
System.out.println(s1.compareTo(s2)); // Negative (A < B)
```

3. String Operations

1. **Splitting Strings**:
o   Splits a string into substrings using a delimiter.
o   Example:

```
String str = "apple,banana,orange";
String[] fruits = str.split(",");
```

2. **Joining Strings**:
o   Combines an array of strings into one string with a delimiter.
o   Example:

```
String[] words = {"Hello", "World"};
String sentence = String.join(" ", words);
```

3. **Trimming Strings**:
o   Removes leading and trailing whitespace.
o   Example:

```
String str = "   Hello   ";
String trimmedStr = str.trim(); // "Hello"
```

Practical Examples with Solutions

Example 1: Demonstrating Immutability

```java
public class StringImmutability {
    public static void main(String[] args) {
        String original = "Immutable";
        String modified = original.concat(" String");

        System.out.println("Original: " + original); // Immutable
        System.out.println("Modified: " + modified); // Immutable String
    }
}
```

Output:

```
Original: Immutable
Modified: Immutable String
```

Example 2: String Comparisons

```java
public class StringComparison {
    public static void main(String[] args) {
        String str1 = "Java";
        String str2 = new String("Java");
        String str3 = "JAVA";

        System.out.println("Using ==: " + (str1 == str2)); // false
        System.out.println("Using equals(): " + str1.equals(str2)); //
true
        System.out.println("Using equalsIgnoreCase(): " +
str1.equalsIgnoreCase(str3)); // true
        System.out.println("Using compareTo(): " + str1.compareTo(str3));
// positive (case-sensitive)
    }
}
```

Output:

```
Using ==: false
Using equals(): true
Using equalsIgnoreCase(): true
Using compareTo(): 32
```

Example 3: Splitting and Joining Strings

```java
public class StringSplitJoin {
    public static void main(String[] args) {
```

```
        String str = "Java,Python,C++";
        String[] languages = str.split(",");

        System.out.println("Languages:");
        for (String lang : languages) {
            System.out.println(lang);
        }

        String joined = String.join(" | ", languages);
        System.out.println("Joined String: " + joined);
    }
}
```

Output:

```
Languages:
Java
Python
C++
Joined String: Java | Python | C++
```

Example 4: Trimming Strings

```
public class StringTrimExample {
    public static void main(String[] args) {
        String str = "   Welcome to Java!   ";
        System.out.println("Before Trim: '" + str + "'");
        System.out.println("After Trim: '" + str.trim() + "'");
    }
}
```

Output:

```
Before Trim: '   Welcome to Java!   '
After Trim: 'Welcome to Java!'
```

Example 5: Combining Multiple Operations

```
public class StringOperations {
    public static void main(String[] args) {
        String str = "  Learn Java Programming  ";

        // Trim the string
        String trimmed = str.trim();

        // Convert to uppercase
        String upper = trimmed.toUpperCase();

        // Replace spaces with hyphens
```

```
        String replaced = upper.replace(" ", "-");

        // Get substring
        String substring = replaced.substring(6, 10);

        System.out.println("Original: " + str);
        System.out.println("Trimmed: " + trimmed);
        System.out.println("Uppercase: " + upper);
        System.out.println("Replaced: " + replaced);
        System.out.println("Substring: " + substring);
    }
}
```

Output:

```
Original:   Learn Java Programming
Trimmed: Learn Java Programming
Uppercase: LEARN JAVA PROGRAMMING
Replaced: LEARN-JAVA-PROGRAMMING
Substring: JAVA
```

2.5 Passing Strings to and from Methods

- **String as a Parameter**: Passing string references.
- Example: Reverse a string using a method.
- **Returning Strings from Methods**:
- Example: Returning substrings or manipulated strings.

2.6 String Buffer Classes

- **Introduction to `StringBuffer` and `StringBuilder`**: Mutable alternatives to `String`.
- **Common Methods**:
- `append()`, `insert()`, `delete()`, `reverse()`, `setLength()`.
- **Performance Comparison**: String vs `StringBuffer` vs `StringBuilder`.
- **Thread Safety**: `StringBuffer` is thread-safe, while `StringBuilder` is not.

1. Introduction to StringBuffer and StringBuilder

- **Definition**:
- `StringBuffer` and `StringBuilder` are **mutable** alternatives to the `String` class in Java, allowing modifications without creating new objects.
- **Key Differences**:
- `StringBuffer`: Thread-safe (synchronized), slightly slower.
- `StringBuilder`: Not thread-safe (unsynchronized), faster.
- **Syntax for Declaration**:

```
StringBuffer sb = new StringBuffer("Hello");
StringBuilder sbuilder = new StringBuilder("World");
```

2. Common Methods of StringBuffer/StringBuilder

1. `append()`:
- Adds a string or other data types to the existing object.
- Example:

```
sb.append(" World"); // Hello World
```

2. `insert()`:
- Inserts a string or value at a specified index.
- Example:

```
sb.insert(5, " Java"); // Hello Java
```

3. `delete()`:
- Removes characters within a specified range.
- Example:

```
sb.delete(5, 9); // Removes " Java"
```

4. `reverse()`:
- Reverses the character sequence.
- Example:

```
sb.reverse(); // "dlroW olleH"
```

5. `setLength()`:
- Sets the length of the string buffer. Truncates or pads with null characters as needed.
- Example:

```
sb.setLength(5); // Truncates to "Hello"
```

3. Performance Comparison: String vs StringBuffer vs StringBuilder

Class	Mutability	Thread Safety	Performance	Use Case
String	Immutable	Yes	Slow (new object creation)	Frequent reads, minimal writes
StringBuffer	Mutable	Yes	Moderate	Thread-safe operations
StringBuilder	Mutable	No	Fast	Single-threaded operations

4. Thread Safety

- `StringBuffer`:
- o Synchronized methods make it safe for multi-threaded environments.
- `StringBuilder`:
- o Non-synchronized, leading to faster execution in single-threaded applications.

Practical Examples with Solutions

Example 1: Using `append()` and `insert()`

```java
public class StringBufferExample {
    public static void main(String[] args) {
        StringBuffer sb = new StringBuffer("Hello");
        sb.append(" World");
        System.out.println("After append: " + sb);

        sb.insert(6, "Java ");
        System.out.println("After insert: " + sb);
    }
}
```

Output:

```
After append: Hello World
After insert: Hello Java World
```

Example 2: Using `delete()` and `reverse()`

```java
public class StringBufferDeleteReverse {
    public static void main(String[] args) {
        StringBuffer sb = new StringBuffer("Programming");
        sb.delete(3, 8); // Removes characters from index 3 to 7
        System.out.println("After delete: " + sb);

        sb.reverse(); // Reverses the string
        System.out.println("After reverse: " + sb);
    }
}
```

Output:

```
After delete: Prong
After reverse: gnorP
```

Example 3: Performance Comparison

```java
public class PerformanceTest {
    public static void main(String[] args) {
        long start, end;

        // String
        String str = "Hello";
        start = System.currentTimeMillis();
        for (int i = 0; i < 10000; i++) {
            str += " World";
        }
        end = System.currentTimeMillis();
        System.out.println("Time with String: " + (end - start) + "ms");

        // StringBuffer
        StringBuffer sb = new StringBuffer("Hello");
        start = System.currentTimeMillis();
        for (int i = 0; i < 10000; i++) {
            sb.append(" World");
        }
        end = System.currentTimeMillis();
        System.out.println("Time with StringBuffer: " + (end - start) +
"ms");

        // StringBuilder
        StringBuilder sbuilder = new StringBuilder("Hello");
        start = System.currentTimeMillis();
        for (int i = 0; i < 10000; i++) {
            sbuilder.append(" World");
        }
        end = System.currentTimeMillis();
        System.out.println("Time with StringBuilder: " + (end - start) +
"ms");
    }
}
```

Output (Approximate):

```
Time with String: 350ms
Time with StringBuffer: 10ms
Time with StringBuilder: 5ms
```

Example 4: Thread Safety with StringBuffer

```java
public class ThreadSafetyTest {
    public static void main(String[] args) {
        StringBuffer sb = new StringBuffer("ThreadSafe");

        Runnable task = () -> {
            for (int i = 0; i < 5; i++) {
                sb.append("!");
            }
```

```
                System.out.println(Thread.currentThread().getName() + ": " +
sb);
        };

        Thread t1 = new Thread(task);
        Thread t2 = new Thread(task);

        t1.start();
        t2.start();
    }
}
```

Output:

```
Thread-0: ThreadSafe!!!!! (output order may vary)
Thread-1: ThreadSafe!!!!!!!!!!
```

Example 5: Using `setLength()`

```
public class SetLengthExample {
    public static void main(String[] args) {
        StringBuffer sb = new StringBuffer("Hello World");

        sb.setLength(5); // Truncate to first 5 characters
        System.out.println("Truncated: " + sb);

        sb.setLength(10); // Expands length and fills with null characters
        System.out.println("Expanded: '" + sb + "'");
    }
}
```

2.7 Simple I/O: Using System.out and Scanner Class

- **Using `System.out` for Output**: Printing messages and variables.
- **Using `Scanner` Class for Input**:
o Methods like `nextInt()`, `nextLine()`, `nextDouble()`.
o Handling whitespace and newline characters.
- **Basic Input Validation**: Using conditions to validate user input.

1. Using System.out for Output

- **Definition**: The `System.out` object in Java is used to output data to the console. Methods like `print()`, `println()`, and `printf()` are available.
- **Methods**:
  - `print()`: Outputs data without adding a newline.
  - `println()`: Outputs data and adds a newline at the end.
  - `printf()`: Formats and prints data using placeholders.
- **Example Usage**:

```
System.out.print("Hello, ");
System.out.println("World!");
System.out.printf("The value of pi is approximately %.2f%n", 3.14159);
```

2. Using Scanner Class for Input

- **Definition**: The `Scanner` class is used for reading input from various sources like the console, files, or strings.
- **Common Methods**:
  - `nextInt()`: Reads an integer.
  - `nextDouble()`: Reads a double.
  - `nextLine()`: Reads a line of text.
  - `next()`: Reads a single word or token.
- **Handling Whitespace**:
  - Use `nextLine()` after `nextInt()` or `nextDouble()` to consume the newline character.
- **Example Usage**:

```
Scanner scanner = new Scanner(System.in);
System.out.print("Enter your name: ");
String name = scanner.nextLine();
System.out.print("Enter your age: ");
int age = scanner.nextInt();
System.out.println("Name: " + name + ", Age: " + age);
```

3. Basic Input Validation

- **Definition**: Input validation ensures that user input meets certain criteria before being processed.
- **Techniques**:
  - Using `if` statements or loops to validate input.
  - Catching exceptions using `try-catch` blocks for invalid data types.
- **Example Usage**:

```
Scanner scanner = new Scanner(System.in);
int age;
do {
```

```
        System.out.print("Enter a valid age (0-120): ");
        age = scanner.nextInt();
} while (age < 0 || age > 120);
System.out.println("Valid age entered: " + age);
```

Practical Examples with Solutions

Example 1: Using `System.out` for Formatted Output

```java
public class OutputExample {
    public static void main(String[] args) {
        int apples = 10;
        double price = 2.5;
        System.out.println("Welcome to the Fruit Store!");
        System.out.printf("You have %d apples, each costing $%.2f%n",
apples, price);
        System.out.println("Total cost: $" + (apples * price));
    }
}
```

Output:

```
Welcome to the Fruit Store!
You have 10 apples, each costing $2.50
Total cost: $25.0
```

Example 2: Using `Scanner` for Input

```java
import java.util.Scanner;

public class InputExample {
    public static void main(String[] args) {
        Scanner scanner = new Scanner(System.in);

        System.out.print("Enter your favorite number: ");
        int number = scanner.nextInt();

        System.out.print("Enter your favorite color: ");
        scanner.nextLine(); // Consume the leftover newline
        String color = scanner.nextLine();

        System.out.println("Your favorite number is " + number + " and
your favorite color is " + color + ".");
    }
}
```

Output:

```
Enter your favorite number: 7
Enter your favorite color: Blue
Your favorite number is 7 and your favorite color is Blue.
```

Example 3: Validating User Input

```java
import java.util.Scanner;

public class ValidationExample {
    public static void main(String[] args) {
        Scanner scanner = new Scanner(System.in);

        int age = -1;
        while (age < 0 || age > 120) {
            System.out.print("Enter a valid age (0-120): ");
            if (scanner.hasNextInt()) {
                age = scanner.nextInt();
                if (age < 0 || age > 120) {
                    System.out.println("Invalid age! Please try again.");
                }
            } else {
                System.out.println("Please enter a number.");
                scanner.next(); // Clear invalid input
            }
        }

        System.out.println("Thank you! Your age is: " + age);
    }
}
```

Output:

```
Enter a valid age (0-120): -5
Invalid age! Please try again.
Enter a valid age (0-120): 130
Invalid age! Please try again.
Enter a valid age (0-120): abc
Please enter a number.
Enter a valid age (0-120): 25
Thank you! Your age is: 25
```

2.8 Byte and Character Streams

- **Streams in Java**:
o Byte Streams (`InputStream` and `OutputStream`) for binary data.
o Character Streams (`Reader` and `Writer`) for text data.
- **Common Classes**:
o `FileInputStream, FileOutputStream, BufferedReader, BufferedWriter`.
- **Difference Between Byte and Character Streams**.

Streams in Java

Java provides two types of stream classes for handling input and output operations:

1. **Byte Streams**:
o Used for handling **binary data** (e.g., images, audio files, etc.).
o They work with raw byte data and are part of the `java.io` package, inheriting from `InputStream` and `OutputStream`.
o Byte streams are suitable for reading and writing all kinds of I/O, especially when data isn't textual.
o **Classes**:
▪ `InputStream`: The superclass for reading byte data.
▪ `OutputStream`: The superclass for writing byte data.
2. **Character Streams**:
o Used for handling **text data** (i.e., characters).
o These streams read and write data in the form of characters rather than bytes, making them more efficient for handling character-based data (like text files).
o They are part of the `java.io` package, inheriting from `Reader` and `Writer`.
o **Classes**:
▪ `Reader`: The superclass for reading character data.
▪ `Writer`: The superclass for writing character data.

Common Classes

1. **FileInputStream and FileOutputStream**:
o **FileInputStream**: Used for reading bytes from a file.
o **FileOutputStream**: Used for writing bytes to a file.

Example of using `FileInputStream` and `FileOutputStream`:

```
import java.io.*;

public class ByteStreamExample {
    public static void main(String[] args) {
        try (FileInputStream fis = new FileInputStream("input.txt");
            FileOutputStream fos = new FileOutputStream("output.txt")) {

            int byteData;
            while ((byteData = fis.read()) != -1) {
                fos.write(byteData);
            }
            System.out.println("File copied successfully using byte
streams.");
        } catch (IOException e) {
            e.printStackTrace();
        }
    }
```

}

Explanation: The `FileInputStream` reads each byte from the file "input.txt", and the `FileOutputStream` writes those bytes to "output.txt". This is a simple file copy operation.

2. **BufferedReader and BufferedWriter**:
o **BufferedReader**: A class used for reading text from a file or other character stream, buffering the input for more efficient reading.
o **BufferedWriter**: A class used for writing text to a file or other character stream, buffering the output for more efficient writing.

Example of using `BufferedReader` and `BufferedWriter`:

```
import java.io.*;

public class CharStreamExample {
    public static void main(String[] args) {
        try (BufferedReader br = new BufferedReader(new
FileReader("input.txt"));
             BufferedWriter bw = new BufferedWriter(new
FileWriter("output.txt"))) {

                String line;
                while ((line = br.readLine()) != null) {
                    bw.write(line);
                    bw.newLine(); // To add a new line after each line
                }
                System.out.println("File copied successfully using character
streams.");
        } catch (IOException e) {
            e.printStackTrace();
        }
    }
}
```

Explanation: The `BufferedReader` reads the file "input.txt" line by line, and the `BufferedWriter` writes each line to "output.txt". This method is more efficient than using `FileReader` and `FileWriter` directly, especially for larger files.

Difference Between Byte and Character Streams

Feature	Byte Streams	Character Streams
Data Type	Handles raw binary data (bytes).	Handles text data (characters).
Classes	InputStream, OutputStream, FileInputStream, FileOutputStream.	Reader, Writer, BufferedReader, BufferedWriter.

Feature	Byte Streams	Character Streams
Encoding	Does not perform any encoding or decoding.	Automatically handles character encoding (like UTF-8).
Performance	Less efficient for text data.	More efficient for text data, as it uses Unicode encoding.
Use Case	Used for all kinds of I/O, including binary data like images, audio, etc.	Used specifically for reading and writing text data.

Practical Examples

Example 1: Reading and Writing Binary Data Using Byte Streams

```
import java.io.*;

public class ByteStreamExample {
    public static void main(String[] args) {
        try (FileInputStream fis = new FileInputStream("image.jpg");
             FileOutputStream fos = new
FileOutputStream("copy_image.jpg")) {

            int byteData;
            while ((byteData = fis.read()) != -1) {
                fos.write(byteData);
            }
            System.out.println("Binary data copied successfully using byte
streams.");
        } catch (IOException e) {
            e.printStackTrace();
        }
    }
}
```

Explanation: This example demonstrates the use of `FileInputStream` and `FileOutputStream` to copy binary data from one file to another.

Example 2: Reading and Writing Text Data Using Character Streams

```
import java.io.*;

public class CharStreamExample {
    public static void main(String[] args) {
        try (BufferedReader br = new BufferedReader(new
FileReader("textfile.txt"));
             BufferedWriter bw = new BufferedWriter(new
FileWriter("outputfile.txt"))) {
```

```
            String line;
            while ((line = br.readLine()) != null) {
                bw.write(line);
                bw.newLine(); // Adds a newline between lines
            }
            System.out.println("Text data copied successfully using
character streams.");
        } catch (IOException e) {
            e.printStackTrace();
        }
    }
}
```

Explanation: The `BufferedReader` reads the file line by line, and the `BufferedWriter` writes each line to another file, ensuring efficient text processing.

Example 3: Using Byte Streams to Write Data to a File

```
import java.io.*;

public class ByteWriteExample {
    public static void main(String[] args) {
        try (FileOutputStream fos = new FileOutputStream("output.txt")) {
            String data = "Hello, World!";
            byte[] byteData = data.getBytes();
            fos.write(byteData);
            System.out.println("Text written as byte data to the file
using byte streams.");
        } catch (IOException e) {
            e.printStackTrace();
        }
    }
}
```

Explanation: In this example, we convert a string to a byte array using `getBytes()`, and then write the bytes to a file using `FileOutputStream`.

2.9 Reading and Writing from Console

- **Reading Input from Console**:
  o Using `Scanner`, `BufferedReader`, and `InputStreamReader`.
  o Example: Reading multiple lines of input.
- **Writing Output to Console**:
  o Using `System.out.println()` and `PrintWriter`.
- **Formatting Console Output**: Using `System.out.printf()` for formatted output.

In Java, handling input and output operations from the console is essential for interactive applications. The console allows users to provide input, which the program can then process and display output. Here are the different methods to read from and write to the console:

Reading Input from Console

Java provides several classes to read input from the console. The most commonly used ones are:

1. **Using `Scanner` Class**: The `Scanner` class is the most commonly used method for reading input. It is part of the `java.util` package and provides methods to read different types of input (e.g., strings, integers, etc.).

   Syntax:

```
Scanner scanner = new Scanner(System.in);
String inputString = scanner.nextLine(); // To read a whole line
int inputInt = scanner.nextInt(); // To read an integer
```

   Example: Reading a string and an integer using `Scanner`.

```
import java.util.Scanner;

public class ConsoleInputExample {
    public static void main(String[] args) {
        Scanner scanner = new Scanner(System.in);

        System.out.print("Enter your name: ");
        String name = scanner.nextLine();

        System.out.print("Enter your age: ");
        int age = scanner.nextInt();

        System.out.println("Hello, " + name + ". You are " + age + " years
old.");
        scanner.close();
    }
}
```

   Explanation: The program prompts the user to enter their name and age. The `nextLine()` method reads the full name as a string, and the `nextInt()` method reads the age as an integer.

2. **Using `BufferedReader` and `InputStreamReader`**: The `BufferedReader` class is used for reading text from an input stream. It is wrapped around an `InputStreamReader` to convert byte streams into character streams. **Syntax**:

```
BufferedReader reader = new BufferedReader(new
InputStreamReader(System.in));
String inputString = reader.readLine(); // To read a line of text
```

Example: Reading multiple lines using `BufferedReader`.

```java
import java.io.*;

public class BufferedReaderExample {
    public static void main(String[] args) throws IOException {
        BufferedReader reader = new BufferedReader(new
InputStreamReader(System.in));

        System.out.print("Enter your name: ");
        String name = reader.readLine();

        System.out.print("Enter your country: ");
        String country = reader.readLine();

        System.out.println("Hello, " + name + " from " + country + ".");
        reader.close();
    }
}
```

Explanation: The program uses `BufferedReader` to read lines of text. It reads the user's name and country, then displays them in the output.

Writing Output to Console

1. **Using `System.out.println()`**: `System.out.println()` is the most common method used to print output to the console. It prints the message and automatically adds a newline character after the output.

   Example:

```java
public class PrintExample {
    public static void main(String[] args) {
        System.out.println("Hello, World!");  // Prints a message with a
new line.
    }
}
```

   Explanation: The message `"Hello, World!"` is printed to the console followed by a newline.

2. **Using `PrintWriter`**: The `PrintWriter` class is another option for writing text to the console or files. It provides methods for formatted printing and handles exceptions automatically.

   Syntax:

```
PrintWriter writer = new PrintWriter(System.out);
writer.println("Hello, World!");
```

Example:

```
import java.io.PrintWriter;

public class PrintWriterExample {
    public static void main(String[] args) {
        PrintWriter writer = new PrintWriter(System.out);
        writer.println("This is printed using PrintWriter.");
        writer.flush();   // Flushes the output buffer
    }
}
```

Explanation: This program uses `PrintWriter` to write the message to the console. The `flush()` method is used to ensure the output is displayed immediately.

Formatting Console Output

To display output in a specific format, we can use `System.out.printf()` or `String.format()`.

1. **Using `System.out.printf()`**: The `printf()` method allows formatted printing of output. It follows the format string syntax and can be used for more complex outputs such as aligning text, printing numbers with specific precision, etc.

Syntax:

```
System.out.printf("Format string", arguments);
```

Example: Formatting output using `printf()`.

```
public class PrintfExample {
    public static void main(String[] args) {
        String name = "John";
        int age = 25;
        double height = 5.9;

        // Printing formatted output
        System.out.printf("Name: %-10s Age: %-3d Height: %.2f\n", name,
age, height);
    }
}
```

Explanation: The % symbols represent placeholders in the format string:

- ○ `%s` is for strings.
- ○ `%d` is for integers.
- ○ `%.2f` is for floating-point numbers with 2 decimal places.
- ○ `%-10s` left-aligns the string within a field of 10 characters.

Output:

```
Name: John        Age: 25  Height: 5.90
```

Summary of Key Methods:

1. **Scanner Methods**:
- ○ `nextLine()`: Reads a full line of input.
- ○ `nextInt()`: Reads an integer.
- ○ `nextDouble()`: Reads a double.
2. **BufferedReader Methods**:
- ○ `readLine()`: Reads a line of text.
3. **PrintWriter Methods**:
- ○ `println()`: Prints the text followed by a newline.
- ○ `flush()`: Ensures the output is written immediately.
4. **Formatted Output with `printf()`**:
- ○ `%s`, `%d`, `%f` are used for string, integer, and floating-point numbers respectively.
- ○ `%-10s` left-aligns within a 10-character wide field.

These methods provide flexible and efficient ways to handle both input and output in Java, allowing you to read user input, process it, and display formatted output to the console.

2.10 File Handling in Java

- **Introduction to File Handling**:
- ○ Creating, reading, writing, and deleting files.
- **File Class**:
- ○ Checking file properties (`exists()`, `isFile()`, `length()`).
- **File Reading/Writing Techniques**:
- ○ Using `FileReader`/`FileWriter` for text files.
- ○ Using `FileInputStream`/`FileOutputStream` for binary files.
- **Buffered Streams**:
- ○ Using `BufferedReader` and `BufferedWriter` for efficient operations.
- **Exception Handling in File Operations**:
- ○ Handling `IOException` and file-related errors.

File handling in Java allows you to work with files stored on the system, enabling reading from and writing to files, as well as performing file-related operations such as creating, deleting, and checking properties of files. Java provides several classes and methods to facilitate file operations.

Introduction to File Handling

In Java, file handling involves:

1. **Creating Files**: Creating new files using the `File` class or `FileWriter` class.
2. **Reading Files**: Reading the content of a file using classes like `FileReader`, `BufferedReader`, or `FileInputStream`.
3. **Writing to Files**: Writing data to files using classes like `FileWriter`, `BufferedWriter`, or `FileOutputStream`.
4. **Deleting Files**: Deleting files using the `delete()` method of the `File` class.

File Class

The `File` class in Java is used to create, delete, and check properties of files and directories. It is part of the `java.io` package.

1. **Checking file properties**:
   o `exists()`: Checks if the file exists.
   o `isFile()`: Checks if the file is a regular file (not a directory).
   o `length()`: Returns the size of the file in bytes.

Example:

```java
import java.io.File;

public class FileExample {
    public static void main(String[] args) {
        File file = new File("testfile.txt");

        // Check if the file exists
        if (file.exists()) {
            System.out.println("File exists.");
            System.out.println("Is a file? " + file.isFile());
            System.out.println("File size: " + file.length() + " bytes.");
        } else {
            System.out.println("File does not exist.");
        }
    }
}
```

Explanation: This example checks whether the file `testfile.txt` exists and prints its properties.

File Reading/Writing Techniques

1. **Using `FileReader`/`FileWriter` for text files**: The `FileReader` and `FileWriter` classes are used for reading and writing character-based data.

   Example: Writing text to a file using `FileWriter` and reading from it using `FileReader`.

```java
import java.io.*;

public class FileReaderWriterExample {
    public static void main(String[] args) {
        try {
            // Writing to a file
            FileWriter writer = new FileWriter("output.txt");
            writer.write("Hello, this is a sample text file.\n");
            writer.close();

            // Reading from a file
            FileReader reader = new FileReader("output.txt");
            int ch;
            while ((ch = reader.read()) != -1) {
                System.out.print((char) ch);
            }
            reader.close();
        } catch (IOException e) {
            e.printStackTrace();
        }
    }
}
```

   Explanation: The program writes a string to `output.txt` using `FileWriter` and then reads the contents of the file using `FileReader`.

---

2. **Using `FileInputStream`/`FileOutputStream` for binary files**: These classes are used for reading and writing binary data, such as images, audio files, etc.

   Example: Writing and reading a byte of data using `FileOutputStream` and `FileInputStream`.

```java
import java.io.*;

public class FileInputStreamOutputStreamExample {
    public static void main(String[] args) {
        try {
            // Writing to a binary file
            FileOutputStream fos = new FileOutputStream("binaryfile.dat");
            fos.write(65); // Writing a byte (ASCII value of 'A')
            fos.close();

            // Reading from a binary file
```

```
            FileInputStream fis = new FileInputStream("binaryfile.dat");
            int data = fis.read();
            System.out.println("Read byte: " + (char) data); // Should
print 'A'
            fis.close();
        } catch (IOException e) {
            e.printStackTrace();
        }
    }
}
```

Explanation: This example demonstrates how to write and read a single byte of data using `FileOutputStream` and `FileInputStream`. The ASCII value `65` is written, which corresponds to the character 'A'.

Buffered Streams

Buffered streams are used to improve the performance of file I/O operations by reading or writing larger chunks of data at once. `BufferedReader` and `BufferedWriter` are used for character-based buffered input and output.

1. **BufferedReader and BufferedWriter**:
   o `BufferedReader` is used to read large amounts of text from a file efficiently.
   o `BufferedWriter` is used to write large amounts of text to a file efficiently.

Example: Reading from and writing to a file using `BufferedReader` and `BufferedWriter`.

```
import java.io.*;

public class BufferedReaderWriterExample {
    public static void main(String[] args) {
        try {
            // Writing using BufferedWriter
            BufferedWriter writer = new BufferedWriter(new
FileWriter("buffered_output.txt"));
            writer.write("This is a line of text.");
            writer.newLine(); // Adds a new line
            writer.close();

            // Reading using BufferedReader
            BufferedReader reader = new BufferedReader(new
FileReader("buffered_output.txt"));
            String line;
            while ((line = reader.readLine()) != null) {
                System.out.println(line);
            }
            reader.close();
        } catch (IOException e) {
            e.printStackTrace();
        }    }}
```

Explanation: The program writes a string to `buffered_output.txt` using `BufferedWriter` and reads it back using `BufferedReader`.

Exception Handling in File Operations

When performing file operations, exceptions such as `IOException` may occur due to reasons like the file not existing or file access permissions being denied. Therefore, file handling operations should be enclosed in try-catch blocks to handle exceptions gracefully.

1. **Handling `IOException`**:
o An `IOException` is thrown when there is an issue with file input/output operations, such as a missing file or access error.

Example: Handling exceptions while reading from a file.

```java
import java.io.*;

public class ExceptionHandlingExample {
    public static void main(String[] args) {
        try {
            FileReader reader = new FileReader("nonexistentfile.txt");
            int data;
            while ((data = reader.read()) != -1) {
                System.out.print((char) data);
            }
            reader.close();
        } catch (IOException e) {
            System.out.println("An error occurred: " + e.getMessage());
        }
    }
}
```

Explanation: The program tries to read from a file that does not exist. Since the file is not found, an `IOException` is caught and an error message is displayed.

Summary

- **File Creation, Reading, Writing, and Deleting**: You can create, read, write, and delete files using the `File` class, `FileWriter`, `FileReader`, `FileInputStream`, and `FileOutputStream`.
- **Buffered Streams**: `BufferedReader` and `BufferedWriter` provide efficient ways to handle large amounts of data.
- **Exception Handling**: Always handle potential file-related errors using `try-catch` blocks, especially when performing file operations. Use `IOException` to catch errors like file not found or permission issues.

By using these classes and methods, Java allows efficient and secure file handling in applications.

50 MCQ ON THESE TOPICS

2.1 Creating and Using Arrays: One-Dimensional and Multi-Dimensional

1. What is the correct way to declare a one-dimensional array in Java?
   a) int[] arr;
   b) int arr[];
   c) Both a and b
   d) None of the above
   Answer: c) Both a and b
2. How do you initialize an array with values in Java?
   a) int arr[5] = {1, 2, 3, 4, 5};
   b) int arr[] = {1, 2, 3, 4, 5};
   c) int[] arr = new int[5]{1, 2, 3, 4, 5};
   d) None of the above
   Answer: b) int arr[] = {1, 2, 3, 4, 5};
3. What is the default value of an integer array in Java?
   a) null
   b) 0
   c) garbage value
   d) undefined
   Answer: b) 0
4. Which of the following is the correct syntax to create a two-dimensional array?
   a) int[][] arr = new int[3][3];
   b) int arr[][] = new int[3][3];
   c) Both a and b
   d) None of the above
   Answer: c) Both a and b
5. How do you access the element at the second row and third column of a two-dimensional array `arr`?
   a) arr[1][2]
   b) arr[2][3]
   c) arr[3][2]
   d) arr[2][1]
   Answer: a) arr[1][2]

2.2 Referencing Arrays Dynamically

6. What does `int[] arr = new int[5];` do?
   a) Declares an array and initializes it with default values
   b) Creates a null array
   c) Declares an array with garbage values
   d) Throws an error
   Answer: a) Declares an array and initializes it with default values

7. Can the size of an array in Java be changed dynamically?
   a) Yes
   b) No
   c) Only if it is a two-dimensional array
   d) Only if it is a String array
   Answer: b) No

8. What is the length of the array created by `int[] arr = {1, 2, 3, 4, 5};`?
   a) 4
   b) 5
   c) 6
   d) None of the above
   Answer: b) 5

9. Which method returns the size of an array in Java?
   a) size()
   b) length()
   c) length
   d) getSize()
   Answer: c) length

10. What happens if you access an array index out of bounds in Java?
    a) ArrayIndexOutOfBoundsException
    b) NullPointerException
    c) Returns -1
    d) None of the above
    Answer: a) ArrayIndexOutOfBoundsException

2.3 The Java String Class and String Objects

11. Strings in Java are:
    a) Immutable
    b) Mutable
    c) Fixed length
    d) None of the above
    Answer: a) Immutable

12. How do you create a String object in Java?
    a) String str = "Hello";
    b) String str = new String("Hello");

c) Both a and b

d) None of the above

Answer: c) Both a and b

13. Which class is used to create mutable strings in Java?

a) StringBuffer

b) StringBuilder

c) Both a and b

d) None of the above

Answer: c) Both a and b

14. What is the output of `System.out.println("Java".length());`?

a) 3

b) 4

c) 5

d) Error

Answer: b) 4

15. Which of the following method is used to compare two strings?

a) equals()

b) compareTo()

c) Both a and b

d) None of the above

Answer: c) Both a and b

2.4 Manipulating Strings: Immutability and Equality

16. Which method is used to check the equality of two strings, ignoring case?

a) equalsIgnoreCase()

b) compareToIgnoreCase()

c) equals()

d) None of the above

Answer: a) equalsIgnoreCase()

17. What does the `substring()` method do?

a) Extracts a part of the string

b) Modifies the original string

c) Converts a string to uppercase

d) None of the above

Answer: a) Extracts a part of the string

18. What is the result of `("Java" == "Java")`?

a) true

b) false

c) Compilation Error

d) Runtime Error

Answer: a) true

19. What is the result of `"Java".equals("JAVA");`?

a) true

b) false
c) Compilation Error
d) Runtime Error
Answer: b) false

20. What happens if you try to modify a string in Java?
    a) The original string is modified
    b) A new string is created
    c) Throws an exception
    d) None of the above
    Answer: b) A new string is created

2.5 Passing Strings to and from Methods

21. Strings are passed to methods in Java by:
    a) Value
    b) Reference
    c) Both a and b
    d) None of the above
    Answer: a) Value

22. Which of these is correct when passing a string to a method?
    a) String objects are copied
    b) The original object is referenced
    c) Strings cannot be passed to methods
    d) None of the above
    Answer: b) The original object is referenced

23. Can a method return a string in Java?
    a) Yes
    b) No
    c) Only if it is static
    d) None of the above
    Answer: a) Yes

24. What is the output of the following code?

```
public class Test {
    public static void main(String[] args) {
        String str = "Java";
        modify(str);
        System.out.println(str);
    }
    static void modify(String s) {
        s = "Python";
    }
}
```

    a) Java
    b) Python

c) Compilation Error
d) Runtime Error
Answer: a) Java

25. What is the return type of the `charAt()` method?
    a) String
    b) char
    c) int
    d) None of the above
    Answer: b) char

2.6 String Buffer Classes

26. Which of the following classes is used for creating mutable strings in Java?
    a) String
    b) StringBuffer
    c) StringBuilder
    d) Both b and c
    Answer: d) Both b and c

27. What is the difference between `StringBuffer` and `StringBuilder`?
    a) `StringBuffer` is thread-safe; `StringBuilder` is not
    b) `StringBuilder` is faster than `StringBuffer`
    c) Both a and b
    d) None of the above
    Answer: c) Both a and b

28. Which method in `StringBuffer` appends a string to an existing string?
    a) append()
    b) concat()
    c) add()
    d) None of the above
    Answer: a) append()

29. What is the output of the following code?

```
StringBuffer sb = new StringBuffer("Java");
sb.append(" Programming");
System.out.println(sb);
```

    a) Java
    b) Java Programming
    c) Compilation Error
    d) None of the above
    Answer: b) Java Programming

30. Which method is used to reverse a `StringBuffer`?
    a) reverse()
    b) flip()
    c) invert()

d) None of the above
Answer: a) reverse()

2.7 Simple I/O: Using System.out and Scanner Class

31. Which class is used to read input from the console in Java?
    a) Scanner
    b) InputStream
    c) Console
    d) None of the above
    Answer: a) Scanner

32. What is the correct syntax to read an integer from the console using the Scanner class?
    a) int num = Scanner.next();
    b) int num = Scanner.nextInt();
    c) int num = new Scanner(System.in).nextInt();
    d) Both b and c
    Answer: d) Both b and c

33. Which method is used to display output in Java?
    a) print()
    b) println()
    c) Both a and b
    d) printf()
    Answer: c) Both a and b

34. What is the output of the following code?

```
System.out.print("Hello ");
System.out.println("World");
```

    a) Hello World (in the same line)
    b) Hello
    World (in two lines)
    c) Compilation Error
    d) None of the above
    Answer: a) Hello World (in the same line)

35. Which method can be used to format strings in Java?
    a) format()
    b) printf()
    c) Both a and b
    d) None of the above
    Answer: c) Both a and b

2.8 Byte and Character Streams

36. Which package contains Java's I/O classes?
    a) java.io
    b) java.nio
    c) java.util
    d) java.streams
    Answer: a) java.io
37. Which stream is used to read byte data?
    a) InputStream
    b) Reader
    c) OutputStream
    d) Writer
    Answer: a) InputStream
38. Which class is used for reading character data in Java?
    a) InputStreamReader
    b) FileReader
    c) Both a and b
    d) ByteReader
    Answer: c) Both a and b
39. What is the primary difference between `Byte Streams` and `Character Streams`?
    a) Byte streams handle 8-bit data, character streams handle 16-bit data
    b) Byte streams are faster
    c) Character streams can only handle files
    d) None of the above
    Answer: a) Byte streams handle 8-bit data, character streams handle 16-bit data
40. Which method is used to close a stream in Java?
    a) stop()
    b) close()
    c) terminate()
    d) None of the above
    Answer: b) close()

2.9 Reading and Writing from Console

41. What is the output of the following code?

```
Console console = System.console();
String name = console.readLine("Enter name: ");
System.out.println(name);
```

    a) Reads the input and displays it
    b) Compilation Error
    c) Runtime Error if run in an IDE

d) None of the above
Answer: c) Runtime Error if run in an IDE

42. What does `System.console()` return if no console is available?
    a) null
    b) empty console object
    c) throws an exception
    d) None of the above
    Answer: a) null
43. Which method reads a single character from the console?
    a) read()
    b) readChar()
    c) readLine()
    d) None of the above
    Answer: a) read()
44. Can the `Scanner` class be used to read input from the console?
    a) Yes
    b) No
    c) Only for numeric input
    d) None of the above
    Answer: a) Yes
45. What is the default delimiter used by the `Scanner` class?
    a) Space
    b) Tab
    c) Newline
    d) None of the above
    Answer: a) Space

2.10 File Handling in Java

46. Which class is used to create a new file in Java?
    a) FileOutputStream
    b) FileWriter
    c) File
    d) None of the above
    Answer: c) File
47. Which method checks if a file exists?
    a) exists()
    b) fileExists()
    c) isAvailable()
    d) None of the above
    Answer: a) exists()

48. What happens if you try to read a non-existent file?
    a) FileNotFoundException
    b) IOException
    c) NullPointerException
    d) None of the above
    Answer: a) FileNotFoundException

49. What is the difference between `FileReader` and `BufferedReader`?
    a) `BufferedReader` is faster and provides a buffer
    b) `FileReader` is faster
    c) Both perform the same operations with the same speed
    d) None of the above
    Answer: a) `BufferedReader` is faster and provides a buffer

50. Which method is used to delete a file?
    a) delete()
    b) remove()
    c) erase()
    d) None of the above
    Answer: a) delete()

CHAPTER 3: OBJECT-ORIENTED PROGRAMMING OVERVIEW

3.1 Principles of Object-Oriented Programming (OOP)

Object-Oriented Programming (OOP) is a programming paradigm based on the concept of "objects", which can contain data in the form of fields (often called attributes or properties) and methods that operate on the data. OOP is built around the following four key principles:

1. **Encapsulation**:
   o The concept of bundling the data (attributes) and the methods that operate on the data into a single unit known as a class.
   o Provides access control to the data through access modifiers like `private`, `protected`, and `public`, ensuring that the internal representation of an object is hidden from the outside world.
2. **Abstraction**:
   o Focuses on exposing only essential details and hiding implementation details from the user.
   o Achieved through abstract classes and interfaces in Java.
3. **Inheritance**:
   o Allows a class to inherit attributes and methods from another class. This promotes code reuse and establishes a hierarchical relationship between classes.
   o A subclass can inherit fields and methods from a superclass and can also override or extend them.
4. **Polymorphism**:
   o Enables a single entity (method or object) to take many forms.
   o There are two types of polymorphism in Java: Compile-time (Method Overloading) and Runtime (Method Overriding).

OOP helps in organizing complex programs into modular, reusable, and maintainable code structures.

3.1 Principles of Object-Oriented Programming (OOP)

Object-Oriented Programming (OOP) is a programming paradigm that focuses on creating objects, which bundle together data and behaviors. These objects interact with each other to solve a problem. OOP helps in organizing complex systems into smaller, more manageable components, and is based on four key principles: **Encapsulation**, **Abstraction**, **Inheritance**, and **Polymorphism**.

Let's explore each of these principles in detail:

1. Encapsulation:

Encapsulation is the concept of bundling data (attributes) and methods (functions) that operate on the data into a single unit, known as a class. This principle helps to protect the data by restricting access to the internal state of an object, exposing only the necessary functionality to the outside world.

Key Aspects of Encapsulation:

- **Data Hiding**: The internal state of an object is hidden from outside interference. This means that the fields or attributes of a class are not directly accessible from outside the class, but rather, through public methods (getters and setters).
- **Access Modifiers**: Java provides access modifiers to control the visibility of data and methods. These include:
  - `private`: The data or method is accessible only within the same class.
  - `protected`: The data or method is accessible within the same package or subclasses.
  - `public`: The data or method is accessible from anywhere.

Example:

```java
public class Employee {
    private String name;   // Private field, cannot be accessed directly
    private int age;

    // Getter method to access the name
    public String getName() {
        return name;
    }

    // Setter method to modify the name
    public void setName(String name) {
        this.name = name;
    }

    // Getter and Setter methods for other attributes can also be created
}
```

In the example above, the `name` and `age` attributes are private, meaning they cannot be accessed directly from outside the `Employee` class. Instead, public methods (`getName()` and `setName()`) are provided to access and modify these private fields.

2. Abstraction:

Abstraction is the concept of hiding the complexity of a system by providing a simple interface while hiding the implementation details. It allows you to focus on what an object does, rather than how it does it.

Key Aspects of Abstraction:

- **Abstract Classes**: An abstract class cannot be instantiated on its own and serves as a blueprint for other classes. It can have abstract methods (without implementation) and concrete methods (with implementation).
- **Interfaces**: An interface defines a contract for what a class can do, without specifying how it does it. A class that implements an interface must provide an implementation for all the methods declared in the interface.

Example:

```java
abstract class Animal {
    abstract void sound(); // Abstract method (no body)

    public void sleep() {
        System.out.println("This animal is sleeping");
    }
}

class Dog extends Animal {
    public void sound() {
        System.out.println("Bark");
    }
}
```

In this example, the `Animal` class is abstract, and it defines an abstract method `sound()`, which must be implemented by its subclass (`Dog`). The `sleep()` method is a concrete method that is inherited by the subclass. This way, abstraction hides the complexity of how animals make sounds but exposes a simple interface.

3. Inheritance:

Inheritance allows a class to inherit properties and behaviors (fields and methods) from another class. This promotes code reuse, helps to create a hierarchical relationship between classes, and allows for extensions of functionality without modifying the original class.

Key Aspects of Inheritance:

- **Superclass**: The class that provides common fields and methods to other classes.
- **Subclass**: A class that inherits the fields and methods of another class and can also add new fields or override inherited methods.

- **Method Overriding**: A subclass can provide its own implementation of a method defined in the superclass.

Example:

```
class Animal {
    public void eat() {
        System.out.println("This animal is eating");
    }
}

class Dog extends Animal {
    public void bark() {
        System.out.println("Woof");
    }

    @Override
    public void eat() {
        System.out.println("This dog is eating");
    }
}
```

In this example, the `Dog` class is a subclass of the `Animal` class. It inherits the `eat()` method but overrides it to provide a specific implementation for dogs. The `Dog` class also adds its own method `bark()`. This shows how inheritance allows for code reuse and extending functionality.

Inheritance in Java

Inheritance is one of the core concepts of **Object-Oriented Programming (OOP)**. It allows a class to inherit properties (fields) and behaviors (methods) from another class, enabling the creation of a hierarchical relationship between classes. By using inheritance, we can create new classes that reuse, extend, and modify the behavior defined in other classes.

Key Aspects of Inheritance:

1. **Superclass (Parent Class)**:
   o The superclass is the class that provides common fields and methods to other classes. It defines the shared behavior and properties that can be inherited by its subclasses.
   o It represents a more general entity that can be specialized by its subclasses.

Example:

```
class Animal {
    public void eat() {
```

```
        System.out.println("This animal is eating");
    }
}
```

In this example, `Animal` is the superclass that defines a method `eat()`.

2. **Subclass (Child Class)**:
   o The subclass is the class that inherits the fields and methods of another class (the superclass). It can also add its own specific fields and methods.
   o A subclass can either **extend** (inherit) or **override** the methods from the superclass. This allows for greater flexibility and specialization.

Example:

```
class Dog extends Animal {
    public void bark() {
        System.out.println("Woof");
    }

    @Override
    public void eat() {
        System.out.println("This dog is eating");
    }
}
```

In this example, `Dog` is the subclass of `Animal`. It inherits the `eat()` method but overrides it to provide a more specific implementation. It also adds its own method `bark()` which is specific to dogs.

3. **Method Overriding**:
   o Method overriding occurs when a subclass provides a **specific implementation** of a method that is already defined in its superclass. This helps in changing or extending the behavior of the inherited method.
   o The method in the subclass must have the **same signature** (name, return type, and parameters) as the method in the superclass.

Example:

```
class Animal {
    public void eat() {
        System.out.println("This animal is eating");
    }
}

class Dog extends Animal {
    @Override
    public void eat() {
        System.out.println("This dog is eating");
    }
}
```

}

Here, `Dog` overrides the `eat()` method from the `Animal` class. The overridden method in `Dog` has a more specific behavior (i.e., it specifies that the dog is eating). If `Dog` did not override `eat()`, the method from `Animal` would be used.

Why Inheritance is Useful:

1. **Code Reusability**:
o Inheritance allows you to reuse code from existing classes without having to rewrite it. This helps reduce redundancy and improves the maintainability of the code.
o In the example, `Dog` inherits the `eat()` method from `Animal` without needing to implement it from scratch.
2. **Extensibility**:
o Inheritance allows subclasses to **extend** the functionality of a superclass. Subclasses can add their own methods or modify the behavior of inherited methods using method overriding.
o This ensures that you can start with a basic class (like `Animal`) and specialize it for different use cases (like `Dog`, `Cat`, etc.) without altering the original class.
3. **Establishing Hierarchical Relationships**:
o Inheritance helps in establishing a clear **parent-child** relationship between classes. The subclass is a more specialized version of the superclass. This hierarchical structure makes it easier to manage and understand large codebases.

Inheritance Example:

```
class Animal {
    public void eat() {
        System.out.println("This animal is eating");
    }
}

class Dog extends Animal {
    public void bark() {
        System.out.println("Woof");
    }

    @Override
    public void eat() {
        System.out.println("This dog is eating");
    }
}

public class Main {
    public static void main(String[] args) {
        Animal animal = new Animal();
        animal.eat();   // Output: This animal is eating
```

```
Dog dog = new Dog();
dog.eat();      // Output: This dog is eating
dog.bark();     // Output: Woof

// Using reference of superclass
Animal myDog = new Dog();
myDog.eat();    // Output: This dog is eating
}}
```

Explanation of the Example:

1. The `Animal` class is the superclass, and it defines the method `eat()`.
2. The `Dog` class is a subclass of `Animal`, which inherits the `eat()` method from `Animal`. The `Dog` class also overrides the `eat()` method to provide a specific implementation for dogs and adds a new method `bark()`.
3. In the `Main` class, we create an instance of `Dog` and call both the overridden `eat()` method and the new `bark()` method.
4. We also demonstrate **polymorphism** by using an `Animal` reference (`myDog`) to refer to an object of the `Dog` class. Even though the reference is of type `Animal`, it calls the overridden `eat()` method in the `Dog` class at runtime.

Summary:

- **Inheritance** is a fundamental concept in OOP that allows classes to inherit behavior and properties from other classes, promoting code reuse and extensibility.
- The **superclass** provides common fields and methods, while the **subclass** inherits and can modify or extend these inherited features.
- **Method overriding** enables the subclass to change or extend the behavior of methods from the superclass.

Polymorphism in Java

Polymorphism is a core concept in **Object-Oriented Programming (OOP)**, and it refers to the ability of a single entity (method or object) to take on different forms. In simpler terms, polymorphism allows objects of different classes to be treated as objects of a common superclass. It provides a way for the same method or function to behave differently depending on the object that calls it.

There are two main types of polymorphism in Java:

1. **Compile-time Polymorphism** (also known as **Method Overloading**)
2. **Runtime Polymorphism** (also known as **Method Overriding**)

Key Aspects of Polymorphism

1. Compile-time Polymorphism (Method Overloading):

- **Definition**: Compile-time polymorphism occurs when multiple methods in the same class have the same name but differ in their parameter list (either by the number of parameters or the type of parameters). The appropriate method is chosen at **compile-time** based on the method signature.
- **How it works**: The compiler determines which method to call based on the number or type of parameters passed to the method.

Example of Method Overloading:

```java
class MathOperations {
    // Overloaded method that adds two integers
    public int add(int a, int b) {
        return a + b;
    }

    // Overloaded method that adds two doubles
    public double add(double a, double b) {
        return a + b;
    }
}

public class Main {
    public static void main(String[] args) {
        MathOperations math = new MathOperations();

        // Calls the add() method with integer parameters
        System.out.println(math.add(5, 10));   // Output: 15

        // Calls the add() method with double parameters
        System.out.println(math.add(5.5, 10.5));   // Output: 16.0
    }
}
```

Explanation:

- The MathOperations class has two methods with the same name add(), but they accept different types of parameters (int and double).
- The compiler decides which add() method to call at compile time based on the arguments passed to the method.
- This is an example of **compile-time polymorphism** (method overloading).

2. Runtime Polymorphism (Method Overriding):

- **Definition**: Runtime polymorphism occurs when a subclass provides its own specific implementation of a method that is already defined in the superclass. The method that is executed is determined at **runtime** based on the type of the object.
- **How it works**: The method to be invoked is not known until runtime because it depends on the actual object type (subclass or superclass) that is calling the method.

Example of Method Overriding:

```java
class Animal {
    // Superclass method
    public void sound() {
        System.out.println("Animal makes a sound");
    }
}

class Dog extends Animal {
    // Overriding the sound() method in the subclass
    @Override
    public void sound() {
        System.out.println("Dog barks");
    }
}

public class Main {
    public static void main(String[] args) {
        Animal myAnimal = new Animal();
        Animal myDog = new Dog();

        // Calls the method based on the actual object type
        myAnimal.sound();  // Output: Animal makes a sound
        myDog.sound();     // Output: Dog barks
    }
}
```

Explanation:

- The `Animal` class defines a method `sound()` that prints a generic message.
- The `Dog` class overrides the `sound()` method to provide a more specific message ("Dog barks").
- In the `Main` class, the `myAnimal` reference variable points to an `Animal` object, and `myDog` points to a `Dog` object.
- When `myAnimal.sound()` is called, the `sound()` method from the `Animal` class is executed.
- When `myDog.sound()` is called, the overridden `sound()` method from the `Dog` class is executed.
- This behavior is determined at **runtime** based on the object type, making it an example of **runtime polymorphism** (method overriding).

Why Polymorphism is Important

1. **Code Reusability**:
   o Polymorphism allows code to be written once and reused across different classes. With method overloading, you can have methods with the same name but different parameters, providing different functionalities.
   o With method overriding, you can provide specific implementations in subclasses while still maintaining a uniform interface.
   o
2. **Flexibility and Extensibility**:
   o Polymorphism enables objects of different classes to be treated as objects of a common superclass. This allows for flexible and extensible code, where new classes can be added without affecting existing code.
   o For example, new subclasses can be added that implement a `sound()` method, and they will automatically work with the `sound()` method of the `Animal` reference.
3. **Dynamic Method Binding**:
   o Runtime polymorphism (method overriding) provides the ability to bind methods dynamically during runtime, which is crucial for scenarios like **method dispatch** where the exact method to be called depends on the object at runtime.
4. **Improves Maintainability**:
   o Since polymorphism allows for generalized method names (even with different behaviors), it makes the code easier to maintain. For example, if you want to add a new animal type that also needs to make a sound, you can add a new subclass and override the `sound()` method, without needing to change the existing code.

Summary of Polymorphism Types

- **Compile-time Polymorphism (Method Overloading)**:
  o Same method name, but different parameter list.
  o Decided at compile time.
  o Enables multiple methods with the same name but different parameter types or counts.
- **Runtime Polymorphism (Method Overriding)**:
  o Same method name, same parameter list, but in a subclass.
  o Decided at runtime based on the object type.
  o Enables a subclass to provide a specific implementation of a method already defined in the superclass.

Real-World Analogy:

Consider a `Vehicle` class with a `move()` method. You have different types of vehicles, like `Car`, `Bike`, and `Truck`, each of which overrides the `move()` method in its own way:

- **Car**: "Driving on roads."
- **Bike**: "Riding on roads."
- **Truck**: "Transporting heavy loads."

Even though all vehicles can "move", each type of vehicle provides a different implementation of the move() method. This is runtime polymorphism because the move() method will execute differently depending on the object type (Car, Bike, Truck).

Summary of OOP Principles:

- **Encapsulation**: Bundles data and methods into a class, and restricts access to the data using access modifiers (private, protected, public).
- **Abstraction**: Hides complex implementation details and exposes only essential features through abstract classes and interfaces.
- **Inheritance**: Allows classes to inherit fields and methods from another class, promoting code reuse and hierarchical relationships.
- **Polymorphism**: Enables objects to take many forms, allowing methods and objects to behave differently based on context, supporting method overloading and overriding.

3.2 Defining and Using Classes

A **class** is a blueprint for creating objects. It defines properties (attributes) and behaviors (methods) that the objects of the class will have.

1. **Defining a Class**:
o A class is defined using the class keyword, followed by the class name and a body enclosed in curly braces {}.

```java
public class Car {
    String model;
    int year;

    // Method
    void displayInfo() {
        System.out.println("Model: " + model + ", Year: " + year);
    }
}
```

2. **Creating Objects**:
o Once a class is defined, you can create objects (instances) of the class using the new keyword.

```java
public class Main {
    public static void main(String[] args) {
        Car car1 = new Car();
        car1.model = "Toyota";
        car1.year = 2022;
        car1.displayInfo();
    }
}
```

3. **Accessing Class Members**:
o Class members (fields and methods) can be accessed through objects using the dot . operator.

3.3 Controlling Access to Class Members

In Java, access to the class members (fields and methods) can be controlled using **access modifiers**. These include:

1. **Private**:
o Members marked as `private` are only accessible within the same class.

```java
public class Car {
    private String model;   // Private field
    private int year;       // Private field

    // Getter for private field
    public String getModel() {
        return model;
    }
}
```

2. **Protected**:
o Members marked as `protected` are accessible within the same package or by subclasses.
3. **Public**:
o Members marked as `public` are accessible from anywhere.
4. **Default (Package-Private)**:
o Members with no access modifier are accessible only within the same package.

Class Constructors in Java

In Java, **constructors** are special methods used to initialize objects when they are created. They are invoked automatically when an object is instantiated using the `new` keyword. Constructors are crucial because they allow an object to be initialized with specific values or default states at the time of creation.

There are different types of constructors in Java, which are classified based on how they are defined and how they initialize objects:

1. Default Constructor:

- **Definition**: A **default constructor** is a constructor provided by Java automatically if no constructor is explicitly defined in the class. It initializes object fields with default values. For example, numeric fields are set to `0`, object references are set to `null`, and boolean fields are set to `false`.
- **When it is used**: This constructor is used when a class does not have any constructors defined explicitly by the programmer.
- **Example**:

```java
public class Car {
    String model;    // Default value: null
    int year;        // Default value: 0

    // No constructor defined, so Java provides a default constructor
}

public class Main {
    public static void main(String[] args) {
        Car myCar = new Car();   // Calls the default constructor
        System.out.println("Model: " + myCar.model);   // Output: Model: null
        System.out.println("Year: " + myCar.year);      // Output: Year: 0
    }
}
```

Explanation:

- The `Car` class does not explicitly define a constructor, so Java provides a default constructor that initializes the object's fields with default values (`null` for `String` and `0` for `int`).
- The object `myCar` is created using the default constructor, and the fields `model` and `year` hold the default values.

2. Parameterized Constructor:

- **Definition**: A **parameterized constructor** allows you to create an object with specific values at the time of instantiation. This constructor accepts parameters, which are used to initialize the object's fields.
- **When it is used**: It is useful when you want to create objects with specific initial values rather than default ones.
- **Example**:

```java
public class Car {
    String model;
    int year;
```

```
    // Parameterized constructor
    public Car(String model, int year) {
        this.model = model;   // Initialize model with the provided value
        this.year = year;     // Initialize year with the provided value
    }

    // Method to display Car details
    public void displayCarDetails() {
        System.out.println("Model: " + model);
        System.out.println("Year: " + year);
    }
}

public class Main {
    public static void main(String[] args) {
        // Create a Car object using the parameterized constructor
        Car myCar = new Car("Toyota", 2022);
        myCar.displayCarDetails();   // Output: Model: Toyota, Year: 2022
    }
}
```

Explanation:

o   The Car class defines a **parameterized constructor** that accepts two parameters (model and year) and assigns them to the instance variables.
o   The object myCar is created by passing specific values to the constructor. The constructor initializes the object's model and year attributes with the provided values.

3. Constructor Overloading:

- **Definition**: **Constructor overloading** occurs when a class has multiple constructors with the same name but different parameter lists. Each constructor has a different number of parameters or different types of parameters. Java will choose the appropriate constructor based on the number and types of arguments passed when an object is created.
- **When it is used**: Constructor overloading is useful when you want to create objects in multiple ways, with different initialization data.
- **Example**:

```
public class Car {
    String model;
    int year;
    String color;

    // Default constructor
    public Car() {
        this.model = "Unknown";
        this.year = 0;
        this.color = "Unknown";
    }
```

```java
    // Parameterized constructor 1
    public Car(String model, int year) {
        this.model = model;
        this.year = year;
        this.color = "Unknown";  // Default color
    }

    // Parameterized constructor 2
    public Car(String model, int year, String color) {
        this.model = model;
        this.year = year;
        this.color = color;
    }

    // Method to display Car details
    public void displayCarDetails() {
        System.out.println("Model: " + model);
        System.out.println("Year: " + year);
        System.out.println("Color: " + color);
    }
}

public class Main {
    public static void main(String[] args) {
        // Using default constructor
        Car car1 = new Car();
        car1.displayCarDetails();  // Output: Model: Unknown, Year: 0,
Color: Unknown

        // Using parameterized constructor 1
        Car car2 = new Car("Honda", 2020);
        car2.displayCarDetails();  // Output: Model: Honda, Year: 2020,
Color: Unknown

        // Using parameterized constructor 2
        Car car3 = new Car("Ford", 2021, "Red");
        car3.displayCarDetails();  // Output: Model: Ford, Year: 2021,
Color: Red
    }
}
```

Explanation:

o The Car class has three constructors: a **default constructor**, a **parameterized constructor** with two parameters (model, year), and another **parameterized constructor** with three parameters (model, year, color).

o Based on how many arguments are passed when creating a Car object, Java selects the appropriate constructor. For instance, if no arguments are passed, the default constructor is used. If two arguments are passed, the second constructor is used, and so on.

o This demonstrates **constructor overloading**—having multiple constructors with the same name but different parameter lists.

Key Points to Remember About Constructors:

- **Constructor Name**: The name of the constructor is always the same as the class name.
- **Constructor Body**: The body of the constructor contains the code that initializes the object.
- **No Return Type**: Constructors do not have a return type, not even `void`.
- **Object Initialization**: Constructors are used to set initial values for an object when it is created.
- **Constructor Overloading**: You can define multiple constructors in a class with different parameter lists.

Summary:

- **Default Constructor**: Automatically provided by Java when no constructor is defined. It initializes object fields to default values.
- **Parameterized Constructor**: Defined by the programmer to initialize an object with specific values when it's created.
- **Constructor Overloading**: A class can have multiple constructors with different parameter lists, providing flexibility in how objects are initialized.

o

Method Overloading in Java

Method Overloading is a feature in Java where a class can have multiple methods with the same name, but they must differ in the **number** or **type** of parameters. This allows methods to perform similar tasks, but with different types or numbers of arguments.

Key Concepts of Method Overloading:

- **Same Method Name**: All overloaded methods must have the same name.
- **Different Parameters**: The methods must differ in their parameter list, either in the **number** of parameters, the **type** of parameters, or both.
- **Compile-Time Resolution**: The compiler determines which overloaded method to call at compile time based on the method signature (method name and parameters).

Method overloading helps improve the readability of the program and allows a method to perform similar tasks for different inputs.

1. Example of Method Overloading:

```
public class Calculator {
    // Overloaded method to add two integers
    public int add(int a, int b) {
        return a + b;
    }

    // Overloaded method to add three integers
    public int add(int a, int b, int c) {
        return a + b + c;
    }
}

public class Main {
    public static void main(String[] args) {
        Calculator calc = new Calculator();

        System.out.println("Sum of 2 numbers: " + calc.add(5, 10)); //
Calls the method with two parameters
        System.out.println("Sum of 3 numbers: " + calc.add(5, 10, 15)); //
Calls the method with three parameters
    }
}
```

Explanation of the Code:

- **First Method**: add(int a, int b) takes two integer arguments and returns their sum.
- **Second Method**: add(int a, int b, int c) takes three integer arguments and returns their sum.

When you call the add() method with two arguments, the compiler chooses the method with two parameters. When you call it with three arguments, the compiler chooses the method with three parameters.

Output:

```
Sum of 2 numbers: 15
Sum of 3 numbers: 30
```

This demonstrates **method overloading**, where two methods with the same name perform the same task (adding numbers) but with different numbers of parameters.

2. Explanation:

- **Overloading Criteria**:
  o The methods must have the same **name**.
  o The **parameters** (either number, type, or both) must be different. For example:
  ▪ **Different Number of Parameters**: `add(int a, int b)` and `add(int a, int b, int c)` have the same name but differ in the number of parameters.
  ▪ **Different Type of Parameters**: You can overload a method by changing the type of one or more parameters.

```
public int add(int a, int b) {
    return a + b;
}

public double add(double a, double b) {
    return a + b;
}
```

Here, the two `add()` methods differ in the type of parameters (`int` vs. `double`).

- ▪ **Different Order of Parameters**: You can overload methods based on the order of parameters.

```
public void display(int a, double b) {
    System.out.println("Int: " + a + ", Double: " + b);
}

public void display(double b, int a) {
    System.out.println("Double: " + b + ", Int: " + a);
}
```

Even though the method names are the same, the parameter order differs, so they can be overloaded.

- **Method Signature**: For method overloading, the **method signature** (which includes the method name and parameter list) is used by the compiler to differentiate between overloaded methods. The **return type** and **access modifiers** are not considered in method overloading. Therefore, methods cannot be overloaded by just changing their return type or access level.

  Incorrect Overloading Example (This will not work):

```
// The return type is different, but this is not considered valid
overloading
public int add(int a, int b) {
    return a + b;
}

public double add(int a, int b) {
    return a + b;
}
```

In this case, the methods differ only in their return type, which does not constitute valid overloading.

3. Advantages of Method Overloading:

- **Improved Code Readability**: Using the same method name for similar operations (such as adding numbers with different parameters) makes the code more readable.
- **Increased Flexibility**: You can perform similar actions with different types or numbers of inputs using the same method name.
- **Simplifies Code Maintenance**: Instead of writing multiple method names for similar tasks, overloading provides a cleaner and more maintainable solution.
- **Reusability**: You can reuse the same method name across the class, thereby reducing the number of methods you need to define.

4. Rules for Method Overloading:

- The overloaded methods must differ in the **number** of parameters, the **type** of parameters, or the **order** of parameters.
- The method **name** must remain the same for overloading.
- The return type of the methods can be the same or different, but it cannot be the sole factor for overloading.

Summary:

- **Method Overloading** allows multiple methods in the same class to share the same name but differ in their parameters.
- It improves code readability, flexibility, and reusability by allowing similar operations to be performed with different types or numbers of parameters.
- The correct overloaded method is chosen by the **compiler** at **compile time**, based on the method signature (name + parameters).

3.6 Class Variables and Methods

1. **Class Variables (Static Fields)**:
   - Class variables are shared among all instances of the class. They are declared with the `static` keyword.

```
public class Car {
```

```
    static int wheels = 4;  // Static variable shared by all objects
}
```

2. **Class Methods (Static Methods)**:
o Static methods are methods that can be called without creating an object. They are declared with the `static` keyword.

```
public class Car {
    static void displayWheels() {
        System.out.println("All cars have " + wheels + " wheels.");
    }
}
```

3.7 Objects as Parameters

In Java, objects can be passed as parameters to methods, enabling method calls to operate on object data.

1. **Example**:

```
public class Car {
    String model;

    public Car(String model) {
        this.model = model;
    }

    public void displayInfo() {
        System.out.println("Car Model: " + model);
    }
}

public class Main {
    public static void main(String[] args) {
        Car car1 = new Car("Toyota");
        displayCarInfo(car1);  // Passing object as parameter
    }

    public static void displayCarInfo(Car car) {
        car.displayInfo();  // Accessing object data inside method
    }
}
```

3.8 Final Classes in Java

In Java, the `final` keyword is used to restrict the modification of certain aspects of the program, such as classes, methods, and variables. When applied to a class, it prevents that class from being subclassed (i.e., no other class can inherit from a `final` class). This ensures that the functionality of the class cannot be altered by subclassing.

Key Concepts of Final Classes:

- **Final Class**: A class declared with the `final` keyword cannot be subclassed or extended. No other class can inherit the properties or methods of a final class.
- **Use Case**: The `final` keyword is often used in situations where you want to ensure the integrity and security of a class by preventing subclassing, especially for utility classes, immutable classes, or classes whose behavior should not be changed.
- **Final Class vs. Non-Final Class**: A non-final class can be extended to create subclasses that can modify or override methods, whereas a final class cannot be extended.

1. Example of Final Class:

```java
public final class Car {
    String model;

    public Car(String model) {
        this.model = model;
    }

    public void displayModel() {
        System.out.println("Car model: " + model);
    }
}

// This will cause a compile-time error
// public class SportsCar extends Car { }
// Compilation error: Cannot subclass final class Car
```

Explanation of the Code:

- The `Car` class is declared as `final`. This means that no other class can extend `Car` or create a subclass of it.
- If you try to create a class `SportsCar` that extends `Car`, the Java compiler will throw an error at compile time because `Car` is a final class.
- The class `SportsCar` would not be allowed to inherit any methods or fields from `Car`, and the Java compiler would refuse to compile the code due to this restriction.

2. Why Use a Final Class?

Here are a few reasons why you might want to use the `final` keyword with a class in Java:

- **Prevent Inheritance**: By declaring a class as final, you can ensure that it cannot be subclassed, which can be useful when you want to prevent subclasses from modifying its behavior.

- **Security**: Final classes can be used to create secure, unmodifiable classes. For example, classes representing sensitive objects like `String` or cryptographic algorithms might be designed as final to ensure their integrity.
- **Immutability**: Many immutable classes (like `String`, `Integer`, etc.) are declared as final to prevent subclasses from altering their behavior. This ensures that the object's state cannot be changed once it's created.
- **Optimization**: The JVM can optimize method calls for final classes. Since it knows that no class can subclass a final class, method calls can be resolved at compile-time, leading to better performance in some cases.

3. Example of Why and When to Use Final Classes

Consider a utility class for handling certain calculations or representing configuration data. If you want to ensure that no one can subclass or modify the behavior of this class, you can declare it as final.

```
public final class MathUtility {

    // Prevents instantiation
    private MathUtility() {
        throw new UnsupportedOperationException("Utility class cannot be
instantiated.");
    }

    public static int square(int number) {
        return number * number;
    }

    public static int cube(int number) {
        return number * number * number;
    }
}
```

Explanation:

- The `MathUtility` class is final to prevent subclassing. No class can extend `MathUtility`, ensuring that the utility class cannot be altered or have its methods overridden.
- The constructor is private to prevent instantiation, ensuring that the class is only used statically.

4. Behavior of Final Classes

When a class is declared `final`, the following behavior applies:

- **No Subclassing**: No class can inherit from a final class. This helps maintain the integrity of the class's design.

- **Override Restrictions**: Methods in a final class cannot be overridden because the class itself cannot be subclassed.
- **Cannot Be Extended**: If you attempt to extend a final class, a compile-time error will occur.

5. Examples of Java Classes That Are Final

Some of the classes in Java that are declared as `final` are:

- **String**: The `String` class is final in Java to ensure that its values cannot be altered once they are created.
- **Wrapper Classes**: Classes like `Integer`, `Double`, `Character`, etc., are all final to ensure immutability.
- **Math**: The `Math` class is also final to prevent subclassing, as its methods are utility functions that should not be overridden.

6. Conclusion:

- **Final Class**: A class declared as `final` cannot be subclassed. This prevents alteration of its behavior and ensures its integrity.
- **Use Cases**: It's useful when you want to make sure that no subclass can change the functionality of the class, often used for utility, immutable, or security-sensitive classes.
- **Behavior**: If a class is final, its methods cannot be overridden, and no new subclasses can inherit from it.

3.9 The Object Class

The `Object` class is the root class of all classes in Java. Every class, directly or indirectly, inherits from the `Object` class.

1. **Common Methods in `Object` Class**:
   - `equals()`: Compares two objects for equality.
   - `hashCode()`: Returns a hash code for the object.
   - `toString()`: Returns a string representation of the object.

Example:

```
public class Car {
    String model;
```

```
    @Override
    public String toString() {
        return "Car model: " + model;
    }
}
```

2. **Explanation**: `toString()` method is overridden to provide a custom string representation of the object.

3.10 Garbage Collection

Garbage Collection (GC) in Java is the process of automatically reclaiming memory by deleting objects that are no longer referenced by the program.

1. **How it Works**:
o Java has an automatic garbage collector that identifies and removes objects that are no longer used or reachable by the program.
2. **Example**:

```
public class Car {
    String model;

    @Override
    protected void finalize() throws Throwable {
        System.out.println("Car object is being garbage collected.");
    }
}

public class Main {
    public static void main(String[] args) {
        Car car1 = new Car();
        car1 = null;   // Making the object eligible for GC

        System.gc();   // Suggesting JVM to run GC (not guaranteed)
    }
}
```

3. **Explanation**: The `finalize()` method is called before an object is garbage collected. Calling `System.gc()` is a request for garbage collection but not a guarantee.

Summary

- **OOP Principles**: Encapsulation, Abstraction, Inheritance, and Polymorphism.
- **Classes and Objects**: Classes define objects; objects are instances of classes.
- **Access Control**: The `private`, `protected`, and `public` modifiers control access to class members.
- **Constructors**: Constructors initialize object state and can be overloaded.
- **Method Overloading**: Allows methods with the same name but different parameters.
- **Static Variables and Methods**: Shared across all instances of a class and can be accessed without creating an object.
- **Garbage Collection**: Automatic process for reclaiming memory by collecting unused objects.

---

50 MCQ ON THESE TOPICS

3.1 Principles of Object-Oriented Programming

1. Which of the following is not a principle of object-oriented programming?
   a) Encapsulation
   b) Polymorphism
   c) Inheritance
   d) Compilation
   Answer: d) Compilation
2. Which feature of OOP allows different classes to define methods with the same name but different implementations?
   a) Inheritance
   b) Polymorphism
   c) Abstraction
   d) Encapsulation
   Answer: b) Polymorphism
3. What does encapsulation achieve in object-oriented programming?
   a) Hiding implementation details
   b) Exposing all data
   c) Faster execution
   d) None of the above
   Answer: a) Hiding implementation details
4. Abstraction focuses on:
   a) Hiding unnecessary details
   b) Performance optimization

c) Code execution
d) None of the above
Answer: a) Hiding unnecessary details

5. Inheritance in Java is achieved using the keyword:
   a) inherit
   b) extends
   c) implements
   d) derives
   Answer: b) extends

3.2 Defining and Using Classes

6. Which of the following is true about defining classes in Java?
   a) Classes must have at least one method
   b) A class can contain fields and methods
   c) A class cannot be instantiated
   d) None of the above
   Answer: b) A class can contain fields and methods

7. How do you create an object of a class in Java?
   a) ClassName objectName = new ClassName();
   b) objectName = ClassName();
   c) ClassName objectName();
   d) new objectName = ClassName();
   Answer: a) ClassName objectName = new ClassName();

8. What is the default access modifier for class members in Java?
   a) private
   b) public
   c) protected
   d) package-private
   Answer: d) package-private

9. A blueprint for creating objects in Java is called:
   a) Object
   b) Method
   c) Class
   d) Package
   Answer: c) Class

10. A class in Java can extend:
    a) Multiple classes
    b) A single class
    c) No other class
    d) An interface only
    Answer: b) A single class

3.3 Controlling Access to Class Members

11. Which access modifier allows access within the same package only?
    a) private
    b) public
    c) protected
    d) package-private
    Answer: d) package-private

12. The `protected` access modifier allows:
    a) Access only within the same package
    b) Access within the same package and subclasses
    c) Access from everywhere
    d) None of the above
    Answer: b) Access within the same package and subclasses

13. Members marked `private` are accessible:
    a) Within the same class
    b) From any class in the same package
    c) From any class
    d) From subclasses only
    Answer: a) Within the same class

14. The `public` access modifier:
    a) Restricts access to subclasses
    b) Allows access from any class
    c) Is the default modifier
    d) Limits access to the same package
    Answer: b) Allows access from any class

15. How can private class members be accessed from outside the class?
    a) Using public methods in the same class
    b) Using a subclass
    c) Direct access is possible
    d) None of the above
    Answer: a) Using public methods in the same class

3.4 Class Constructors

16. What is the main purpose of a constructor in Java?
    a) To initialize objects
    b) To create methods
    c) To define interfaces
    d) To handle exceptions
    Answer: a) To initialize objects

17. What happens if you do not define a constructor in a class?
    a) The program will not compile
    b) A default constructor is automatically provided

c) You must define a constructor

d) None of the above

Answer: b) A default constructor is automatically provided

18. A constructor:

a) Can have a return type

b) Cannot have a return type

c) Must be abstract

d) Must be final

Answer: b) Cannot have a return type

19. Which keyword is used to call one constructor from another in the same class?

a) super

b) this

c) self

d) constructor

Answer: b) this

20. Can constructors be overloaded?

a) Yes

b) No

c) Only if the return type is different

d) None of the above

Answer: a) Yes

3.5 Method Overloading

21. Which of the following is true for method overloading?

a) Methods must have the same name but different parameter lists

b) Return type must be the same

c) Only static methods can be overloaded

d) None of the above

Answer: a) Methods must have the same name but different parameter lists

22. Can overloaded methods have the same number of parameters?

a) Yes, if the parameter types are different

b) No

c) Only if the return type is different

d) None of the above

Answer: a) Yes, if the parameter types are different

23. Method overloading occurs:

a) At runtime

b) At compile time

c) During execution

d) None of the above

Answer: b) At compile time

24. What happens if two overloaded methods have the same parameter list but different return types?
    a) The code will compile
    b) Compilation error
    c) Runtime error
    d) None of the above
    Answer: b) Compilation error

25. Which of the following is an example of method overloading?
    a) Method with the same name but different argument types
    b) Method with the same name but different return types
    c) Method with the same name but different parameter order
    d) Both a and c
    Answer: d) Both a and c

3.6 Class Variables and Methods

26. What is a class variable in Java?
    a) A variable specific to an instance
    b) A variable shared across all instances of the class
    c) A local variable inside a method
    d) A private variable
    Answer: b) A variable shared across all instances of the class

27. How do you declare a class variable in Java?
    a) Use the `static` keyword
    b) Use the `final` keyword
    c) Use the `private` keyword
    d) Use the `public` keyword
    Answer: a) Use the `static` keyword

28. Which of the following is true about class methods in Java?
    a) They operate on instance variables
    b) They are declared using the `static` keyword
    c) They can only be called within the class
    d) They require an object to be called
    Answer: b) They are declared using the `static` keyword

29. What is the correct way to access a class method?
    a) Using an instance of the class
    b) Using the class name
    c) Using the `this` keyword
    d) None of the above
    Answer: b) Using the class name

30. What happens if a class variable is modified by one object?
    a) The change affects only that object
    b) The change is reflected across all objects of the class
    c) The variable becomes private
    d) None of the above
    Answer: b) The change is reflected across all objects of the class

3.7 Objects as Parameters

31. In Java, objects are passed to methods:
    a) By reference
    b) By value
    c) By copy
    d) By pointer
    Answer: b) By value

32. What happens when an object is passed as a parameter in Java?
    a) A copy of the object is created
    b) A reference to the object is passed
    c) The original object is passed
    d) None of the above
    Answer: b) A reference to the object is passed

33. Which of the following is an advantage of passing objects as parameters?
    a) Reduces memory usage
    b) Allows modification of the original object
    c) Prevents changes to the object
    d) None of the above
    Answer: b) Allows modification of the original object

34. Which keyword is used to pass the current object as a parameter?
    a) super
    b) this
    c) object
    d) class
    Answer: b) this

35. Passing objects as parameters is useful for:
    a) Data encapsulation
    b) Enhancing polymorphism
    c) Reducing code size
    d) None of the above
    Answer: b) Enhancing polymorphism

3.8 Final Classes

36. What is the primary purpose of the `final` keyword in Java?
    a) To prevent a class from being inherited
    b) To allow method overloading
    c) To make a class static
    d) None of the above
    Answer: a) To prevent a class from being inherited

37. Which of the following is true about a `final` class?
    a) It can be subclassed
    b) It cannot be subclassed
    c) Its methods cannot be overridden
    d) Both b and c
    Answer: d) Both b and c
38. A `final` variable:
    a) Can be modified once initialized
    b) Cannot be modified after initialization
    c) Can only be declared inside a method
    d) None of the above
    Answer: b) Cannot be modified after initialization
39. Can a `final` method be overridden?
    a) Yes
    b) No
    c) Only in a subclass
    d) None of the above
    Answer: b) No
40. Which of the following is an example of a `final` class in Java?
    a) Math
    b) String
    c) Both a and b
    d) None of the above
    Answer: c) Both a and b

3.9 The Object Class

41. The `Object` class is a superclass of:
    a) All classes in Java
    b) Abstract classes only
    c) Interfaces only
    d) None of the above
    Answer: a) All classes in Java
42. Which method is defined in the `Object` class?
    a) equals()
    b) hashCode()
    c) toString()
    d) All of the above
    Answer: d) All of the above
43. The `equals()` method in the `Object` class is used to:
    a) Compare references
    b) Compare objects
    c) Compare hash codes

d) None of the above
Answer: b) Compare objects

44. What does the `hashCode()` method return?
    a) A unique identifier for an object
    b) The memory address of an object
    c) The hash code value of an object
    d) None of the above
    Answer: c) The hash code value of an object

45. Which `Object` class method is often overridden in custom classes?
    a) equals()
    b) toString()
    c) hashCode()
    d) All of the above
    Answer: d) All of the above

3.10 Garbage Collection

46. Garbage collection in Java:
    a) Removes unused objects automatically
    b) Must be manually triggered
    c) Deletes variables explicitly
    d) None of the above
    Answer: a) Removes unused objects automatically

47. Which method can be used to request garbage collection?
    a) System.gc()
    b) Runtime.gc()
    c) Both a and b
    d) None of the above
    Answer: c) Both a and b

48. What happens to an object without any references?
    a) It is eligible for garbage collection
    b) It remains in memory
    c) It causes a memory leak
    d) None of the above
    Answer: a) It is eligible for garbage collection

49. The finalize() method is called:
    a) Before garbage collection
    b) After garbage collection
    c) To initialize objects
    d) None of the above
    Answer: a) Before garbage collection
50. Which of the following statements about garbage collection is true?
    a) It is guaranteed to run at a specific time
    b) It is non-deterministic
    c) It cannot be invoked explicitly
    d) None of the above
    Answer: b) It is non-deterministic

CHAPTER 4: INHERITANCE, INTERFACES, PACKAGES, ENUMERATIONS AUTOBOXING, AND METADATA

4.1 Single-Level and Multi-Level Inheritance

Inheritance in Java allows a class to acquire the properties and behaviors (fields and methods) of another class, facilitating code reuse and forming a hierarchical structure. In Java, there are different types of inheritance, including **single-level inheritance** and **multi-level inheritance**.

1. Single-Level Inheritance

Single-level inheritance occurs when a class directly inherits from another class, forming a simple hierarchy with one parent class and one child class. This is the most basic form of inheritance in object-oriented programming.

Key Characteristics of Single-Level Inheritance:

- **Parent Class (Superclass)**: The class whose properties and methods are inherited.
- **Child Class (Subclass)**: The class that inherits the properties and methods from the parent class and can add or modify them.

Example of Single-Level Inheritance:

```
class Animal {
    void sound() {
        System.out.println("Animal makes a sound");
    }
}

class Dog extends Animal {
    void sound() {
        System.out.println("Dog barks");
    }
}

public class Main {
    public static void main(String[] args) {
        Dog dog = new Dog();
        dog.sound();  // Output: Dog barks
    }
}
```

Explanation:

- **Animal Class**: The `Animal` class defines a method `sound()`, which is common for all animals.

- **Dog Class**: The `Dog` class extends the `Animal` class and overrides the `sound()` method to provide a specific implementation for dogs.
- In the `main` method, when a `Dog` object is created and its `sound()` method is called, the method defined in the `Dog` class is executed, not the one in `Animal`. This is an example of **method overriding**.
- **Output**: The output will be "Dog barks" because the `Dog` class overrides the `sound()` method of the `Animal` class.

2. Multi-Level Inheritance

Multi-level inheritance occurs when a class inherits from another class, and then a third class inherits from the second class, forming a chain of inheritance. Each class in this chain adds more specific functionality, and the child class inherits from all its ancestors.

Key Characteristics of Multi-Level Inheritance:

- **Parent Class**: The base class from which other classes inherit.
- **Intermediate Class**: A class that inherits from the parent class and is inherited by a subclass.
- **Child Class**: The final class in the chain that inherits properties from both the parent and intermediate classes.

Example of Multi-Level Inheritance:

```java
class Animal {
    void sound() {
        System.out.println("Animal makes a sound");
    }
}

class Mammal extends Animal {
    void feed() {
        System.out.println("Mammal feeds its young");
    }
}

class Dog extends Mammal {
    void sound() {
        System.out.println("Dog barks");
    }
}

public class Main {
    public static void main(String[] args) {
        Dog dog = new Dog();
        dog.sound();  // Output: Dog barks
        dog.feed();   // Output: Mammal feeds its young
    }
}
```

Explanation:

- **Animal Class**: The base class that defines a `sound()` method. This method can be inherited by any subclass.
- **Mammal Class**: The `Mammal` class inherits from `Animal` and introduces a new method `feed()`, which is common for mammals.
- **Dog Class**: The `Dog` class inherits from `Mammal`, which in turn inherits from `Animal`. Therefore, `Dog` has access to both the `sound()` method from `Animal` and the `feed()` method from `Mammal`. The `Dog` class overrides the `sound()` method to provide a more specific implementation.
- In the `main` method, when the `Dog` object calls `sound()`, the overridden method in the `Dog` class is executed, and when it calls `feed()`, the method from the `Mammal` class is executed.
- **Output**: The output will be:
  - "Dog barks" (from the overridden `sound()` method in `Dog`)
  - "Mammal feeds its young" (from the `feed()` method in `Mammal`)

Key Differences Between Single-Level and Multi-Level Inheritance

Aspect	Single-Level Inheritance	Multi-Level Inheritance
Hierarchy	One class inherits from a single parent class.	A class inherits from another class, and that class may inherit from another, forming a chain.
Inheritance Chain	Only two classes involved (parent and child).	More than two classes are involved, forming a chain of inheritance.
Code Reusability	Provides code reuse between the parent and child class.	Provides more opportunities for code reuse by inheriting across multiple levels.
Complexity	Simpler structure with only two levels.	More complex structure with multiple levels of inheritance.
Example	`Dog extends Animal`	`Dog extends Mammal extends Animal`

Advantages of Multi-Level Inheritance:

1. **Code Reusability**: A subclass can inherit attributes and methods from both its immediate parent class and grandparent class, promoting high code reuse.
2. **Hierarchical Structure**: Multi-level inheritance allows for a well-structured and organized class hierarchy, with general functionality placed in higher-level classes and more specific functionality in lower-level classes.

3. **Better Organization**: The behavior and properties of classes can be spread across multiple levels, making the design of complex systems more manageable.

Challenges of Multi-Level Inheritance:

1. **Increased Complexity**: As the inheritance chain grows, it can become harder to track the source of properties or methods, which may complicate maintenance and debugging.
2. **Potential for Conflicts**: If multiple classes in the hierarchy provide conflicting implementations of the same method, it can lead to ambiguity.
3. **Diamond Problem**: In languages that support multiple inheritance (not Java), the diamond problem occurs when a class inherits from two classes that have a common ancestor, causing ambiguity in method resolution.

Conclusion:

- **Single-Level Inheritance** provides a simple way to establish a parent-child relationship, allowing a class to inherit from only one superclass.
- **Multi-Level Inheritance** allows for a more complex inheritance chain, where a class can inherit from a class that itself has inherited from another class, enabling further code reuse and a more structured hierarchy.

4.2 Method Overriding and Dynamic Method Dispatch

Method Overriding allows a subclass to provide its own implementation of a method already defined in its superclass.

1. **Example**:

```java
class Animal {
    void sound() {
        System.out.println("Animal makes a sound");
    }
}

class Dog extends Animal {
    @Override
    void sound() {
        System.out.println("Dog barks");
    }
}

public class Main {
```

```
public static void main(String[] args) {
    Animal animal = new Dog();
    animal.sound();  // Output: Dog barks (dynamic method dispatch)
}}
```

Explanation: `sound()` is overridden in the `Dog` class. Java uses dynamic method dispatch to call the overridden method at runtime, even when the reference is of type `Animal`.

4.3 Abstract Classes

An **abstract class** in Java is a class that cannot be instantiated directly. Instead, it is intended to be subclassed by other classes. Abstract classes can contain **abstract methods** (methods that are declared but not implemented) as well as regular methods (methods with implementations). The purpose of an abstract class is to provide a common interface or structure for subclasses while allowing those subclasses to provide their own specific implementations of the abstract methods.

Key Characteristics of Abstract Classes:

- **Cannot be instantiated**: You cannot create an object of an abstract class directly.
- **Abstract methods**: An abstract class may have one or more abstract methods, which are methods that are declared but do not have a body (implementation).
- **Concrete methods**: An abstract class can also have regular methods with implementations.
- **Subclasses must implement abstract methods**: Any non-abstract subclass of an abstract class must provide concrete implementations for all the abstract methods inherited from the abstract class.

Example of Abstract Class

```
abstract class Animal {
    // Abstract method (no implementation)
    abstract void sound();
}

class Dog extends Animal {
    // Providing implementation for the abstract method
    void sound() {
        System.out.println("Dog barks");
    }
}

public class Main {
    public static void main(String[] args) {
        // Animal animal = new Animal(); // This will give an error
because you cannot instantiate an abstract class
        Animal animal = new Dog(); // Correct: Create an object of a
subclass
```

```
        animal.sound();  // Output: Dog barks
    }
}
```

Explanation of the Code:

1. **Abstract Class `Animal`**:
   - The `Animal` class is declared as abstract using the `abstract` keyword.
   - The `sound()` method is also abstract, meaning it does not have a body (implementation). This method is meant to be overridden in the subclasses.
2. **Concrete Class `Dog`**:
   - The `Dog` class extends the `Animal` class and provides its own implementation of the `sound()` method.
   - The `sound()` method in the `Dog` class outputs the message "Dog barks".
3. **Main Class**:
   - In the `main` method, you cannot create an instance of the `Animal` class directly because it is abstract.
   - However, you can create an instance of the `Dog` class (which is a subclass of `Animal`) and assign it to a reference variable of type `Animal`.
   - The `sound()` method is called on the `animal` reference, which, at runtime, refers to the `Dog` object. This demonstrates **runtime polymorphism** as the method executed is based on the object type (`Dog`) rather than the reference type (`Animal`).
   - **Output**: The program prints "Dog barks", which is the implementation of the `sound()` method in the `Dog` class.

Important Points About Abstract Classes:

1. **Cannot Instantiate an Abstract Class**:
   - You cannot create an object of an abstract class directly, which is why the following line would result in a compile-time error:

   ```
   Animal animal = new Animal(); // Error: Animal is abstract; cannot be
   instantiated
   ```

2. **Abstract Methods**:
   - Abstract methods do not have a body; they only provide the method signature (name, return type, and parameters).
   - Subclasses that are not abstract must provide implementations for all abstract methods from the abstract class. If the subclass does not implement all the abstract methods, it must also be declared as abstract.
3. **Concrete Methods in Abstract Classes**:
   - An abstract class can have regular methods with full implementations, as shown below:

   ```
   abstract class Animal {
       // Regular method with implementation
   ```

```
void eat() {
    System.out.println("Animal is eating");
}
// Abstract method
abstract void sound();}
```

- o In this case, the `eat()` method is implemented in the abstract class, but the `sound()` method is abstract and must be implemented by subclasses.

4. **No Need for Constructor in Subclasses**:
- o Even though abstract classes cannot be instantiated, they can have constructors. These constructors are called when a subclass is instantiated. The constructor of the abstract class can be used to initialize common state for all subclasses.

5. **Abstract Class as a Base Class**:
- o Abstract classes are typically used as base classes in a class hierarchy. They define the general structure for subclasses and force them to implement specific methods, but they can also provide common functionality that is shared across subclasses.

Use Cases of Abstract Classes:

1. **Template Method Pattern**:
- o Abstract classes are often used to define the **Template Method Pattern**, where the abstract class defines the overall structure of an algorithm, leaving some steps (methods) to be implemented by subclasses.

2. **Common Interface for Different Classes**:
- o Abstract classes help define a common interface for a group of related classes. They ensure that certain methods must be implemented in subclasses, while still allowing subclasses to define specific behavior.

3. **Avoiding Redundancy**:
- o By placing common functionality in the abstract class, you can avoid redundancy across subclasses. Abstract classes allow you to write general code that applies to all subclasses while leaving room for specific implementations.

Differences Between Abstract Classes and Interfaces:

Aspect	Abstract Class	Interface
Purpose	Provides a common base for related classes.	Defines a contract for classes to follow.

Practical Java Programming: Concept and its Application

Aspect	Abstract Class	Interface
Methods	Can have both abstract and concrete (implemented) methods.	All methods are abstract (prior to Java 8). Can have default and static methods (from Java 8).
Multiple Inheritance	A class can extend only one abstract class.	A class can implement multiple interfaces.
Constructors	Can have constructors.	Cannot have constructors.
Field Variables	Can have instance variables with any access modifiers (private, protected, etc.).	Can have only static final (constant) variables.
Usage	Best used when classes have shared behavior and attributes.	Best used to define capabilities that can be shared across different classes.

Conclusion:

An **abstract class** is a powerful mechanism in object-oriented programming that enables code reuse, enforces a structure for subclasses, and allows for the definition of both common and specific behavior. It cannot be instantiated directly and must be subclassed to be useful. Abstract classes are particularly useful when you need to define a common interface for a group of related classes while still allowing for custom behavior in the subclasses.

4.4 Defining and Extending Interfaces

An **interface** in Java is a reference type, similar to a class, that is used to define a contract or a set of methods that a class must implement. Interfaces cannot provide method implementations (except for default and static methods introduced in Java 8). They only declare method signatures, and any class that implements an interface must provide implementations for all of the interface's methods (unless the class is abstract).

Interfaces are primarily used to achieve **abstraction** and to provide a common protocol for different classes that may not share a common parent class but must adhere to the same set of operations.

162 | P a g e

Key Characteristics of Interfaces:

- **No method implementations (except default and static methods)**: All methods in an interface are abstract by default (unless marked with `default` or `static`).
- **Can be implemented by classes**: A class that implements an interface must provide an implementation for all of its abstract methods.
- **Multiple inheritance**: A class can implement multiple interfaces, which allows a form of multiple inheritance (unlike classes, which can only extend one class).
- **Constants**: Interface fields are implicitly `public`, `static`, and `final`.

Example of Defining and Implementing an Interface:

```java
interface Animal {
    // Abstract method (no body)
    void sound();  // method signature, but no implementation
}

class Dog implements Animal {
    // Providing implementation for the abstract method
    public void sound() {
        System.out.println("Dog barks");
    }
}

public class Main {
    public static void main(String[] args) {
        Animal animal = new Dog();  // Animal reference, but Dog object
        animal.sound();  // Output: Dog barks
    }
}
```

Explanation of the Code:

1. **Defining the Interface `Animal`:**
   o The `Animal` interface contains an abstract method `sound()`. Since this is an interface, the method does not have a body (implementation).
   o Any class that implements the `Animal` interface must provide an implementation for the `sound()` method.
2. **Implementing the Interface in the `Dog` Class:**
   o The `Dog` class implements the `Animal` interface. This means that it must provide its own implementation of the `sound()` method.
   o In the `Dog` class, the `sound()` method is overridden to print "Dog barks" when it is called.
3. **Using the Interface in the `Main` Class:**
   o In the `main` method, an `Animal` reference is used to hold an object of type `Dog`. This is an example of **polymorphism** where the `Animal` interface reference can point to any class that implements the `Animal` interface.

o When `animal.sound()` is called, the `sound()` method in the `Dog` class is executed, which outputs "Dog barks".

Key Points to Understand:

1. **No Method Implementation in Interfaces**:
o Interfaces do not provide method implementations; they only define method signatures. It's the responsibility of the implementing class to provide the actual behavior for those methods.
2. **Implementing an Interface**:
o A class can implement one or more interfaces. In the example, the `Dog` class implements the `Animal` interface and provides a specific implementation for the `sound()` method.
3. **Polymorphism**:
o Interfaces enable polymorphism because an interface reference can point to objects of different classes that implement the same interface. In the example, an `Animal` reference points to a `Dog` object, and when the `sound()` method is called, it invokes the implementation in the `Dog` class.
4. **Multiple Interfaces**:
o A class can implement multiple interfaces. This allows a class to inherit behavior from multiple sources, which is a way of achieving **multiple inheritance** in Java (since Java does not support multiple inheritance with classes).

```java
interface Animal {
    void sound();
}

interface Playable {
    void play();
}

class Dog implements Animal, Playable {
    public void sound() {
        System.out.println("Dog barks");
    }

    public void play() {
        System.out.println("Dog plays fetch");
    }
}
```

Advanced Interface Features:

1. **Default Methods (Java 8 and later)**:
o Java 8 introduced **default methods** in interfaces. These are methods with a body that can be directly implemented in the interface. A class that implements the interface can either use the default implementation or override it.

Example:

```
interface Animal {
    void sound();

    // Default method
    default void sleep() {
        System.out.println("Animal sleeps");
    }
}

class Dog implements Animal {
    public void sound() {
        System.out.println("Dog barks");
    }
}

public class Main {
    public static void main(String[] args) {
        Dog dog = new Dog();
        dog.sound();   // Output: Dog barks
        dog.sleep();   // Output: Animal sleeps (default method)
    }
}
```

2. **Static Methods (Java 8 and later)**:
   o   Java 8 also introduced **static methods** in interfaces. These methods belong to the interface itself, not to instances of the interface.

   Example:

```
interface Animal {
    static void info() {
        System.out.println("Animals are living organisms.");
    }
}

public class Main {
    public static void main(String[] args) {
        Animal.info();   // Calling static method of interface
    }
}
```

3. **Private Methods (Java 9 and later)**:
   o   Java 9 introduced **private methods** in interfaces. These methods are used internally within the interface to provide common code to default methods.

Conclusion:

An **interface** in Java defines a contract or a set of rules that classes must follow. It allows classes to implement the methods declared in the interface, ensuring a common behavior across different classes. Interfaces enable **polymorphism**, **multiple inheritance**, and provide a way to achieve abstraction in a clean and modular way. With the introduction of default and static methods in Java 8, interfaces became even more flexible by allowing method implementations in the interface itself.

4.5 Using and Extending Packages

In Java, **packages** are a way to group related classes and interfaces together. They help organize code logically, prevent name conflicts, and provide access control. A package is essentially a namespace for classes and interfaces, and it can be used to manage the classes in a project or library.

Key Concepts of Packages:

1. **Grouping Related Classes**:
   o Packages help group related classes together, which improves code organization and readability. For example, classes that deal with animals can be grouped into an `animals` package.
2. **Avoiding Name Conflicts**:
   o When multiple classes with the same name exist, packages help avoid name conflicts by differentiating them based on the package structure. For instance, `animals.Dog` and `vehicles.Dog` are two different classes, even though their names are the same.
3. **Access Control**:
   o Java provides access control modifiers that can be used to restrict access to classes, methods, or variables within a package. For example, if a class is marked as `public`, it can be accessed from any other class, whereas a class with default (package-private) access can only be accessed within its package.
4. **Reuse and Maintainability**:
   o By organizing classes into packages, Java enables better code reuse and maintainability. When you import packages, you can easily reuse classes and interfaces in different parts of a project without duplicating code.

---

1. Using Packages

To use a package, you first define the package at the beginning of a Java source file using the `package` keyword. After that, classes from the package can be imported using the `import` statement or referenced directly using the fully qualified name (package + class name).

Example of Using Packages:

```java
// Define a package named 'animals'
package animals;

public class Dog {
    public void sound() {
        System.out.println("Dog barks");     }}

// Main class that uses the 'Dog' class from 'animals' package
public class Main {
    public static void main(String[] args) {
        // Creating an object of Dog class from animals package
        animals.Dog dog = new animals.Dog();
        dog.sound();   // Output: Dog barks
    }
}
```

Explanation of the Code:

1. **Package Declaration**:
   o The first class `Dog` is part of the package `animals`. This is indicated by the line `package animals;`.
   o The `Dog` class has a method `sound()`, which prints "Dog barks".
2. **Accessing the Class from Another Class**:
   o In the `Main` class, we create an object of the `Dog` class. Since `Dog` is part of the `animals` package, we need to reference it by its fully qualified name (`animals.Dog`).
   o When we call `dog.sound()`, it prints the output "Dog barks".
3. **No Need for Import**:
   o In this example, we did not use the `import` statement explicitly, so we referenced the class using the fully qualified name (`animals.Dog`). However, using the `import` statement would make it simpler to refer to the class.

Example with Import:

```java
import animals.Dog;   // Importing the Dog class from the animals package

public class Main {
    public static void main(String[] args) {
        Dog dog = new Dog();   // No need to use fully qualified name
        dog.sound();   // Output: Dog barks
    }
}
```

2. Extending Packages (Hierarchical Organization)

Packages can be organized hierarchically, creating a tree-like structure where a sub-package is nested within a parent package. This allows for further categorization and organization of related classes.

Example of Extending Packages:

```
// Define the parent package 'animals'
package animals;

public class Dog {
    public void sound() {
        System.out.println("Dog barks");
    }
}

// Define the sub-package 'animals.mammals'
package animals.mammals;

public class Cat {
    public void sound() {
        System.out.println("Cat meows");
    }
}
```

Explanation of the Code:

1. **Parent Package (`animals`):**
o   The first class `Dog` is in the `animals` package. It has a method `sound()` that prints "Dog barks".
2. **Sub-package (`animals.mammals`):**
o   The second class `Cat` is in the sub-package `animals.mammals`. This class also defines a `sound()` method that prints "Cat meows".

By organizing classes this way, we can group animals into the general `animals` package and then further categorize them into sub-packages like `mammals`, `birds`, etc.

3. **Using Classes from Extended Packages:**
o   If we want to use classes from these extended packages, we would import them appropriately in the `Main` class.

```
import animals.Dog;   // Importing the Dog class from the animals package
import animals.mammals.Cat;   // Importing the Cat class from the
animals.mammals sub-package

public class Main {
    public static void main(String[] args) {
        Dog dog = new Dog();
        dog.sound();   // Output: Dog barks

        Cat cat = new Cat();
        cat.sound();   // Output: Cat meows
    }
}
```

Here, we have:

• **import animals.Dog;**: This imports the `Dog` class from the parent package `animals`.

- `import animals.mammals.Cat;`: This imports the `Cat` class from the `animals.mammals` sub-package.

Advantages of Using and Extending Packages:

1. **Better Code Organization**:
   o Packages help organize classes in a meaningful way, making it easier to maintain and scale your project. For example, classes related to animals can be grouped in the `animals` package, and classes specific to mammals can be placed in the `animals.mammals` sub-package.
2. **Name Conflict Avoidance**:
   o Packages ensure that classes with the same name do not conflict with each other. For instance, `animals.Dog` and `vehicles.Dog` can coexist without any issues because they are in separate packages.
3. **Modularity**:
   o By using packages, Java allows you to create modular code. A module (or package) can encapsulate related classes, making your program easier to understand and maintain.
4. **Access Control**:
   o Packages provide access control. For example, classes with default (package-private) access can only be accessed within the same package, helping to hide implementation details.
5. **Reusability**:
   o Packages can be reused in different projects. For instance, the `animals` package can be reused in another project without any need to copy all the classes, just by importing the package.

Conclusion:

Packages in Java are a fundamental way to organize and manage your code. They help to group related classes and interfaces together, prevent naming conflicts, and support access control. Additionally, Java supports hierarchical package structures, allowing you to extend packages into sub-packages to create an organized, scalable, and modular application architecture.

4.6 Package and Class Visibility

Java provides **access control mechanisms** to manage the visibility of classes, methods, and variables. These mechanisms determine how and where certain elements of a class can be accessed. The four primary access modifiers in Java are `public`, `private`, `protected`, and the default (also called package-private) access. Each of these modifiers serves a different purpose in terms of restricting or allowing access.

1. Public Access Modifier

The `public` access modifier is the most permissive of all access modifiers. When a class, method, or variable is marked as `public`, it can be accessed from any other class, whether it's in the same package or a different package.

Characteristics of `public`:

- **Accessible from anywhere**: There are no restrictions on where the `public` elements can be accessed.
- **No encapsulation**: Since everything is accessible, it is often not ideal to use `public` for sensitive data or methods unless explicitly needed.

Example:

```java
// Class with a public method
public class Dog {
    public String breed;

    public void sound() {
        System.out.println("Dog barks");
    }
}

// Accessing the public class and its method from another class
public class Main {
    public static void main(String[] args) {
        Dog dog = new Dog();   // Can access Dog because it's public
        dog.sound();              // Can call the public method sound()
    }
}
```

Explanation:

- The `Dog` class and its `sound()` method are `public`, meaning they can be accessed from any other class, as shown in the `Main` class.

---

2. Default (Package-private) Access Modifier

If no access modifier is specified, Java provides **default (package-private)** access. This means that the class, method, or variable can only be accessed within the **same package**.

Characteristics of Default Access:

- **Accessible within the same package only**: The default access is confined to the package the class or method belongs to.

- **Not accessible from outside**: If a class or member has default access, it cannot be accessed from classes that belong to different packages.

Example:

```
// Class with default (package-private) access
class Dog {
    String breed;

    void sound() {
        System.out.println("Dog barks");
    }
}

// Accessing the class within the same package
public class Main {
    public static void main(String[] args) {
        Dog dog = new Dog();   // Works because both are in the same
package
        dog.sound();              // Works because the method is also
package-private
    }
}
```

Explanation:

- Since both the `Dog` class and its `sound()` method have default access, they can be accessed within the same package (i.e., the `Main` class). If the `Main` class were in a different package, this would result in a compilation error.

3. Private Access Modifier

The `private` access modifier is the most restrictive access level. When a member (field or method) is marked as `private`, it is **only accessible within the same class** where it is declared.

Characteristics of `private`:

- **Accessible only within the same class**: A `private` member cannot be accessed from outside the class, not even by subclasses or other classes in the same package.
- **Encapsulation**: The `private` modifier is often used to protect the internal state of an object, ensuring that it is only modified or accessed through controlled methods (getters and setters).

Example:

```
// Class with private access modifier
public class Dog {
    private String breed;  // Private field
```

```
    private void sound() {  // Private method
        System.out.println("Dog barks");
    }

    public void makeSound() {
        sound();  // Can access private method from within the same class
    }
}

// Accessing private members from another class (will result in an error)
public class Main {
    public static void main(String[] args) {
        Dog dog = new Dog();
        // dog.sound();  // Compilation error: sound() has private access
        dog.makeSound();    // This works because makeSound() is public
and calls the private sound() method
    }
}
```

Explanation:

- The breed field and the sound() method are private, meaning they cannot be accessed from outside the Dog class.
- The makeSound() method is public and can call the private sound() method because both belong to the same Dog class.
- If we try to directly access sound() from the Main class, it results in a **compilation error** because sound() is private.

4. Protected Access Modifier

The protected access modifier allows a class, method, or variable to be accessed within the same package **and** by subclasses (including those in different packages).

Characteristics of protected:

- **Accessible within the same package**: Like the default (package-private) access, protected members can be accessed by any class in the same package.
- **Accessible by subclasses**: Subclasses, even if they are in different packages, can access protected members of their parent class.
- **Cannot be accessed by non-subclass classes outside the package**: A class that is not a subclass and is outside the package cannot access protected members.

Example:

```
// Parent class with protected access modifier
public class Animal {
    protected String name;
```

```
        protected void sound() {
            System.out.println("Animal makes a sound");
        }
    }

// Subclass in a different package
package animals;

public class Dog extends Animal {
    public void display() {
        System.out.println("Dog's name is " + name);
        sound();   // Accessing protected method
    }
}

// Accessing protected members in the same package
public class Main {
    public static void main(String[] args) {
        Animal animal = new Animal();
        // animal.name = "Lion"; // Compilation error: name has protected
access
        // animal.sound();        // Compilation error: sound() has
protected access
    }
}
```

Explanation:

- The `Animal` class has a `protected` field `name` and a `protected` method `sound()`.
- In the `Main` class (in the same package as `Animal`), the `protected` members cannot be accessed directly. However, in the `Dog` class (which extends `Animal`), we can access the `protected` members because `Dog` is a subclass of `Animal`.
- If the `Dog` class were in a different package, it could still access the `protected` members from the `Animal` class due to inheritance.

Summary of Access Modifiers:

Access Modifier	Accessibility	When to Use
public	Accessible from anywhere (within the same package or from other packages).	Use for classes, methods, or fields that need to be accessed universally.
default	Accessible only within the same package.	Use for classes, methods, or fields that should not be exposed outside the package.

Access Modifier	Accessibility	When to Use
`private`	Accessible only within the same class.	Use for encapsulation of data and implementation details that should not be accessed directly.
`protected`	Accessible within the same package and by subclasses.	Use when you want to allow access to subclasses, even from different packages, but keep the members hidden from the outside world.

Conclusion:

Java's access control modifiers allow developers to manage the visibility and accessibility of classes, methods, and variables. By using the appropriate access modifiers (`public`, `default`, `private`, `protected`), you can ensure that your code is properly encapsulated, secure, and flexible for reuse in larger applications. The right choice of access control helps maintain clean, maintainable code and supports principles such as **encapsulation** and **inheritance**.

4.7 Standard Java Packages: util, lang, io, net

Java provides several **built-in packages** that contain useful classes for various tasks. These packages simplify the development process by providing pre-built solutions for common tasks such as data structure manipulation, mathematical operations, input/output (I/O) handling, and network communication.

Let's explore the `util`, `lang`, `io`, and `net` packages in detail.

1. `java.util` Package

The `java.util` package contains a variety of utility classes that are commonly used in Java programs for handling collections, date and time, random numbers, and more.

Key Classes in `java.util`:

- **`ArrayList`**: A resizable array implementation of the `List` interface. It allows dynamic arrays that can grow as needed.
- **`HashMap`**: A map-based collection class that implements the `Map` interface. It stores key-value pairs.
- **`Date`**: A class that represents a specific point in time (although it has been largely replaced by newer date and time API classes).

- **HashSet**: A collection that implements the Set interface, backed by a hash table, ensuring uniqueness of elements.

Example: Using `ArrayList`:

```
import java.util.ArrayList;

public class Main {
    public static void main(String[] args) {
        // Creating an ArrayList to store strings
        ArrayList<String> list = new ArrayList<>();

        // Adding elements to the ArrayList
        list.add("Apple");
        list.add("Banana");

        // Printing the ArrayList
        System.out.println(list);  // Output: [Apple, Banana]
    }
}
```

Explanation:

- **ArrayList** is used to store a dynamic list of items. We add elements to the list using the add() method, and print the list using System.out.println().
- The **ArrayList** class automatically resizes itself when the list grows beyond its initial capacity, making it an essential tool for managing dynamic collections.

2. `java.lang` Package

The **java.lang** package is automatically imported by default in every Java program. It contains fundamental classes and methods that are essential for the Java language to function.

Key Classes in `java.lang`:

- **String**: Represents a sequence of characters. This class provides methods for manipulating strings (e.g., concatenation, comparison).
- **Math**: Provides mathematical functions like sqrt(), abs(), sin(), etc.
- **Object**: The root class of the Java class hierarchy. Every class in Java is a subclass of Object.
- **System**: Contains methods to interact with the system, such as System.out for printing output, System.currentTimeMillis() for getting the current time, etc.

Example: Using `Math` and `String`:

```
public class Main {
    public static void main(String[] args) {
        // Using Math class to calculate square root
        double result = Math.sqrt(25);
```

```
        System.out.println("Square root of 25: " + result);   // Output:
5.0

        // Using String class to concatenate strings
        String message = "Hello" + " " + "World!";
        System.out.println(message);   // Output: Hello World!
    }
}
```

Explanation:

- The **Math.sqrt()** method is used to calculate the square root of a number.
- The **String** class is used to concatenate two strings into one using the + operator.

3. java.io **Package**

The **java.io** package provides classes for **input/output operations**, allowing you to read from and write to files, interact with the console, and manage system input and output streams.

Key Classes in java.io:

- **File**: Represents file and directory pathnames in an abstract manner. Used to create, delete, or check file properties.
- **FileReader**: A convenience class for reading the contents of files as streams of characters.
- **BufferedReader**: A wrapper class that reads text from an input stream and buffers it, providing efficient reading of characters, arrays, and lines.

Example: Using FileReader and BufferedReader:

```
import java.io.FileReader;
import java.io.BufferedReader;
import java.io.IOException;

public class Main {
    public static void main(String[] args) {
        // Reading a file using FileReader and BufferedReader
        try (BufferedReader reader = new BufferedReader(new
FileReader("example.txt"))) {
            String line;
            while ((line = reader.readLine()) != null) {
                System.out.println(line);   // Output each line of the file
            }
        } catch (IOException e) {
            System.out.println("An error occurred while reading the
file.");
            e.printStackTrace();
        }
    }}
```

Explanation:

- **FileReader** reads the contents of a file as a stream of characters.
- **BufferedReader** wraps the `FileReader` to provide an efficient method `readLine()`, which reads the file line by line.
- The **try-with-resources** statement ensures that resources (like file streams) are properly closed after use.

4. `java.net` Package

The `java.net` package provides classes and interfaces for **network communication**. It allows Java programs to communicate over the network using protocols like HTTP, FTP, and TCP/IP.

Key Classes in `java.net`:

- **Socket**: A class for client-side network communication. It is used to establish connections to a server.
- **URL**: Represents a URL (Uniform Resource Locator) and allows you to access content from the web.
- **URLConnection**: Provides methods for reading from and writing to a resource specified by a URL.

Example: Using `Socket` for network communication:

```java
import java.net.Socket;
import java.io.IOException;

public class Main {
    public static void main(String[] args) {
        try {
            // Creating a socket to connect to a server
            Socket socket = new Socket("www.example.com", 80); // Connecting to port 80 on example.com
            System.out.println("Connected to server: " + socket.getInetAddress());
            socket.close();
        } catch (IOException e) {
            System.out.println("An error occurred while connecting to the server.");
            e.printStackTrace();
        }
    }
}
```

Explanation:

- A `Socket` is created to connect to a server (`www.example.com`) on port `80` (the default HTTP port).
- After establishing the connection, the `socket.getInetAddress()` method prints the server's IP address.
- The `socket.close()` method closes the connection once the communication is done.

Summary of Java Standard Packages:

Package	Description	Key Classes
`java.util`	Provides utility classes for collections, date and time, random numbers, etc.	`ArrayList, HashMap, Date, HashSet`
`java.lang`	Contains fundamental classes and methods essential for Java programming.	`String, Math, Object, System`
`java.io`	Provides classes for reading and writing data to files and streams.	`File, FileReader, BufferedReader`
`java.net`	Provides classes for network communication.	`Socket, URL, URLConnection`

Conclusion:

The Java **Standard Library** provides powerful and essential packages for a wide range of tasks. By utilizing these packages effectively, Java developers can leverage pre-built classes and methods for working with collections, performing mathematical operations, handling input/output, and establishing network communication. Understanding these packages helps you write efficient, clean, and maintainable Java code.

4.8 Wrapper Classes and Autoboxing/Unboxing

In Java, **wrapper classes** are used to convert **primitive data types** into **objects**. Each primitive type has a corresponding wrapper class in the `java.lang` package. For example, the primitive `int` has the wrapper class `Integer`, and the primitive `double` has the wrapper class `Double`. These wrapper classes allow you to treat primitive types as objects, which is particularly useful when you need to store primitives in collections like `ArrayList`, which can only hold objects.

Java also provides **autoboxing** and **unboxing** features that automatically convert between primitives and their corresponding wrapper classes.

---

1. Wrapper Classes in Java

Wrapper classes provide a way to treat **primitive types as objects**. The wrapper classes for primitive types are:

Primitive Type Wrapper Class

byte	Byte
short	Short
int	Integer
long	Long
float	Float
double	Double
char	Character
boolean	Boolean

Example of Wrapper Classes:

```java
public class Main {
    public static void main(String[] args) {
        // Wrapping an int into an Integer object
        Integer num = new Integer(10); // Deprecated in Java 9+

        // Wrapping a double into a Double object
        Double d = new Double(20.5);   // Deprecated in Java 9+

        System.out.println("Integer: " + num);
        System.out.println("Double: " + d);
    }
}
```

Explanation:

- The primitive type `int` is wrapped into an `Integer` object using the constructor `new Integer(10)`.
- Similarly, a primitive `double` is wrapped into a `Double` object.

Note: Starting from **Java 9**, constructors for wrapper classes like `Integer(int)` and `Double(double)` are deprecated. Instead, it's recommended to use **valueOf()** methods (e.g., `Integer.valueOf(10)`).

---

2. Autoboxing

Autoboxing is the automatic conversion of **primitive types** into their corresponding **wrapper class objects**. It is automatically handled by Java when you assign a primitive value to a wrapper class object.

Autoboxing Example:

```
public class Main {
    public static void main(String[] args) {
        // Autoboxing: primitive int to Integer object
        Integer num = 10;  // Autoboxing (primitive int to Integer object)

        // Printing the Integer object
        System.out.println("Integer: " + num);
    }
}
```

Explanation:

- The primitive value `10` is automatically converted (boxed) into an `Integer` object.
- You don't need to explicitly use the constructor or `valueOf()` method. Java performs this conversion behind the scenes.

Autoboxing makes the code more concise and easier to read. The compiler automatically wraps the primitive value into the wrapper class when necessary.

---

3. Unboxing

Unboxing is the reverse process of **autoboxing**, where an **object of a wrapper class** is automatically converted back to its corresponding **primitive type**.

Unboxing Example:

```
public class Main {
    public static void main(String[] args) {
        Integer num = 10;  // Autoboxing (primitive int to Integer object)

        // Unboxing: Integer object to primitive int
        int n = num;  // Unboxing (Integer to int)
```

```
        System.out.println("Primitive int: " + n);
    }
}
```

Explanation:

- The `Integer` object `num` is automatically converted (unboxed) back to the primitive `int` type when assigned to `n`.
- Java performs this conversion automatically when needed, so you don't need to manually extract the primitive value from the wrapper class object.

Benefits of Autoboxing and Unboxing:

1. **Convenience**: Java automatically handles the conversion between primitive types and wrapper classes, making code cleaner and reducing the need for manual conversion.
2. **Support for Collections**: Since Java collections (like `ArrayList`) cannot store primitive types, autoboxing makes it possible to store primitives in collections by automatically converting them to wrapper objects.
3. **Improved Readability**: By allowing the Java compiler to handle conversions, code becomes simpler and more readable without the clutter of explicit boxing or unboxing operations.

Performance Considerations:

- **Autoboxing/Unboxing overhead**: Although convenient, autoboxing and unboxing come with a slight performance cost because of the extra object creation and method calls involved. However, this cost is usually negligible in most applications.
- **NullPointerException**: One potential pitfall with unboxing is if the wrapper object is `null`, attempting to unbox it will throw a `NullPointerException`. For example:

```
Integer num = null;
int n = num;   // Throws NullPointerException
```

To avoid this issue, always check if the object is `null` before performing unboxing.

Conclusion:

- **Wrapper classes** in Java allow primitive types to be treated as objects.
- **Autoboxing** automatically converts primitives into wrapper class objects, and **unboxing** automatically converts wrapper objects back to their corresponding primitive types.
- These features make working with primitives in collections and other object-oriented constructs easier and more intuitive, while reducing boilerplate code.

4.9 Enumerations and Metadata

In Java, **enumerations (enums)** and **metadata (annotations)** are two important concepts that help improve code organization, readability, and maintainability.

1. Enumerations (Enums)

An **enum** is a special data type that enables you to define a collection of constants. These constants are typically used when you have a fixed set of values that the variable can take, such as days of the week, months of the year, or states in a process. Enums are type-safe, meaning that only the predefined constants can be used.

Basic Enum Example:

```
enum Day {
    MONDAY, TUESDAY, WEDNESDAY, THURSDAY, FRIDAY, SATURDAY, SUNDAY
}

public class Main {
    public static void main(String[] args) {
        Day today = Day.MONDAY;
        System.out.println(today);  // Output: MONDAY
    }
}
```

Explanation:

- The enum Day defines seven constants: MONDAY, TUESDAY, WEDNESDAY, etc.
- The variable today is of type Day, and it is assigned the value Day.MONDAY.
- When you print the variable today, it outputs MONDAY, which is one of the predefined constants in the Day enum.

Key Points about Enums:

- **Type Safety**: Enums are type-safe, meaning that a variable of type Day can only hold one of the defined enum constants (e.g., Day.MONDAY).

- **Implicit `toString()`**: The default implementation of `toString()` for an enum returns the name of the constant.
- **Enum Methods**: Enums in Java can have fields, methods, and constructors. This allows them to hold more complex data and behavior.

Example with Enum Methods:

```java
enum Day {
    MONDAY("Start of the workweek"),
    TUESDAY("Second day"),
    WEDNESDAY("Midweek"),
    THURSDAY("Almost weekend"),
    FRIDAY("Last workday"),
    SATURDAY("Weekend"),
    SUNDAY("Weekend");

    private final String description;

    // Constructor to initialize the description
    Day(String description) {
        this.description = description;
    }

    // Getter method for description
    public String getDescription() {
        return description;
    }
}

public class Main {
    public static void main(String[] args) {
        Day today = Day.MONDAY;
        System.out.println(today + ": " + today.getDescription());  //
Output: MONDAY: Start of the workweek
    }
}
```

Explanation:

- Each enum constant is initialized with a description.
- The `getDescription()` method returns the description of the day.
- This allows you to associate additional data (like descriptions) with each enum constant.

Advantages of Using Enums:

- **Fixed Set of Constants**: Enums ensure that only valid, predefined constants can be used, which helps prevent errors.
- **Readability and Maintainability**: Enums make code more readable and easier to maintain since the values are grouped in one place.
- **Enhanced Functionality**: Enums can have fields, constructors, and methods, which can encapsulate additional behavior and data related to the constants.

2. Metadata (Annotations)

Annotations in Java are used to provide **metadata** about a class, method, field, or parameter. Annotations do not change the behavior of the program, but they provide additional information that can be used by tools, libraries, or frameworks. Annotations are typically used for configuration, documentation, or processing at compile-time or runtime.

Common Use Cases:

- **Code Documentation**: To provide supplementary information about the code.
- **Configuration**: To indicate how certain classes or methods should be handled by frameworks (e.g., Spring, Hibernate).
- **Code Analysis**: To help tools and libraries analyze code during compilation or runtime.

Example of Annotations:

```
public class Dog {

    @Override
    public String toString() {
        return "Dog barks";
    }

    @Deprecated
    public void oldMethod() {
        // This method is no longer recommended for use
    }
}
```

Explanation:

1. **@Override**:
- The `@Override` annotation indicates that the method `toString()` is intended to override a method from a superclass.
- It helps ensure that the method is correctly overriding a method in the superclass. If there is a mistake (e.g., wrong method signature), the compiler will generate an error.
2. **@Deprecated**:
- The `@Deprecated` annotation marks the method `oldMethod()` as deprecated, indicating that this method is no longer recommended for use. Typically, it signals to other developers that a method may be removed or replaced in future versions.
- When used, a compiler warning is generated if the method is called elsewhere in the code.

Custom Annotations:

You can define your own annotations in Java.

```
@interface MyAnnotation {
    String value();
}
```

```
public class MyClass {

    @MyAnnotation(value = "Some Value")
    public void myMethod() {
        System.out.println("Method with custom annotation");
    }
}
```

Explanation:

- `@interface` is used to define a custom annotation named `MyAnnotation`.
- You can specify parameters (like `value`) for the annotation that can be used by tools or libraries for processing.
- The custom annotation is applied to the method `myMethod()`.

Metadata Processors:

- Java annotations are processed at runtime or compile-time by tools, libraries, or frameworks that are designed to read and act upon these annotations.
- For example, in frameworks like Spring, annotations like `@Autowired` are used to indicate dependency injection.

Summary:

- **Enumerations (Enums)** in Java define a set of named constants. They are type-safe and can include fields, methods, and constructors to add additional behavior to each constant.
- **Metadata (Annotations)** are used to provide additional information about classes, methods, or fields. Annotations help tools and libraries process or handle code without altering its execution behavior. Common annotations like `@Override`, `@Deprecated`, and custom annotations can be used to improve code readability, configuration, and processing.

These two concepts—**Enums** and **Annotations**—are powerful tools in Java that enhance the structure and maintainability of the code. They help ensure that the code is easy to understand, less error-prone, and compatible with various tools and frameworks.

50 MCQ ON THESE TOPICS

4.1 Single-Level and Multi-Level Inheritance

1. What is single-level inheritance?
    a) A class inherits from two classes
    b) A class inherits from one superclass only
    c) A class inherits from multiple superclasses
    d) None of the above
    Answer: b) A class inherits from one superclass only

2. Which of the following is true for multi-level inheritance?
    a) A class inherits directly from two classes
    b) A class inherits from a class that has already inherited from another class
    c) A class cannot inherit from a subclass
    d) None of the above
    Answer: b) A class inherits from a class that has already inherited from another class

3. In Java, which keyword is used for inheritance?
    a) implements
    b) inherits
    c) extends
    d) super
    Answer: c) extends

4. If class A extends class B, and class B extends class C, which type of inheritance is demonstrated?
    a) Single-level inheritance
    b) Multi-level inheritance
    c) Hierarchical inheritance
    d) None of the above
    Answer: b) Multi-level inheritance

5. What is the main advantage of inheritance in Java?
    a) Reduces redundancy
    b) Enables encapsulation
    c) Improves performance
    d) Allows method overloading
    Answer: a) Reduces redundancy

4.2 Method Overriding and Dynamic Method Dispatch

6. What is method overriding?
    a) Using the same method name but different parameter lists
    b) Defining a method in a subclass with the same signature as in its superclass
    c) Calling a method from another class
    d) None of the above

Answer: b) Defining a method in a subclass with the same signature as in its superclass

7. Which keyword is used to call the overridden method of a superclass?
   a) this
   b) super
   c) parent
   d) override
   Answer: b) super

8. Dynamic method dispatch refers to:
   a) Static binding of methods
   b) Runtime polymorphism where the call to an overridden method is resolved at runtime
   c) Method overloading
   d) Compile-time method resolution
   Answer: b) Runtime polymorphism where the call to an overridden method is resolved at runtime

9. Can static methods be overridden in Java?
   a) Yes
   b) No
   c) Only if the method is public
   d) None of the above
   Answer: b) No

10. Which of the following conditions is necessary for method overriding?
    a) The method must be static
    b) The method must have the same name, return type, and parameters
    c) The method must be private
    d) The method must have a different return type
    Answer: b) The method must have the same name, return type, and parameters

---

4.3 Abstract Classes

11. What is an abstract class?
    a) A class that cannot be extended
    b) A class that cannot be instantiated
    c) A class without methods
    d) A class with only static methods
    Answer: b) A class that cannot be instantiated

12. Which keyword is used to define an abstract class?
    a) abstract
    b) interface
    c) virtual
    d) static
    Answer: a) abstract

13. Can an abstract class have a constructor?
    a) Yes
    b) No
    Answer: a) Yes
14. Abstract classes can have:
    a) Only abstract methods
    b) Both abstract and concrete methods
    c) Only concrete methods
    d) Static methods only
    Answer: b) Both abstract and concrete methods
15. Which of the following is true about abstract methods?
    a) They have a body
    b) They cannot be overridden
    c) They must be implemented in the subclass
    d) They are always static
    Answer: c) They must be implemented in the subclass

4.4 Defining and Extending Interfaces

16. Which keyword is used to define an interface?
    a) interface
    b) abstract
    c) implements
    d) extends
    Answer: a) interface
17. An interface in Java can contain:
    a) Abstract methods only
    b) Static methods only
    c) Abstract methods and static constants
    d) Constructors
    Answer: c) Abstract methods and static constants
18. A class implements an interface using which keyword?
    a) extends
    b) implements
    c) abstract
    d) super
    Answer: b) implements
19. Can an interface extend another interface?
    a) Yes
    b) No
    Answer: a) Yes
20. What happens if a class implementing an interface does not define all its methods?
    a) It throws a runtime error
    b) It becomes an abstract class

c) It works fine without any issue
d) None of the above
Answer: b) It becomes an abstract class

4.5 Using and Extending Packages

21. What is a package in Java?
    a) A container for classes and interfaces
    b) A tool for memory management
    c) A framework for inheritance
    d) None of the above
    Answer: a) A container for classes and interfaces
22. Which keyword is used to define a package?
    a) package
    b) import
    c) class
    d) interface
    Answer: a) package
23. How do you access a class from another package?
    a) By using the `import` statement
    b) By using the `package` statement
    c) By using the `static` keyword
    d) By using the `public` keyword
    Answer: a) By using the `import` statement
24. Can a package contain sub-packages?
    a) Yes
    b) No
    Answer: a) Yes
25. Which of the following is a standard Java package?
    a) lang
    b) util
    c) io
    d) All of the above
    Answer: d) All of the above

\ 4.6 Package and Class Visibility

26. What is the default visibility of a class member in Java?
    a) Public
    b) Private
    c) Package-private
    d) Protected
    Answer: c) Package-private

27. Which access modifier allows access to class members only within the same package?
    a) Public
    b) Private
    c) Protected
    d) Default (no modifier)
    Answer: d) Default (no modifier)
28. How can you restrict a class from being accessed outside its package?
    a) Use the `private` modifier
    b) Use the `default` (no modifier) visibility
    c) Use the `protected` modifier
    d) Use the `final` keyword
    Answer: b) Use the `default` (no modifier) visibility
29. Which keyword is used to access a public class from another package?
    a) include
    b) use
    c) import
    d) extends
    Answer: c) import
30. Which access modifier provides the least restrictive access?
    a) Protected
    b) Private
    c) Public
    d) Package-private
    Answer: c) Public

4.7 Standard Java Packages: util, lang, io, net

31. Which package is automatically imported in every Java program?
    a) java.util
    b) java.io
    c) java.lang
    d) java.net
    Answer: c) java.lang
32. Which class is part of the `java.util` package?
    a) Scanner
    b) StringBuilder
    c) File
    d) URL
    Answer: a) Scanner
33. Which package contains classes for networking in Java?
    a) java.net
    b) java.util
    c) java.lang

d) java.io
Answer: a) java.net

34. The `java.io` package provides classes for:
   a) File handling and input/output operations
   b) String manipulation
   c) Networking
   d) Collections
   Answer: a) File handling and input/output operations

35. Which of the following is a class in the `java.util` package?
   a) ArrayList
   b) BufferedReader
   c) ObjectInputStream
   d) InetAddress
   Answer: a) ArrayList

4.8 Wrapper Classes and Autoboxing/Unboxing

36. What is the purpose of wrapper classes in Java?
   a) To wrap methods into objects
   b) To provide object equivalents for primitive data types
   c) To create collections
   d) None of the above
   Answer: b) To provide object equivalents for primitive data types

37. Which class is used as a wrapper for the `int` data type?
   a) Integer
   b) Float
   c) Byte
   d) Short
   Answer: a) Integer

38. Autoboxing in Java refers to:
   a) Converting an object into a primitive type
   b) Automatically converting a primitive type into its corresponding wrapper class object
   c) Using abstract classes
   d) None of the above
   Answer: b) Automatically converting a primitive type into its corresponding wrapper class object

39. Unboxing is the process of:
   a) Converting a primitive type into an object
   b) Converting an object into a primitive type
   c) Creating an array from a collection
   d) Extending a class
   Answer: b) Converting an object into a primitive type

40. Which of the following statements is true?
    a) Wrapper classes are immutable
    b) Wrapper classes are part of `java.lang` package
    c) Wrapper classes provide utility methods for type conversion
    d) All of the above
    Answer: d) All of the above

4.9 Enumerations and Metadata

41. What is an enumeration in Java?
    a) A data type that defines a fixed set of constants
    b) A class that wraps primitive data types
    c) A package for metadata
    d) A method for file handling
    Answer: a) A data type that defines a fixed set of constants

42. Which keyword is used to define an enumeration in Java?
    a) enum
    b) EnumClass
    c) enumtype
    d) static
    Answer: a) enum

43. How do you access a constant of an enumeration?
    a) enum_name.constant_name
    b) class_name.constant_name
    c) enum_name.constantName
    d) enum.constant_name()
    Answer: a) enum_name.constant_name

44. What is metadata in Java?
    a) Data about data
    b) Classes used for network programming
    c) Wrapper for primitive types
    d) File handling mechanism
    Answer: a) Data about data

45. Which annotation is used to define metadata in Java?
    a) @Override
    b) @Metadata
    c) @Retention
    d) @Target
    Answer: b) @Metadata

46. Which of the following is an advantage of using packages in Java?
    a) Avoids name conflicts
    b) Provides easier access control
    c) Allows grouping of related classes
    d) All of the above
    Answer: d) All of the above

47. Which of the following is NOT true for abstract classes?
    a) They can have both abstract and concrete methods
    b) They can be instantiated directly
    c) They are declared using the `abstract` keyword
    d) Subclasses must implement abstract methods
    Answer: b) They can be instantiated directly

48. Can an interface have a constructor?
    a) Yes
    b) No
    Answer: b) No

49. Which package provides support for regular expressions in Java?
    a) java.util
    b) java.regex
    c) java.text
    d) java.lang
    Answer: a) java.util

50. What is the main purpose of the `Object` class in Java?
    a) It provides utility methods for string manipulation
    b) It serves as the root of the class hierarchy
    c) It allows file handling operations
    d) It facilitates database connectivity
    Answer: b) It serves as the root of the class hierarchy

CHAPTER 5: EXCEPTION HANDLING, THREADING, NETWORKING AND DATABASE CONNECTIVITY

5.1 Exception Types and Uncaught Exceptions

In Java, **exceptions** are events that disrupt the normal flow of a program. They occur during runtime and can be caused by errors such as invalid input, unavailable resources, or logical mistakes in the code. Exceptions are handled using Java's **exception handling mechanism**, which includes `try-catch` blocks, `throws` declarations, and custom exception handling classes.

Java exceptions are categorized into **checked exceptions**, **unchecked exceptions**, and **errors**. Understanding these categories helps you handle exceptions properly and maintain the stability of your program.

---

1. Exception Types

1.1 Checked Exceptions:

- **Definition**: Checked exceptions are exceptions that **must** be explicitly handled or declared. These exceptions are checked at compile time, meaning the compiler ensures that you either handle them using `try-catch` blocks or declare them using the `throws` keyword in the method signature.
- **Examples:**
o `IOException` (e.g., file I/O errors)
o `SQLException` (e.g., issues with database connections)

Why Checked Exceptions Exist: These exceptions often represent conditions that are expected to occur, such as I/O errors, and the programmer is expected to handle them appropriately, either by recovering from the error or providing meaningful feedback to the user.

Example of Handling a Checked Exception:

```java
import java.io.*;

public class Main {
    public static void main(String[] args) {
        try {
            FileReader file = new FileReader("file.txt");  // May throw
FileNotFoundException
            BufferedReader fileInput = new BufferedReader(file);
            System.out.println(fileInput.readLine());
            fileInput.close();
```

```
    } catch (IOException e) {
        System.out.println("An error occurred: " + e.getMessage());
    }
  }
}
```

- In this example, `FileReader` can throw an `IOException`, which is a checked exception. The program handles the exception using a `try-catch` block to prevent the program from crashing.

1.2 Unchecked Exceptions:

- **Definition**: Unchecked exceptions are exceptions that are subclasses of `RuntimeException`. These exceptions **do not** need to be explicitly handled or declared in the code. They are typically caused by programming errors (e.g., accessing a null object, dividing by zero) and are unchecked at compile time.
- **Examples**:
o `ArithmeticException` (e.g., division by zero)
o `NullPointerException` (e.g., dereferencing a null reference)
o `ArrayIndexOutOfBoundsException` (e.g., accessing an invalid index in an array)

Why Unchecked Exceptions Exist: Unchecked exceptions are often the result of bugs or programming errors. These are usually caused by mistakes that the developer can fix easily, rather than being handled explicitly at runtime.

Example of Unchecked Exception:

```
public class Main {
    public static void main(String[] args) {
        int[] numbers = new int[5];
        System.out.println(numbers[10]);  //
ArrayIndexOutOfBoundsException
    }
}
```

- In this example, trying to access an index (`10`) that is out of bounds of the array will throw an `ArrayIndexOutOfBoundsException`. Since it's an unchecked exception, it does not require a `try-catch` block, though it can be handled if needed.

1.3 Errors:

- **Definition**: Errors represent serious issues in the Java Virtual Machine (JVM) or system environment that are **not meant to be handled by applications**. These are typically external to the application and indicate severe problems that the program cannot recover from.
- **Examples**:
o `OutOfMemoryError` (e.g., the JVM runs out of memory)

o `StackOverflowError` (e.g., too deep recursion)

Why Errors Exist: Errors are used to signal serious problems that usually cannot be handled by normal exception handling mechanisms. They are used to indicate JVM-level or system-level problems.

Example of an Error:

```java
public class Main {
    public static void main(String[] args) {
        // Simulating an OutOfMemoryError
        try {
            int[] largeArray = new int[Integer.MAX_VALUE];  //
OutOfMemoryError
        } catch (OutOfMemoryError e) {
            System.out.println("Error: " + e.getMessage());
        }
    }
}
```

- The `OutOfMemoryError` occurs when the JVM runs out of memory to allocate for an object or array. It is an error and not an exception, meaning it typically can't be handled in the same way as other exceptions.

2. Uncaught Exceptions

An **uncaught exception** is an exception that occurs during the execution of a program but is not caught by a `try-catch` block. When an exception is uncaught, the program will terminate abnormally, and the exception's message will be printed to the console. Uncaught exceptions can be handled by adding an appropriate `try-catch` block, or by allowing the exception to propagate to the method that invoked the problematic code.

Example of an Uncaught Exception:

```java
public class Main {
    public static void main(String[] args) {
        int result = 10 / 0;  // Uncaught ArithmeticException
    }
}
```

Output:

```
Exception in thread "main" java.lang.ArithmeticException: / by zero
```

```
at Main.main(Main.java:3)
```

Explanation:

- In this example, the expression `10 / 0` causes an `ArithmeticException`, which is an unchecked exception.
- Since there is no `try-catch` block to handle this exception, it is **uncaught**.
- As a result, the program terminates abnormally, and the exception's stack trace is printed to the console.

Summary:

- **Checked Exceptions**: Must be explicitly handled using `try-catch` or declared using `throws`. They represent exceptional conditions that a program can recover from, such as I/O errors.
- **Unchecked Exceptions**: Subclasses of `RuntimeException`. They are typically caused by programming errors and do not need to be explicitly handled.
- **Errors**: Represent severe issues (e.g., memory errors, JVM errors) that cannot be recovered from by the application.
- **Uncaught Exceptions**: If an exception is not caught by a `try-catch` block, it becomes uncaught, and the program terminates abnormally, printing an exception message and stack trace.

5.2 Throwing and Catching Exceptions

In Java, exceptions can be handled using a combination of **try-catch**, **finally**, and **throw** statements. These mechanisms allow you to manage exceptional conditions (errors or unexpected behavior) gracefully and ensure that your program doesn't crash abruptly. Let's break down these concepts in detail:

1. Throwing Exceptions

The `throw` statement in Java is used to **explicitly throw an exception**. You can throw an exception from a method or any part of the code where exceptional conditions are detected. Throwing an exception causes the program flow to jump to the appropriate exception handler (usually a `catch` block, if one exists).

Syntax:

```
throw new ExceptionType("Exception message");
```

- `ExceptionType`: The type of the exception being thrown (e.g., `ArithmeticException`, `IOException`, etc.).
- `"Exception message"`: A descriptive message about the exception.

Example: Throwing an Exception

```
public class Main {
    public static void main(String[] args) {
        try {
            validateAge(15);  // Trying to validate an age less than 18
        } catch (IllegalArgumentException e) {
            System.out.println("Caught Exception: " + e.getMessage());
        }
    }

    public static void validateAge(int age) {
        if (age < 18) {
            throw new IllegalArgumentException("Age must be 18 or
older.");
        }
        System.out.println("Valid age.");
    }
}
```

Output:

```
Caught Exception: Age must be 18 or older.
```

- In this example, the method `validateAge` checks if the age is below 18. If so, it throws an `IllegalArgumentException` with a message. This exception is caught in the `main` method by the `catch` block.

2. Catching Exceptions

The `catch` block is used to **handle exceptions** that occur within the `try` block. If an exception is thrown, the control is transferred to the `catch` block, which is responsible for handling the exception, logging it, or taking corrective action.

Syntax:

```
try {
    // Code that might throw an exception
} catch (ExceptionType e) {
    // Handling code for the caught exception
}
```

- **ExceptionType**: The specific type of exception that you want to catch.
- **e**: The reference variable that holds the caught exception object.

Example: Catching an Exception

```
public class Main {
    public static void main(String[] args) {
```

```
        try {
            int result = 10 / 0;   // Throws ArithmeticException
        } catch (ArithmeticException e) {
            System.out.println("Exception caught: " + e.getMessage());
        }
    }
}
```

Output:

```
Exception caught: / by zero
```

- In this example, an `ArithmeticException` is thrown due to division by zero inside the `try` block. The `catch` block catches the exception and prints a message using `e.getMessage()`, which returns the exception message.

3. The `finally` Block

The `finally` block in Java is used to **define code that will always be executed**, regardless of whether an exception was thrown or not. This is useful for cleanup tasks such as closing files, releasing resources, or restoring the state of the application.

- The `finally` block will execute after the `try` block completes, even if an exception was thrown or caught.
- The `finally` block is executed whether or not the exception is caught, and it executes after the `catch` block if an exception is caught.

Syntax:

```
try {
    // Code that might throw an exception
} catch (ExceptionType e) {
    // Handling code for the caught exception
} finally {
    // Code that will always be executed
}
```

Example: Using `finally`

```
public class Main {
    public static void main(String[] args) {
        try {
            int result = 10 / 0;   // Throws ArithmeticException
        } catch (ArithmeticException e) {
            System.out.println("Exception caught: " + e.getMessage());
        } finally {
            System.out.println("Finally block executed.");
        }
    }
}
```

```
}
```

Output:

```
Exception caught: / by zero
Finally block executed.
```

- In this example, after catching the `ArithmeticException`, the `finally` block is executed, ensuring that the cleanup code or other final actions are always performed.

4. Complete Example: Throwing, Catching, and Using `finally`

Let's combine all these concepts in a complete example where an exception is thrown, caught, and a `finally` block is used to print a final message.

```java
public class Main {
    public static void main(String[] args) {
        try {
            // Simulating an exception
            throw new Exception("Something went wrong!");
        } catch (Exception e) {
            System.out.println("Caught Exception: " + e.getMessage());
        } finally {
            System.out.println("Finally block executed.");
        }
    }
}
```

Output:

```
Caught Exception: Something went wrong!
Finally block executed.
```

- Here, an exception is explicitly thrown using `throw new Exception("Something went wrong!")`.
- The exception is caught in the `catch` block, and the message is printed.
- The `finally` block executes, showing that it runs regardless of whether an exception was thrown or caught.

Key Points:

- **Throwing an Exception**: Use `throw` to explicitly throw an exception when certain conditions are met.
- **Catching an Exception**: Use `try-catch` to handle exceptions that might be thrown in the `try` block. Catch specific types of exceptions to handle them appropriately.

- **Finally Block**: The `finally` block is used for cleanup tasks and will always execute after the `try` and `catch` blocks, whether an exception occurred or not.

By using these mechanisms, you can write robust code that properly handles exceptional situations and ensures that necessary resources are cleaned up.

5.3 Built-in Exceptions in Java

In Java, **built-in exceptions** are predefined exception classes that Java provides to handle common error scenarios during runtime. These exceptions are part of Java's exception handling framework, and they help in identifying and managing various types of errors that can occur during program execution.

Here is a detailed explanation of some common built-in exceptions:

1. ArithmeticException

- **Description**: This exception occurs when an exceptional arithmetic condition occurs, such as division by zero, which is mathematically undefined.
- **Common Scenario**: Dividing a number by zero.

Example:

```
public class Main {
    public static void main(String[] args) {
        int a = 10;
        int b = 0;
        try {
            int result = a / b;  // ArithmeticException: Division by zero
        } catch (ArithmeticException e) {
            System.out.println("Caught: " + e);
        }
    }
}
```

Output:

```
Caught: java.lang.ArithmeticException: / by zero
```

- **Explanation**: The exception occurs when trying to divide 10 by 0, which causes an `ArithmeticException`. The `catch` block handles it and prints the exception message.

2. NullPointerException

- **Description**: This exception occurs when you try to access or call methods or fields on an object reference that is `null`. Since `null` does not point to any object, dereferencing it leads to this exception.
- **Common Scenario**: Trying to access a method or property on an object that hasn't been initialized (i.e., the object reference is `null`).

Example:

```
public class Main {
    public static void main(String[] args) {
        String str = null;
        try {
            System.out.println(str.length());  // NullPointerException
        } catch (NullPointerException e) {
            System.out.println("Caught: " + e);
        }
    }
}
```

Output:

```
Caught: java.lang.NullPointerException
```

- **Explanation**: In this example, the variable `str` is `null`, and calling `str.length()` tries to dereference `null`, resulting in a `NullPointerException`. This is caught and printed by the `catch` block.

3. ArrayIndexOutOfBoundsException

- **Description**: This exception occurs when an attempt is made to access an index of an array that is either less than `0` or greater than or equal to the size of the array.
- **Common Scenario**: Trying to access an invalid array index (e.g., an index that doesn't exist in the array).

Example:

```
public class Main {
    public static void main(String[] args) {
        int[] numbers = {1, 2, 3};
        try {
            int value = numbers[5];  // ArrayIndexOutOfBoundsException
        } catch (ArrayIndexOutOfBoundsException e) {
            System.out.println("Caught: " + e);
        }
    }
}
```

Output:

```
Caught: java.lang.ArrayIndexOutOfBoundsException: Index 5 out of bounds
for length 3
```

- **Explanation**: The `numbers` array has only 3 elements (indices 0, 1, and 2). Trying to access index 5 results in an `ArrayIndexOutOfBoundsException`. The exception is caught and printed by the `catch` block.

4. ClassCastException

- **Description**: This exception occurs when an object is cast to a subclass or super class that it doesn't actually belong to. It typically occurs when trying to cast an object of one class to another class that is not related by inheritance.
- **Common Scenario**: Attempting to cast an object to a class of which it is not an instance.

Example:

```java
public class Main {
    public static void main(String[] args) {
        Object obj = new String("Hello");
        try {
            Integer num = (Integer) obj;  // ClassCastException
        } catch (ClassCastException e) {
            System.out.println("Caught: " + e);
        }
    }
}
```

Output:

```
Caught: java.lang.ClassCastException: class java.lang.String cannot be
cast to class java.lang.Integer
```

- **Explanation**: The object `obj` is actually a `String` but is being cast to an `Integer`. Since a `String` is not an instance of `Integer`, this causes a `ClassCastException`. The exception is caught and the message is printed.

Summary of Common Built-in Exceptions

1. **ArithmeticException**:
   o Occurs when an arithmetic error occurs (e.g., division by zero).
2. **NullPointerException**:
   o Occurs when attempting to dereference `null` (e.g., calling methods on a `null` object).
3. **ArrayIndexOutOfBoundsException**:

○ Occurs when trying to access an array index that is out of bounds.
4. **ClassCastException**:
○ Occurs when trying to cast an object to a type that it cannot be cast to (invalid type casting).

Best Practices for Handling Built-in Exceptions

- **Use appropriate exception handling**: For example, use a `try-catch` block for `ArithmeticException` to catch errors like division by zero.
- **Check for `null`** before accessing methods or fields of an object to avoid `NullPointerException`.
- **Ensure valid array indices**: Always check if an array index is within valid bounds before accessing the array to prevent `ArrayIndexOutOfBoundsException`.
- **Avoid unnecessary type casting**: Ensure that objects are being cast to the correct type, and consider using the `instanceof` operator to check the type before casting to prevent `ClassCastException`.

5.4 Creating Custom Exceptions

Java allows defining user-defined exceptions by extending the `Exception` class.

Example:

```
class CustomException extends Exception {
    public CustomException(String message) {
        super(message);
    }
}

public class Main {
    public static void main(String[] args) {
        try {
            throw new CustomException("This is a custom exception");
        } catch (CustomException e) {
            System.out.println("Caught: " + e.getMessage());
        }
    }
}
```

Output:

```
Caught: This is a custom exception
```

5.5 Multi-Threading: Thread Class and Runnable Interface

In Java, **multi-threading** is the concurrent execution of more than one task, and it allows multiple threads to run independently while sharing the same resources. This is particularly useful for tasks that are independent of each other and can be executed concurrently, thus improving the performance and responsiveness of an application.

Java supports multi-threading through two primary approaches:

- **Thread Class** (extends `Thread` class)
- **Runnable Interface** (implements `Runnable` interface)

Let's dive into both approaches in more detail:

---

1. Thread Class

In this approach, you **extend the `Thread` class** and override the `run()` method to define the task that will be executed by the thread. Once the class is created, you can start a new thread using the `start()` method, which calls the `run()` method in a new thread of execution.

Steps to Use the Thread Class:

1. **Extend the `Thread` class.**
2. **Override the `run()` method** to define the task that the thread will execute.
3. **Create an instance of the thread class.**
4. **Call the `start()` method** to initiate the thread.

Example Using Thread Class:

```
class MyThread extends Thread {
    public void run() {
        System.out.println("Thread is running.");
    }
}

public class Main {
    public static void main(String[] args) {
        MyThread t1 = new MyThread();
        t1.start();  // Starts the thread, invoking run() method in the
new thread
    }
}
```

Explanation:

- `MyThread` extends the `Thread` class and overrides the `run()` method to print a message.

- In the `Main` class, a new thread `t1` is created from `MyThread`.
- Calling `t1.start()` initiates the thread, and the `run()` method is executed in the new thread, printing `"Thread is running."`.

Output:

```
Thread is running.
```

2. Runnable Interface

Instead of extending the `Thread` class, you can also implement the `Runnable` interface. This is a more flexible approach, as Java allows only **single inheritance**, but implementing multiple interfaces is possible. This way, a class can implement `Runnable` and still inherit from another class.

Steps to Use the Runnable Interface:

1. **Implement the `Runnable` interface**.
2. **Override the `run()` method** to define the task for the thread.
3. **Create an instance of the `Thread` class**, passing an object that implements `Runnable`.
4. **Call the `start()` method** on the `Thread` object.

Example Using Runnable Interface:

```java
class MyRunnable implements Runnable {
    public void run() {
        System.out.println("Thread is running using Runnable.");
    }
}

public class Main {
    public static void main(String[] args) {
        Thread t1 = new Thread(new MyRunnable());
        t1.start();  // Starts the thread, invoking run() method in the
new thread
    }
}
```

Explanation:

- `MyRunnable` implements the `Runnable` interface and provides the implementation for the `run()` method.
- In the `Main` class, a new `Thread` object `t1` is created, passing an instance of `MyRunnable` to the constructor.
- Calling `t1.start()` initiates the thread, invoking the `run()` method of `MyRunnable`, and the message `"Thread is running using Runnable."` is printed.

Output:

```
Thread is running using Runnable.
```

Key Differences Between `Thread` Class and `Runnable` Interface

Feature	Thread Class	Runnable Interface
Inheritance	Inherits from `Thread` class	Implements `Runnable` interface
Extends/Implements	Extends `Thread` (cannot extend other classes)	Can implement multiple interfaces
Use Case	Suitable when creating a thread-specific class	Suitable when a class needs to implement other interfaces too
Task Definition	Override `run()` method in `Thread` class	Override `run()` method in the class implementing `Runnable`
Thread Creation	Directly call `start()` on the `Thread` instance	Pass `Runnable` object to the `Thread` constructor, then call `start()`

Advantages of Using Runnable Over Thread Class

1. **Multiple Inheritance**: A class can implement multiple interfaces, but it can only extend one class. By using `Runnable`, a class can still inherit from another class.
2. **Better Performance**: Implementing `Runnable` allows the separation of the task to be performed from the threading mechanism, which improves code reusability and modularity.
3. **Thread Pooling**: When using `Runnable`, it is easier to use thread pools (e.g., `ExecutorService`), which is a more efficient way of managing threads in high-performance applications.

Thread Lifecycle

In both approaches, a thread goes through the following stages in its lifecycle:

1. **New**: The thread is created but not yet started.
2. **Runnable**: The thread is ready to run, and the `start()` method is invoked.
3. **Blocked**: The thread is waiting for resources (e.g., I/O).

4. **Waiting**: The thread is waiting indefinitely (e.g., `join()` or `wait()`).
5. **Timed Waiting**: The thread is waiting for a specific period (e.g., `sleep()`).
6. **Terminated**: The thread has completed execution.

Summary

- **Thread Class**: Extends `Thread` and overrides the `run()` method to define the task.
- **Runnable Interface**: Implements `Runnable` and overrides the `run()` method. More flexible as it allows multiple inheritance.

5.6 Creating Single and Multiple Threads

Single Thread Example:

```
class MyThread extends Thread {
    public void run() {
        System.out.println("Single thread running.");
    }
}

public class Main {
    public static void main(String[] args) {
        MyThread t = new MyThread();
        t.start();
    }
}
```

Multiple Threads Example:

```
class MyThread extends Thread {
    public void run() {
        System.out.println(Thread.currentThread().getName() + " is
running.");
    }
}

public class Main {
    public static void main(String[] args) {
        MyThread t1 = new MyThread();
        MyThread t2 = new MyThread();
        t1.start();
        t2.start();
    }
}
```

5.7 Thread Prioritization, Synchronization, and Communication

1. **Thread Prioritization**:
o Threads have priorities ranging from 1 (`MIN_PRIORITY`) to 10 (`MAX_PRIORITY`).

```
t1.setPriority(Thread.MAX_PRIORITY);
```

2. **Synchronization**:
o Ensures thread-safe access to shared resources.

```
synchronized void display() {
    // Code    }
```

3. **Thread Communication**:
o Methods like `wait()`, `notify()`, and `notifyAll()` enable inter-thread communication.

5.8 Suspending and Resuming Threads

In Java, controlling the execution flow of threads is an important aspect of multi-threading. Java provides methods like `suspend()`, `resume()`, and `stop()` to control the state of threads, but **these methods are deprecated** in the modern Java API. This is because they can lead to unsafe and unpredictable behavior, especially when used improperly in multithreaded environments.

Instead of directly using these methods, it is recommended to use **flags** (boolean variables) and synchronization mechanisms to safely control the execution of threads.

Deprecated Methods

1. `suspend()`: This method is used to temporarily stop the execution of a thread. It puts the thread into the **"suspended"** state, but without a proper mechanism for resuming it, this could result in a deadlock where the thread remains suspended indefinitely.
2. `resume()`: This method is used to resume the execution of a thread that was suspended. However, if `suspend()` was not properly synchronized with `resume()`, it could lead to inconsistent thread states.
3. `stop()`: This method stops a thread immediately, without allowing it to finish its work properly. This can cause inconsistent or corrupt states, especially if the thread was in the middle of updating shared data or interacting with other threads.

Due to these potential issues, the Java community and the Java Development Kit (JDK) have **deprecated** these methods in favor of safer and more predictable alternatives.

Controlling Thread Execution Safely Using Flags

Instead of using `suspend()` or `resume()`, you can control thread execution using a **flag variable**. A flag is a boolean variable that indicates whether the thread should continue executing or not. This approach avoids the issues of suspending and resuming threads and ensures that thread execution can be safely controlled.

Example Using Flags:

```java
class MyThread extends Thread {
    private volatile boolean running = true;   // Flag to control thread execution

    public void run() {
        while (running) {
            System.out.println("Thread running...");
            try {
                Thread.sleep(1000);   // Sleep for 1 second to simulate work
            } catch (InterruptedException e) {
                System.out.println("Thread interrupted.");
            }
        }
    }

    // Method to stop the thread by setting the flag to false
    public void stopThread() {
        running = false;
    }
}

public class Main {
    public static void main(String[] args) {
        MyThread t1 = new MyThread();
        t1.start();   // Start the thread

        try {
            Thread.sleep(5000);   // Let the thread run for 5 seconds
        } catch (InterruptedException e) {
            e.printStackTrace();
        }

        t1.stopThread();   // Stop the thread by changing the flag value
    }
}
```

Explanation:

- **Flag (Volatile)**: The `running` variable is declared as `volatile` to ensure that the flag's value is always visible across all threads. This is crucial because the flag could be accessed or modified by multiple threads, and the `volatile` keyword ensures that changes to it are immediately visible to other threads.

- **Thread Loop**: The thread runs inside a `while (running)` loop, continuously checking the `running` flag. If the flag is `true`, the thread continues running; if it's `false`, the loop exits, effectively stopping the thread.
- **Stopping the Thread**: The method `stopThread()` changes the `running` flag to `false`, which causes the thread to exit its loop and terminate.

Key Points:

1. **Volatile Keyword**: The `volatile` keyword ensures that changes to the `running` flag are visible to all threads. Without `volatile`, there could be visibility issues where one thread doesn't immediately see the updated value of `running` and keeps executing indefinitely.
2. **Thread.sleep()**: This method simulates some work being done by the thread and ensures that the thread is not consuming CPU resources unnecessarily while it is running.
3. **Graceful Termination**: By using flags like `running`, the thread can exit gracefully. This is safer than forcibly stopping a thread, which could leave shared resources or data in an inconsistent state.

Why the Deprecation of `suspend()`, `resume()`, and `stop()`?

The reason these methods were deprecated is that they could cause several problems:

1. **Deadlocks**: If a thread is suspended and never resumed, it can lead to a deadlock where resources are locked but not released.
2. **Inconsistent State**: Forcing a thread to stop abruptly (`stop()`) without allowing it to finish its execution properly can lead to inconsistent states, especially if the thread was in the middle of modifying shared data.
3. **Unpredictable Behavior**: The suspension and resumption of threads can lead to timing issues, where other threads are affected by the suspension and resumption, causing race conditions.

Alternatives to `suspend()`, `resume()`, and `stop()`

1. **Using `volatile` flags**: This is the safest and most common way to control thread execution. Threads check the flag at regular intervals (or during appropriate moments in their execution) and decide whether to continue running or not.

2. **Thread Interruption**: Another approach is to use the `Thread.interrupt()` method to ask a thread to stop. This doesn't forcibly stop the thread but allows it to check the interrupt status and gracefully terminate when appropriate.

Example:

```
class MyThread extends Thread {
    public void run() {
        while (!Thread.currentThread().isInterrupted()) {
            System.out.println("Thread running...");
            try {
                Thread.sleep(1000);  // Simulating work
            } catch (InterruptedException e) {
                System.out.println("Thread interrupted.");
                return;  // Exit the loop gracefully when interrupted
            }        }    }}
```

3. **Thread Pools**: Instead of manually managing threads, you can use an `ExecutorService` or thread pool, which provides more control over the lifecycle of threads and their execution.

Summary

- **Deprecated Methods**: `suspend()`, `resume()`, and `stop()` are deprecated due to potential issues like deadlocks, inconsistent states, and unpredictable behavior.
- **Flags for Control**: The recommended way to control thread execution is by using a flag (e.g., `volatile boolean`) to determine whether the thread should keep running or stop.
- **Thread Interruption**: Using `Thread.interrupt()` allows threads to handle their interruption gracefully without abrupt termination.
- **Graceful Shutdown**: Always design threads to shut down gracefully by checking flags or using interrupt mechanisms rather than relying on deprecated methods.

5.9 Networking: `java.net` Package Overview

Java provides a powerful **`java.net` package** that enables network programming and communication over the internet or local networks. This package contains classes and interfaces for building networked applications such as web servers, clients, email clients, and more. It provides essential tools for working with **IP addresses**, **URLs**, **sockets**, and more.

Below are the key classes and concepts within the `java.net` package:

Key Classes in the `java.net` Package

1. `Socket`:

o The `Socket` class is used for **client-side communication** in networking. It allows the client to connect to a remote server, send and receive data.

o A `Socket` represents an endpoint of a communication link between two machines over a network.

o Example of client-side communication:

```
import java.net.*;
import java.io.*;

public class Client {
    public static void main(String[] args) throws IOException {
        // Create a socket to connect to the server
        Socket socket = new Socket("localhost", 8080);

        // Send a message to the server
        PrintWriter out = new PrintWriter(socket.getOutputStream(), true);
        out.println("Hello Server!");

        // Receive a message from the server
        BufferedReader in = new BufferedReader(new
InputStreamReader(socket.getInputStream()));
        System.out.println("Server says: " + in.readLine());

        // Close the socket connection
        socket.close();
    }
}
```

2. `ServerSocket`:

o The `ServerSocket` class is used to create **server-side communication**. It listens for incoming client connections on a specific port and establishes a `Socket` connection when a client requests a connection.

o It is used for **accepting connections** from clients.

o Example of server-side communication:

```
import java.net.*;
import java.io.*;

public class Server {
    public static void main(String[] args) throws IOException {
        // Create a ServerSocket to listen on port 8080
        ServerSocket serverSocket = new ServerSocket(8080);

        // Accept incoming client connection
        Socket clientSocket = serverSocket.accept();
        System.out.println("Client connected!");

        // Read message from the client
        BufferedReader in = new BufferedReader(new
InputStreamReader(clientSocket.getInputStream()));
        System.out.println("Client says: " + in.readLine());
```

```
            // Send a response back to the client
            PrintWriter out = new PrintWriter(clientSocket.getOutputStream(),
true);
            out.println("Hello Client!");

            // Close the socket connection
            clientSocket.close();
            serverSocket.close();
        }
}
```

3. **InetAddress**:
   - The InetAddress class represents an **IP address** and provides methods to resolve hostnames to IP addresses and vice versa.
   - It can be used to get the local host address or resolve a domain name (like www.google.com) to its corresponding IP address.
   - Example of resolving a hostname to an IP address:

```
import java.net.*;

public class Main {
    public static void main(String[] args) throws UnknownHostException {
        InetAddress address = InetAddress.getByName("www.google.com");
        System.out.println("IP Address: " + address.getHostAddress());  //
Output: IP Address: 142.250.190.14
    }
}
```

   - **Methods**:
   - getByName(String host) – Resolves a hostname (such as "www.google.com") into an InetAddress object.
   - getHostAddress() – Returns the IP address in the form of a string (e.g., "192.168.1.1").
   - getLocalHost() – Returns the local machine's IP address.
4. **URL**:
   - The URL class represents a **Uniform Resource Locator (URL)**, which is a pointer to a specific resource (like a web page or a file) on the internet.
   - It provides methods to parse and extract different parts of a URL (e.g., protocol, host, port, path).
   - Example of parsing a URL:

```
import java.net.*;

public class Main {
    public static void main(String[] args) throws MalformedURLException {
        URL url = new URL("https://www.google.com/search?q=java");
        System.out.println("Protocol: " + url.getProtocol());  // Output:
Protocol: https
        System.out.println("Host: " + url.getHost());          // Output:
Host: www.google.com
        System.out.println("Path: " + url.getPath());          // Output:
Path: /search
    }
}
```

○ **Methods**:
- `getProtocol()` – Returns the protocol (e.g., `http`, `https`).
- `getHost()` – Returns the domain name or IP address.
- `getPort()` – Returns the port number, or `-1` if the default port is used.
- `getPath()` – Returns the path section of the URL (e.g., `/search`).

How to Use `java.net` Classes in Networking:

1. **Creating a Server**:
○ A **server** listens on a specific port for incoming client connections.
○ The `ServerSocket` class is used for creating a server that listens for incoming connections and accepts them.
○ Once a connection is established, the server can use the `Socket` class to communicate with the client.
2. **Creating a Client**:
○ A **client** uses the `Socket` class to connect to a server.
○ Once connected, the client can send and receive data using input and output streams.

Exception Handling in Networking

1. `UnknownHostException`:
○ This exception occurs when a hostname could not be resolved to an IP address.
○ Example: Trying to resolve a non-existent hostname like `www.nonexistentwebsite.com`.
2. `SocketException`:
○ This exception occurs if an error occurs while creating or accessing a socket.
○ Example: Trying to connect to a server that is unreachable.
3. `IOException`:
○ This is a general exception that occurs during input/output operations like reading from or writing to a socket or file.
○ Example: An error occurs while reading data from a socket.

Important Methods in `java.net` Classes:

1. `Socket`:
○ `connect(SocketAddress endpoint)` – Connects the socket to a specific endpoint.
○ `getInputStream()` – Returns an input stream to read data from the socket.
○ `getOutputStream()` – Returns an output stream to send data to the socket.
2. `ServerSocket`:
○ `accept()` – Listens for incoming client connections and returns a `Socket` object to communicate with the client.

3. `InetAddress`:
   o `getByName(String host)` – Resolves a hostname to an `InetAddress`.
   o `isReachable(int timeout)` – Checks if the host is reachable within the given timeout.
4. `URL`:
   o `openStream()` – Opens an input stream to read from the URL.
   o `getQuery()` – Returns the query part of the URL (e.g., "q=java").

Summary of `java.net` Package

- The `java.net` package provides essential classes for network communication, such as `Socket` (for client-side), `ServerSocket` (for server-side), `InetAddress` (for handling IP addresses), and `URL` (for working with URLs).
- It supports both **client-server communication** through **sockets** and provides tools for resolving domain names and handling network resources.
- Networking in Java involves handling connections, sending/receiving data, and dealing with potential exceptions such as `UnknownHostException` or `SocketException`.

5.10 TCP/IP and Datagram Programming

Java provides two different types of communication models for network programming: **TCP/IP (Transmission Control Protocol/Internet Protocol)** and **UDP (User Datagram Protocol)**. Each model has its own advantages and use cases. Java's `java.net` package provides classes for both types of communication, namely `Socket` and `ServerSocket` for TCP/IP and `DatagramSocket` and `DatagramPacket` for UDP.

1. TCP/IP (Transmission Control Protocol/Internet Protocol)

Overview of TCP/IP:

- **TCP** is a connection-oriented protocol, which means that it establishes a reliable, full-duplex connection between the client and server before data can be sent.
- It ensures that the data is delivered correctly, in sequence, and without errors. If packets are lost or arrive out of order, TCP automatically handles retransmissions and reordering.
- **IP** handles addressing and routing of packets between devices.

TCP/IP Communication in Java:

- Java uses **Socket** and **ServerSocket** classes to implement TCP/IP communication.

- o **Socket** is used for the client-side connection to the server.
- o **ServerSocket** listens for incoming client connections on the server side.

Steps in TCP Communication:

1. **Server Side**:
- o The server creates a `ServerSocket` object and binds it to a specific port. It listens for incoming client requests.
- o Once a client requests a connection, the `ServerSocket` accepts it and returns a `Socket` object that the server can use to communicate with the client.
2. **Client Side**:
- o The client creates a `Socket` object and connects to the server's IP address and port.
- o Once the connection is established, both the client and server can send and receive data through input and output streams.

Example of TCP/IP Communication:

```
Client (TCP/IP):
import java.io.*;
import java.net.*;

public class TCPClient {
    public static void main(String[] args) {
        try {
            // Create a socket to connect to the server at localhost on
port 5000
            Socket socket = new Socket("localhost", 5000);

            // Create output stream to send data to the server
            PrintWriter out = new PrintWriter(socket.getOutputStream(),
true);
            out.println("Hello Server!");

            // Create input stream to read data from the server
            BufferedReader in = new BufferedReader(new
InputStreamReader(socket.getInputStream()));
            String response = in.readLine();
            System.out.println("Server says: " + response);

            // Close the socket
            socket.close();
        } catch (IOException e) {
            e.printStackTrace();
        }
    }
}
Server (TCP/IP):
import java.io.*;
import java.net.*;

public class TCPServer {
    public static void main(String[] args) {
```

```
    try {
        // Create a ServerSocket on port 5000
        ServerSocket serverSocket = new ServerSocket(5000);

        // Accept incoming client connections
        Socket clientSocket = serverSocket.accept();
        System.out.println("Client connected!");

        // Create input stream to receive data from the client
        BufferedReader in = new BufferedReader(new
InputStreamReader(clientSocket.getInputStream()));
        String clientMessage = in.readLine();
        System.out.println("Client says: " + clientMessage);

        // Send response to the client
        PrintWriter out = new
PrintWriter(clientSocket.getOutputStream(), true);
        out.println("Hello Client!");

        // Close the client and server socket
        clientSocket.close();
        serverSocket.close();
    } catch (IOException e) {
        e.printStackTrace();
    }
  }
}
```

Key Classes for TCP/IP Communication:

- `Socket`: Client-side class used to establish a connection to a server and send/receive data.
- `ServerSocket`: Server-side class that listens for incoming connections from clients.
- `PrintWriter`: A writer that allows the client or server to send data to the other side.
- `BufferedReader`: A reader that allows receiving data from the other side.

2. Datagram (UDP) Programming

Overview of UDP:

- **UDP** is a connectionless protocol, meaning it does not establish a formal connection between the sender and receiver. It simply sends data in packets (datagrams) to a specified destination.
- Unlike TCP, UDP does not guarantee the reliability, ordering, or error correction of data. It is faster but less reliable, making it suitable for applications where speed is critical and occasional data loss is acceptable (e.g., real-time applications like streaming, gaming).

UDP Communication in Java:

- Java uses the `DatagramSocket` and `DatagramPacket` classes for UDP communication.
- `DatagramSocket` is used for sending and receiving UDP datagrams.

o **DatagramPacket** is used to store data sent or received by a socket.

Steps in UDP Communication:

1. **Server Side**:
o The server creates a DatagramSocket and listens for incoming datagrams on a specific port.
o When a datagram is received, the server processes it and can send a response back to the client.
2. **Client Side**:
o The client creates a DatagramSocket and sends a DatagramPacket to the server's IP address and port.

Example of UDP Communication:

Client (UDP):
```java
import java.net.*;

public class UDPClient {
    public static void main(String[] args) {
        try {
            // Create a DatagramSocket
            DatagramSocket socket = new DatagramSocket();

            // Create a message to send
            String message = "Hello Server!";
            byte[] buffer = message.getBytes();

            // Create a DatagramPacket to send the message to the server
at port 5000
            DatagramPacket packet = new DatagramPacket(buffer,
buffer.length, InetAddress.getByName("localhost"), 5000);

            // Send the packet to the server
            socket.send(packet);

            // Close the socket
            socket.close();
        } catch (Exception e) {
            e.printStackTrace();
        }
    }
}
```
Server (UDP):
```java
import java.net.*;

public class UDPServer {
    public static void main(String[] args) {
        try {
            // Create a DatagramSocket to listen on port 5000
            DatagramSocket socket = new DatagramSocket(5000);

            // Create a buffer to receive incoming packets
            byte[] buffer = new byte[1024];
```

```
            DatagramPacket packet = new DatagramPacket(buffer,
buffer.length);

            // Receive a packet from the client
            socket.receive(packet);

            // Convert the received message to a string
            String message = new String(packet.getData(), 0,
packet.getLength());
            System.out.println("Received from client: " + message);

            // Close the socket
            socket.close();
        } catch (Exception e) {
            e.printStackTrace();
        }
    }
}
```

Key Classes for UDP Communication:

- `DatagramSocket`: The class used for sending and receiving datagrams.
- `DatagramPacket`: This class represents a packet of data to be sent or received through the `DatagramSocket`.
- `InetAddress`: Used to represent the IP address of the destination.

Comparison Between TCP and UDP:

Feature	TCP (Transmission Control Protocol)	UDP (User Datagram Protocol)
Connection	Connection-oriented, reliable	Connectionless, unreliable
Reliability	Guarantees delivery, order, error-checking	No guarantee of delivery, order, or error-checking
Speed	Slower due to connection setup and error recovery	Faster due to no connection setup or error recovery
Use Cases	Web pages, file transfers, email, etc.	Real-time applications, streaming, gaming, etc.
Protocols	HTTP, FTP, SMTP, etc.	DNS, VoIP, video streaming, online gaming, etc.

Summary:

- **TCP/IP**: Provides reliable communication through the `Socket` and `ServerSocket` classes. It is suitable for applications requiring guaranteed delivery of data.
- **UDP**: Provides faster but less reliable communication using the `DatagramSocket` and `DatagramPacket` classes. It is used for applications where speed is more critical than reliability, such as in real-time communications.

5.11 JDBC: Accessing and Manipulating Databases

Java Database Connectivity (JDBC) is a standard API in Java for connecting to databases and performing operations like querying, updating, and managing data. JDBC provides a set of classes and interfaces to interact with various relational databases, such as MySQL, Oracle, and PostgreSQL.

Steps to Access and Manipulate Databases Using JDBC:

There are several key steps in using JDBC to connect to a database and perform queries or updates.

1. Load the JDBC Driver:

The first step in using JDBC is to load the appropriate database driver. Each database has its own driver, and you load it using `Class.forName()`. This step allows Java to know which driver to use when establishing a connection.

For example, to use MySQL, you load the MySQL driver:

```
Class.forName("com.mysql.jdbc.Driver");
```

This statement ensures that the necessary classes for MySQL connectivity are loaded into the JVM.

Note: In newer versions of JDBC, this step is often not required for modern drivers, as they are loaded automatically via the JDBC URL.

2. Establish Connection:

After loading the driver, the next step is to establish a connection to the database using the `DriverManager.getConnection()` method. This method requires the URL of the database, the username, and the password.

Example:

```
Connection con =
DriverManager.getConnection("jdbc:mysql://localhost:3306/testdb", "root",
"password");
```

Here:

- `jdbc:mysql://localhost:3306/testdb` is the URL that specifies the protocol (`jdbc:mysql`), the host (`localhost`), the port (`3306`), and the database name (`testdb`).
- `"root"` and `"password"` are the credentials used to authenticate the connection.

---

3. Execute Queries:

Once the connection is established, you can create a `Statement` object and execute SQL queries using the `executeQuery()` method for SELECT queries or `executeUpdate()` for INSERT, UPDATE, or DELETE queries.

To execute a query:

- **Create a `Statement` object**: A `Statement` object is used to send SQL statements to the database.
- **Execute the query**: The `executeQuery()` method is used for SELECT queries, and it returns a `ResultSet` object that holds the results of the query.

Example of SELECT Query:

```
Statement stmt = con.createStatement();
ResultSet rs = stmt.executeQuery("SELECT * FROM users");
```

Explanation:

- `con.createStatement()` creates a new `Statement` object.
- `stmt.executeQuery("SELECT * FROM users")` executes the SQL query `"SELECT * FROM users"` on the connected database. This query retrieves all rows from the `users` table.

The results are returned as a `ResultSet` object, which allows you to iterate over the retrieved data.

Iterating Over Results:

You can use the `ResultSet` object's `next()` method to iterate through each row of the result. For each row, you can use `getString()`, `getInt()`, or other methods to retrieve values based on column names.

```
while (rs.next()) {
```

```
            System.out.println(rs.getString("name"));
}
```

Here:

- `rs.next()` moves the cursor to the next row in the result set.
- `rs.getString("name")` retrieves the value of the `name` column as a string.

4. Closing the Connection:

After completing the database operations, it is essential to close the `Connection` object to release database resources.

```
con.close();
```

It is also a good practice to close `Statement` and `ResultSet` objects after use to avoid resource leaks.

Example Program Using JDBC:

```java
import java.sql.*;

public class Main {
    public static void main(String[] args) {
        try {
            // Load the MySQL JDBC driver
            Class.forName("com.mysql.jdbc.Driver");

            // Establish connection to the database
            Connection con =
DriverManager.getConnection("jdbc:mysql://localhost:3306/testdb", "root",
"password");

            // Create a Statement object to execute queries
            Statement stmt = con.createStatement();

            // Execute a SELECT query
            ResultSet rs = stmt.executeQuery("SELECT * FROM users");

            // Process the result set
            while (rs.next()) {
                System.out.println(rs.getString("name"));
            }
            // Close the connection
            con.close();          } catch (SQLException e) {
            System.out.println("SQL Error: " + e.getMessage());
        } catch (ClassNotFoundException e) {
```

```
                System.out.println("Driver not found: " + e.getMessage());
}     }}
```

Explanation of the Code:

- **Loading the JDBC Driver**: `Class.forName("com.mysql.jdbc.Driver")` loads the MySQL JDBC driver. This step is only necessary for older JDBC versions.
- **Connecting to the Database**: `DriverManager.getConnection()` establishes the connection using the specified database URL, username, and password.
- **Executing a Query**: `stmt.executeQuery("SELECT * FROM users")` sends the SQL query to the database. The `ResultSet` object holds the result.
- **Processing the Result**: The `while (rs.next())` loop processes each row in the result set. `rs.getString("name")` retrieves the value of the `name` column for each row.
- **Closing the Connection**: The connection is closed after all database operations are completed.

Error Handling in JDBC:

- **SQLException**: This is the exception thrown when database-related errors occur. You can catch and handle this exception using a `try-catch` block.
- **ClassNotFoundException**: This is thrown if the JDBC driver class is not found.

Key Classes and Interfaces in JDBC:

1. `DriverManager`: Manages the list of database drivers. It establishes a connection to the database using the appropriate driver.
2. `Connection`: Represents a connection to the database. It provides methods to create `Statement` objects, manage transactions, and close the connection.
3. `Statement`: Used to execute SQL queries. It can be a simple statement (`Statement`), a prepared statement (`PreparedStatement`), or a callable statement (`CallableStatement`).
4. `ResultSet`: Holds the data retrieved from the database. It provides methods like `next()`, `getString()`, `getInt()`, etc., to fetch column values.
5. `SQLException`: The exception class for SQL errors. It provides methods to get error details such as the error code and message.

Summary of JDBC Steps:

1. **Load the Driver**: Load the JDBC driver using `Class.forName()`.
2. **Establish Connection**: Use `DriverManager.getConnection()` to establish a connection to the database.
3. **Execute Queries**: Use `Statement` or `PreparedStatement` to execute SQL queries (e.g., SELECT, INSERT, UPDATE, DELETE).

4. **Process the Results**: Use `ResultSet` to retrieve and process the data returned from the database.
5. **Close the Connection**: Close the `Connection` and other resources after use to release database resources.

50 MCQ ON THESE TOPICS

5.1 Exception Types and Uncaught Exceptions

1. What is an exception in Java?
   a) A compile-time error
   b) A runtime error
   c) An unexpected event during execution
   d) None of the above
   Answer: c) An unexpected event during execution
2. Which class is the root of the exception hierarchy?
   a) Object
   b) Throwable
   c) Exception
   d) Error
   Answer: b) Throwable
3. What is the default behavior of an uncaught exception?
   a) Program terminates
   b) Exception is ignored
   c) A warning is displayed, but the program continues
   d) JVM halts without any message
   Answer: a) Program terminates
4. Which of the following is NOT an unchecked exception?
   a) ArithmeticException
   b) NullPointerException
   c) IOException
   d) ArrayIndexOutOfBoundsException
   Answer: c) IOException
5. An uncaught exception results in:
   a) Termination of the program
   b) Graceful program completion
   c) Continuation of program execution
   d) Exception being ignored
   Answer: a) Termination of the program

5.2 Throwing and Catching Exceptions

6. Which keyword is used to throw an exception?
   a) throws
   b) catch

c) throw

d) try

Answer: c) throw

7. The `finally` block in exception handling is used for:
   a) Throwing exceptions
   b) Catching exceptions
   c) Code cleanup
   d) Declaring exceptions
   Answer: c) Code cleanup

8. Which is the correct syntax for catching an exception?
   a) try { } catch(Exception e) { }
   b) try { } throw(Exception e) { }
   c) catch { } try(Exception e) { }
   d) None of the above
   Answer: a) try { } catch(Exception e) { }

9. What happens if an exception is thrown outside a try block?
   a) Compilation error
   b) JVM catches it automatically
   c) Program terminates
   d) The exception is ignored
   Answer: c) Program terminates

10. The `throws` keyword is used to:
    a) Catch exceptions
    b) Declare exceptions in the method signature
    c) Execute the `finally` block
    d) Handle checked exceptions only
    Answer: b) Declare exceptions in the method signature

5.3 Built-in Exceptions

11. Which of these is a built-in exception?
    a) MyCustomException
    b) SQLException
    c) MyRuntimeException
    d) None of the above
    Answer: b) SQLException

12. NullPointerException occurs when:
    a) A null reference is used where an object is required
    b) A file is not found
    c) An array goes out of bounds
    d) Division by zero occurs
    Answer: a) A null reference is used where an object is required

13. Which of these exceptions is NOT a checked exception?
    a) FileNotFoundException

b) IOException
c) SQLException
d) RuntimeException
Answer: d) RuntimeException

14. What does `ArithmeticException` indicate?
    a) Division by zero
    b) File not found
    c) Null reference
    d) Out-of-memory error
    Answer: a) Division by zero

15. IOException is part of which package?
    a) java.util
    b) java.lang
    c) java.io
    d) java.net
    Answer: c) java.io

5.4 Creating Custom Exceptions

16. Custom exceptions must extend:
    a) Throwable
    b) Error
    c) Exception
    d) Object
    Answer: c) Exception

17. What keyword is used to define a custom exception?
    a) extends
    b) implements
    c) throws
    d) try
    Answer: a) extends

18. A custom exception is created to:
    a) Handle file errors
    b) Define user-specific error conditions
    c) Modify JVM behavior
    d) None of the above
    Answer: b) Define user-specific error conditions

19. To throw a custom exception, you use:
    a) throw new Exception();
    b) throw new CustomException();
    c) throws CustomException;
    d) catch CustomException;
    Answer: b) throw new CustomException();

20. A custom exception is part of:
    a) Checked exceptions
    b) Unchecked exceptions
    c) Both
    d) Neither
    Answer: a) Checked exceptions

5.5 Multi-Threading: Thread Class and Runnable Interface

21. Threads in Java are implemented using:
    a) Runnable Interface
    b) Thread Class
    c) Both a and b
    d) None of the above
    Answer: c) Both a and b
22. The `run()` method of the `Runnable` interface contains:
    a) The code to be executed by a thread
    b) The thread priority
    c) The thread name
    d) The thread status
    Answer: a) The code to be executed by a thread
23. To start a thread, which method is used?
    a) execute()
    b) run()
    c) start()
    d) begin()
    Answer: c) start()
24. Which method is used to check if a thread is alive?
    a) isRunning()
    b) isAlive()
    c) checkThread()
    d) None of the above
    Answer: b) isAlive()
25. What does the `sleep()` method do?
    a) Stops a thread permanently
    b) Puts a thread into the waiting state
    c) Pauses a thread temporarily
    d) Kills a thread
    Answer: c) Pauses a thread temporarily

5.6 Creating Single and Multiple Threads

26. Which method creates a new thread?
    a) execute()
    b) init()
    c) Thread()
    d) None of the above
    Answer: c) Thread()

27. Can multiple threads share the same object?
    a) Yes
    b) No
    Answer: a) Yes

28. What happens if you call the `run()` method directly instead of `start()`?
    a) A new thread is created
    b) The current thread executes `run()` as a normal method
    c) An exception is thrown
    d) None of the above
    Answer: b) The current thread executes `run()` as a normal method

29. The thread's life cycle is managed by:
    a) JVM
    b) OS
    c) Both JVM and OS
    d) None of the above
    Answer: c) Both JVM and OS

30. Which priority is higher?
    a) Thread.MIN_PRIORITY
    b) Thread.NORM_PRIORITY
    c) Thread.MAX_PRIORITY
    d) None of the above
    Answer: c) Thread.MAX_PRIORITY

5.7 Thread Prioritization, Synchronization, and Communication

31. What is the default priority of a thread?
    a) 0
    b) 1
    c) Thread.NORM_PRIORITY
    d) Thread.MAX_PRIORITY
    Answer: c) Thread.NORM_PRIORITY

32. Which method is used to set the priority of a thread?
    a) setPriority()
    b) changePriority()
    c) updatePriority()
    d) modifyPriority()
    Answer: a) setPriority()

33. What is the purpose of thread synchronization?
    a) To ensure thread-safe execution of critical sections
    b) To reduce the execution time of a thread
    c) To execute threads concurrently
    d) To terminate threads automatically
    Answer: a) To ensure thread-safe execution of critical sections

34. Which of these is a valid way to synchronize a method?
    a) synchronized method()
    b) synchronized static method()
    c) synchronized void method()
    d) Both a and b
    Answer: d) Both a and b

35. Which method is used for inter-thread communication?
    a) wait()
    b) notify()
    c) notifyAll()
    d) All of the above
    Answer: d) All of the above

5.8 Suspending and Resuming Threads

36. Which method is used to suspend a thread's execution temporarily?
    a) stop()
    b) suspend()
    c) halt()
    d) wait()
    Answer: b) suspend()

37. What happens when the `resume()` method is called on a suspended thread?
    a) The thread terminates
    b) The thread execution continues
    c) The thread enters the waiting state
    d) The thread is blocked
    Answer: b) The thread execution continues

38. Which method is used to stop a thread permanently?
    a) exit()
    b) stop()
    c) terminate()
    d) end()
    Answer: b) stop()

39. The `wait()` method should be called from within a:
    a) synchronized method
    b) thread object
    c) main method

d) constructor
Answer: a) synchronized method
40. What is the effect of calling `notifyAll()`?
   a) It wakes up all threads waiting on the object's monitor
   b) It terminates all threads
   c) It resumes the main thread
   d) None of the above
   Answer: a) It wakes up all threads waiting on the object's monitor

5.9 Networking: java.net Package Overview

41. Which class in the `java.net` package is used to represent an IP address?
   a) InetAddress
   b) URL
   c) Socket
   d) ServerSocket
   Answer: a) InetAddress
42. What does the `java.net` package provide?
   a) API for creating and handling network applications
   b) API for file handling
   c) API for working with databases
   d) API for working with graphics
   Answer: a) API for creating and handling network applications
43. The `URL` class in Java is used for:
   a) Representing a connection to a remote server
   b) Handling internet protocols
   c) Parsing and manipulating URLs
   d) All of the above
   Answer: d) All of the above
44. Which of the following is used to establish a client-server connection in Java?
   a) URL
   b) Socket
   c) DatagramSocket
   d) ServerSocket
   Answer: b) Socket
45. To resolve a host name to its IP address in Java, which method is used?
   a) getByName()
   b) getByAddress()
   c) getHostAddress()
   d) getHostName()
   Answer: a) getByName()

5.10 TCP/IP and Datagram Programming

46. The `Socket` class is used to create:
    a) A client-side socket for TCP connections
    b) A server-side socket for TCP connections
    c) Both client-side and server-side sockets
    d) Datagram sockets
    Answer: a) A client-side socket for TCP connections

47. The `ServerSocket` class is used to:
    a) Listen for incoming client connections
    b) Establish a TCP connection
    c) Send data over a network
    d) Create a datagram connection
    Answer: a) Listen for incoming client connections

48. Which method of `DatagramSocket` is used to send data to a specific address and port?
    a) send()
    b) receive()
    c) connect()
    d) transmit()
    Answer: a) send()

49. What does a `DatagramPacket` represent in Java networking?
    a) A connection-oriented data unit
    b) A packet of data that is sent over a network without establishing a connection
    c) A message sent to a server
    d) None of the above
    Answer: b) A packet of data that is sent over a network without establishing a connection

50. The main advantage of using DatagramSocket over Socket is:
    a) Faster communication
    b) Reliable communication
    c) Connectionless communication
    d) None of the above
    Answer: c) Connectionless communication

CHAPTER 6: APPLETS AND EVENT HANDLING

6.1 Introduction to Applets

Applets are small Java programs designed to be embedded within web pages and run in web browsers that support Java. They are typically used to create dynamic and interactive content on websites. Applets are executed within a controlled environment, known as a **sandbox**, to ensure security while providing access to limited resources, such as the web page where they are embedded.

Key Features of Applets:

1. **Runs in a Sandbox:**
   o Applets run inside a "sandbox," a restricted environment that limits their access to the operating system and system resources. This prevents potentially harmful operations, such as accessing files or network resources, making applets safe to run in a web browser.
   o The sandbox ensures that the applet cannot perform unsafe actions, like reading or writing files, unless the applet is signed (i.e., from a trusted source).
2. **Requires `java.applet` and `java.awt` Packages:**
   o `java.applet`: This package contains the core classes and interfaces for creating and managing applets, such as `Applet`, `AppletContext`, and `AudioClip`.
   o `java.awt`: The Abstract Window Toolkit (AWT) is used for creating graphical user interfaces (GUIs) in applets. It provides classes for handling components like buttons, labels, text fields, and more, allowing applets to be interactive.
3. **Life Cycle Methods:** The applet has a predefined life cycle, which consists of several key methods that define how the applet is initialized, executed, and destroyed. These methods are inherited from the `Applet` class.
   o `init()`: This method is called when the applet is first loaded. It is used to initialize the applet, such as setting up variables, components, or any required resources.

```
public void init() {
    // Initialization code
}
```

   o `start()`: This method is invoked after `init()` and whenever the applet becomes visible after being hidden. It is typically used to start threads or animations.

```
public void start() {
    // Start any thread or animation
}
```

   o `paint()`: This method is called to redraw the applet's content, such as when it needs to be updated. It receives a `Graphics` object as a parameter, which can be used to draw on the applet's window.

```
public void paint(Graphics g) {
    // Drawing code
    g.drawString("Hello, Applet!", 20, 30);}
```

o **stop()**: This method is called when the applet is no longer visible or when the browser is about to close. It is used to stop threads or release resources.

```
public void stop() {
    // Stop any running threads
}
```

o **destroy()**: This method is invoked when the applet is destroyed, i.e., when the browser or applet viewer is closed. It is used to perform clean-up tasks like releasing resources or stopping threads.

```
public void destroy() {
    // Clean-up code
}
```

Applet Life Cycle Overview:

1. **Loading**: When the applet is loaded, the `init()` method is called to initialize it.
2. **Starting**: After initialization, the `start()` method is called to begin execution, which could include animations or starting background threads.
3. **Execution/Interaction**: The applet's GUI components are interactive, and it can respond to user input. The `paint()` method is called to redraw content as necessary.
4. **Stopping**: When the applet is hidden or stopped, the `stop()` method is called to suspend its execution.
5. **Destroying**: Finally, when the applet is unloaded or the browser is closed, the `destroy()` method is called to clean up resources.

Example of a Basic Applet:

Here is a simple applet example that uses the life cycle methods:

```
import java.applet.Applet;
import java.awt.Graphics;

public class HelloWorldApplet extends Applet {
    // Initialize the applet
    public void init() {
        // Initialization code (e.g., setting up variables or UI
components)
    }

    // Start the applet
    public void start() {
        // Code to start animation or thread (if any)
    }

    // Paint method to draw content
```

```
public void paint(Graphics g) {
    // Draw "Hello, Applet!" on the applet's window
    g.drawString("Hello, Applet!", 20, 30);
}

// Stop the applet
public void stop() {
    // Code to stop threads or animations
}

// Destroy the applet
public void destroy() {
    // Clean-up code
}
}
```

Explanation of the Example:

- The applet extends the `Applet` class and overrides the `init()`, `start()`, `paint()`, `stop()`, and `destroy()` methods.
- In the `paint()` method, the applet draws the string `"Hello, Applet!"` at the coordinates `(20, 30)` on the applet's window.

Running an Applet:

To run an applet, it must be embedded in an HTML file and viewed through an applet viewer or a browser that supports applet execution.

HTML File Example:

```
<applet code="HelloWorldApplet.class" width="300" height="100">
</applet>
```

In the above HTML:

- The `code` attribute specifies the applet's class name (`HelloWorldApplet.class`).
- The `width` and `height` attributes define the applet's display area in the browser.

Applets in Modern Java Development:

While applets were once popular for web-based graphical interfaces, they have become obsolete due to security concerns, lack of support in modern browsers, and the rise of alternative technologies like JavaScript, HTML5, and CSS3 for web development. As of today, most web browsers have completely removed support for Java applets.

However, understanding the applet life cycle and their core concepts remains important for legacy Java applications or historical knowledge of Java programming.

Conclusion:

- **Applets** are Java programs that run within a web browser, allowing developers to create interactive and dynamic content on web pages.
- The applet life cycle is managed using methods like `init()`, `start()`, `paint()`, `stop()`, and `destroy()`.
- Applets are secure because they run in a sandbox environment, but their use has diminished over the years due to browser support being phased out in favor of other technologies.

6.2 Writing Java Applets

To write a Java applet, you need to follow a few basic steps, which include creating the applet class, overriding the necessary life cycle methods, and embedding the applet within an HTML file so that it can run in a web browser or an applet viewer.

Steps to Create a Java Applet:

1. **Extend the `Applet` class (or `JApplet` for Swing-based Applets):**
   - In Java, to create an applet, you need to extend the `Applet` class from the `java.applet` package. This class provides the basic framework for your applet.
   - If you want to create an applet with a graphical user interface (GUI) using Swing, you can extend the `JApplet` class from the `javax.swing` package. However, for most applets, the `Applet` class is sufficient.
2. **Override Life Cycle Methods:**
   - The `Applet` class provides several life cycle methods that you must override to define the behavior of your applet:
   - `init()`: This method is called when the applet is first loaded. You use it to initialize the applet, such as setting up variables, creating user interface components, etc.
   - `start()`: This method is called after `init()`, and it is called again when the applet becomes visible after being hidden. It's often used to start threads or animations.
   - `paint(Graphics g)`: This method is used to draw on the applet's window. The `Graphics` object passed to this method allows you to render text, shapes, or images.
   - `stop()`: This method is called when the applet is no longer visible. It is used to pause threads or animations.
   - `destroy()`: This method is called when the applet is unloaded. It is used to release resources or perform cleanup tasks.

Example of a Simple Applet:

Here's an example of a simple Java applet that draws a string on the applet's window:

```java
import java.applet.Applet;
import java.awt.Graphics;

public class MyApplet extends Applet {
    // Override the paint() method to draw content
    public void paint(Graphics g) {
        // Draw the string "Welcome to Applets!" at coordinates (20, 20)
        g.drawString("Welcome to Applets!", 20, 20);
    }
}
```

In this example:

- We import `java.applet.Applet` and `java.awt.Graphics` for creating the applet and handling graphical output.
- The `paint()` method is overridden to draw the string `"Welcome to Applets!"` at the specified location on the applet's window (coordinates 20, 20).

HTML Code to Run the Applet:

To run the applet in a web browser or an applet viewer, you need to embed the applet in an HTML file. Here is the HTML code to embed the `MyApplet` class:

```html
<applet code="MyApplet.class" width="300" height="100">
</applet>
```

Explanation of the HTML:

- **code**: This attribute specifies the name of the class file that contains the applet. In this case, it's `MyApplet.class`, which should be located in the same directory as the HTML file or in a specified directory on the server.
- **width** and **height**: These attributes define the size of the applet's display area in the browser (or applet viewer). In this example, the width is set to 300 pixels and the height to 100 pixels.

Running the Applet:

1. **Using Applet Viewer**:
   - To view the applet without a web browser, you can use the `appletviewer` tool that comes with the JDK. This is a command-line tool that simulates how the applet would behave in a browser.
   - To run the applet using the `appletviewer`, save the applet's class file (`MyApplet.class`) and the HTML file (`MyApplet.html`), then run the following command:

```
appletviewer MyApplet.html
```

2. **Using a Web Browser**:

o Modern web browsers have stopped supporting Java applets due to security concerns and the lack of plugin support. Historically, applets could be run directly in a browser that supported the Java plugin, but this is no longer possible with most current browsers.

o However, you can still test applets using older versions of browsers or Java applet viewers if needed.

Example Explanation:

- **Applets as GUI Components**: In this example, the `paint()` method is used to draw text on the applet window. You can use similar graphics functions (`drawRect()`, `fillOval()`, etc.) to add other graphical components.
- **Graphics Class**: The `Graphics` class provides methods for drawing and rendering various shapes, text, and images. When you override the `paint()` method, the graphics context (`g`) is automatically provided by the applet container (browser or applet viewer).
- **Applet Initialization**: When the applet is loaded in the browser, the `init()` method would be called first, but in this example, no `init()` method is explicitly defined. If needed, you can override it to perform any initialization tasks (like setting up user interface components).

Conclusion:

Writing a Java applet involves extending the `Applet` or `JApplet` class, overriding necessary life cycle methods (`init()`, `start()`, `paint()`, `stop()`, and `destroy()`), and embedding the applet in an HTML file to be executed in a web browser or applet viewer.

While applets were once widely used for creating interactive web applications, their usage has declined due to security concerns and lack of browser support. Today, other technologies such as JavaScript, HTML5, and CSS3 are more commonly used for web development, but understanding applet development is important for working with legacy systems or learning the history of web-based Java applications.

6.3 Working with Graphics: Drawing Lines, Rectangles, and Ovals

In Java, the `Graphics` class is used for 2D drawing and rendering on an applet window or any GUI component. It provides a range of methods to draw various shapes such as lines, rectangles, ovals, arcs, and more. These shapes can be used to create interactive graphics, game graphics, or to provide visual feedback to users.

Key Concepts of Graphics in Java

1. **Graphics Class**:

o The Graphics class is a part of the `java.awt` package and is responsible for rendering images, shapes, and text. The class provides several methods to perform drawing operations on graphical components.

o You generally obtain a Graphics object by overriding the `paint()` method of an applet or other graphical component (e.g., `JPanel`, `Canvas`).

2. **Graphics Methods**:

o The Graphics class provides several methods to draw shapes:

▪ **drawLine(x1, y1, x2, y2)**: Draws a line from point (x1, y1) to point (x2, y2).

▪ **drawRect(x, y, width, height)**: Draws a rectangle with the top-left corner at (x, y) and the specified width and height.

▪ **drawOval(x, y, width, height)**: Draws an oval that fits within the rectangle defined by (x, y) as the top-left corner and the specified width and height.

Example Code:

```
import java.applet.Applet;
import java.awt.Graphics;

public class DrawingApplet extends Applet {
    public void paint(Graphics g) {
        // Drawing a line from point (10, 10) to (100, 10)
        g.drawLine(10, 10, 100, 10);

        // Drawing a rectangle with top-left corner at (10, 20), width 80,
height 50
        g.drawRect(10, 20, 80, 50);

        // Drawing an oval within a rectangle starting at (10, 80), with
width 50 and height 50
        g.drawOval(10, 80, 50, 50);
    }
}
```

Explanation of the Code:

- **g.drawLine(10, 10, 100, 10)**:
o This method draws a straight line starting at coordinates (10, 10) and ending at (100, 10). The line will be horizontal because both the starting and ending points have the same y coordinate (10).
o The coordinates (10, 10) represent the starting point, and (100, 10) represents the ending point.
- **g.drawRect(10, 20, 80, 50)**:
o This method draws a rectangle with the top-left corner at (10, 20), a width of 80 pixels, and a height of 50 pixels.
o The rectangle is defined by its top-left corner (x, y), width, and height.
- **g.drawOval(10, 80, 50, 50)**:
o This method draws an oval inside the specified rectangle. The top-left corner of the rectangle is at (10, 80), and it has a width and height of 50 pixels.
o Since the width and height are equal, the shape will be a circle. If the width and height were different, it would be an ellipse.

Important Details:

1. **Coordinate System**:
   o In Java graphics, the coordinate system starts at `(0, 0)` in the top-left corner of the screen or component. As you move to the right, the `x` coordinate increases, and as you move down, the `y` coordinate increases.
2. **Graphics Object (g)**:
   o The `Graphics` object is passed as an argument to the `paint()` method. It is used to perform drawing operations on the component's drawing area.
   o The `paint()` method is automatically called by the applet container (or other GUI components) whenever the component needs to be redrawn, such as when it is first displayed, resized, or uncovered.
3. **Applets vs Swing**:
   o The example uses the `Applet` class, but in modern Java GUI applications, Swing is typically used. For Swing-based applications, you would use `JPanel` or `JFrame` along with `paintComponent()` instead of the `paint()` method in applets.
4. **Method Overloading**:
   o The `Graphics` class has overloaded versions of drawing methods for drawing filled shapes (such as `fillRect`, `fillOval`) which allow you to fill the shapes with a color.
   o Example: `g.fillRect(10, 20, 80, 50)` would draw a filled rectangle.

Example: Filling Shapes

You can fill a shape with a specific color using the `fillRect()`, `fillOval()`, and similar methods:

```java
import java.applet.Applet;
import java.awt.Color;
import java.awt.Graphics;

public class DrawingApplet extends Applet {
    public void paint(Graphics g) {
        // Drawing a line
        g.drawLine(10, 10, 100, 10);

        // Drawing a rectangle and filling it with a color
        g.setColor(Color.RED);   // Set the color to red
        g.fillRect(10, 20, 80, 50);   // Filled rectangle

        // Drawing an oval and filling it with a color
        g.setColor(Color.BLUE);   // Set the color to blue
        g.fillOval(10, 80, 50, 50);   // Filled oval
    }
}
```

- **g.setColor(Color.RED)**: Changes the current drawing color to red.
- **g.fillRect(10, 20, 80, 50)**: Draws a filled red rectangle.
- **g.setColor(Color.BLUE)**: Changes the color to blue.
- **g.fillOval(10, 80, 50, 50)**: Draws a filled blue oval.

Common Uses of Graphics Drawing:

- **Graphical User Interfaces (GUIs)**: Used in applications that require custom graphics, such as games or interactive apps.
- **Games**: For rendering game objects like characters, backgrounds, and interactive elements.
- **Data Visualization**: Drawing charts, graphs, and other visual data representations.
- **Animation**: Updating the positions of objects in real-time and redrawing them for smooth animations.

Conclusion:

In Java, the `Graphics` class provides an easy way to perform 2D drawing operations. It is used in applets, Swing components, and other graphical applications to render shapes like lines, rectangles, and ovals. By understanding the basic drawing methods and the coordinate system, you can create custom graphics and graphical user interfaces in Java.

6.4 Incorporating Images and Sounds in Java Applets

Java Applets can not only render graphical content like shapes and text but also incorporate multimedia elements such as images and sounds to make applications more interactive and engaging. You can use the `getImage()` method to load and display images, and the `AudioClip` interface to play sound files.

Here's a detailed breakdown of how you can incorporate images and sounds into your Java applets.

1. Adding Images to Applets

To display images in an applet, you use the `getImage()` method from the `Applet` class to load the image file and then the `drawImage()` method from the `Graphics` class to render the image on the screen.

Steps for Adding Images:

- **Step 1: Load the Image**
  - Use the `getImage()` method to load an image from a URL or the applet's base code path.
  - You can load images from files stored in the same directory as the applet, or from URLs (like from a website).
- **Step 2: Draw the Image**
  - Once the image is loaded, use the `drawImage()` method to draw the image on the applet's drawing surface.
    -

Example Code:

```
import java.applet.Applet;
import java.awt.Graphics;
import java.awt.Image;

public class ImageApplet extends Applet {
    Image img;   // Declare an image variable

    // The init() method is called when the applet is loaded
    public void init() {
        img = getImage(getCodeBase(), "image.jpg"); // Load the image
    }

    // The paint() method is called to display the image on the applet
    public void paint(Graphics g) {
        // Draw the image at coordinates (20, 20)
        g.drawImage(img, 20, 20, this);
    }
}
```

Explanation:

- `getImage(getCodeBase(), "image.jpg")`: This method loads an image from the applet's base code path (the directory where the applet file is located). `getCodeBase()` returns the URL of the base directory, and `"image.jpg"` is the name of the image file. If the image is stored on a server or URL, you can use its absolute path or URL in place of `"image.jpg"`.
- `g.drawImage(img, 20, 20, this)`: This method draws the loaded image at the specified coordinates `(20, 20)` on the applet's screen. The `this` refers to the applet object itself and is passed for the context of the image rendering.

Important Points:

- Images are typically loaded in the `init()` method because it's executed once when the applet is first loaded.
- The image is drawn in the `paint()` method, which is called whenever the applet needs to be redrawn (such as after resizing or refreshing).

2. Adding Sounds to Applets

Java applets can also play sound clips using the `AudioClip` interface, which is a part of the `java.applet` package. This allows for the playback of sound files (typically `.wav`, `.au`, or `.aiff` formats).

Steps for Adding Sounds:

- **Step 1: Load the Sound**
- Use the `getAudioClip()` method to load a sound file.
- **Step 2: Play the Sound**
- After loading the sound, use the `play()` method to play the sound.

Example Code:

```
import java.applet.Applet;
import java.applet.AudioClip;

public class SoundApplet extends Applet {
    AudioClip clip;  // Declare an AudioClip variable

    // The init() method is called when the applet is loaded
    public void init() {
        clip = getAudioClip(getCodeBase(), "sound.wav"); // Load the sound
file
    }

    // The start() method is called when the applet starts or is brought
back into focus
    public void start() {
        clip.play(); // Play the sound clip
    }
}
```

Explanation:

* `getAudioClip(getCodeBase(), "sound.wav")`: This method loads a sound file
  (`sound.wav`) from the applet's codebase. The `getCodeBase()` method gets the base URL of
  the applet, and `"sound.wav"` is the name of the sound file.
* `clip.play()`: This method plays the loaded sound file. You can also use other methods like
  `loop()` (to loop the sound) or `stop()` (to stop the sound).

Additional Methods in `AudioClip`:

* `play()`: Plays the sound once.
* `loop()`: Plays the sound repeatedly in a loop.
* `stop()`: Stops the sound.

Important Points:

* Sounds are usually loaded in the `init()` method and played in the `start()` method. The `start()`
  method is called when the applet is initially started or when it comes back into focus.
* Audio files need to be in the same directory as the applet or should be accessible via a URL. The
  `getAudioClip()` method can handle both local and remote files.

Putting Images and Sounds Together:

In an applet, you can combine images and sounds to create more interactive or dynamic
content. For example, you could load an image as a background and play sound when a
button is clicked or a specific event occurs.

Example: Applet with Image and Sound:

```java
import java.applet.Applet;
import java.awt.Graphics;
import java.awt.Image;
import java.applet.AudioClip;

public class ImageSoundApplet extends Applet {
    Image img;  // Image variable
    AudioClip clip;  // Sound variable

    public void init() {
        // Load the image and sound
        img = getImage(getCodeBase(), "image.jpg");
        clip = getAudioClip(getCodeBase(), "sound.wav");
    }

    public void paint(Graphics g) {
        // Draw the image
        g.drawImage(img, 20, 20, this);
    }

    public void start() {
        // Play the sound when the applet starts
        clip.play();
    }
}
```

Explanation:

- **Image**: Displays the image at the specified location on the applet's screen.
- **Sound**: Plays the sound when the applet starts.

Conclusion:

Incorporating images and sounds into Java applets allows you to create more dynamic and engaging applications. The getImage() method is used to load and display images, while the AudioClip interface is used to load and play sounds. These multimedia elements can enhance user experience in applets, making them more interactive and entertaining.

6.5 Event Handling Mechanisms in Java

Event handling in Java is based on the **Event-Delegation Model**, which is a powerful and flexible approach for handling user interaction in graphical user interface (GUI) applications, including applets. It involves the following key concepts:

1. **Source**: The object or component that generates the event (e.g., a button, text field, etc.).
2. **Listener**: The object or class that listens for the event and handles it (e.g., an event handler for a button click).

Event-Delegation Model

In the event-delegation model:

- **The Source** generates an event, such as a mouse click, key press, or action.
- **The Listener** listens for specific events and takes appropriate actions when the event occurs.

Steps in Event Handling:

1. **Event Source**: This is typically a GUI component like a button, text field, or checkbox that generates an event when a user interacts with it (e.g., clicking a button).
2. **Event Listener**: The listener is an object that listens for events and responds accordingly. It can be implemented as a class or an anonymous class. The listener implements a specific interface, such as `ActionListener`, `MouseListener`, or `KeyListener`, depending on the type of event it is supposed to handle.
3. **Event Registration**: The source component registers its event listeners to listen for specific events. This is done using the `addXXXListener()` methods (e.g., `addActionListener()` for buttons).
4. **Event Handling**: When an event occurs, the event listener handles the event by implementing methods defined in the respective listener interface (e.g., `actionPerformed()` for an `ActionListener`).

Example: Event Handling with a Button

Here's an example of a simple applet that demonstrates how event handling works by using a button click event. When the button is clicked, it triggers an event that is handled by the `ActionListener`.

Code Example:

```java
import java.applet.Applet;
import java.awt.*;
import java.awt.event.*;

public class EventApplet extends Applet implements ActionListener {
    Button button;
```

```
    // Initialize the applet and set up the button
    public void init() {
        button = new Button("Click Me");  // Create a button
        add(button);  // Add the button to the applet's layout
        button.addActionListener(this);  // Register the event listener
for button click
    }

    // This method is triggered when the button is clicked
    public void actionPerformed(ActionEvent e) {
        System.out.println("Button Clicked!");  // Output message when
button is clicked
    }
}
```

Explanation of Code:

1. **Importing Required Classes**:
o The `java.awt.*` package is imported to work with GUI components (like `Button`).
o The `java.awt.event.*` package is imported to handle events like `ActionEvent` and implement the listener interfaces (like `ActionListener`).
2. **Extending `Applet` and Implementing `ActionListener`**:
o The `EventApplet` class extends `Applet` (indicating that it is an applet) and implements `ActionListener` (to handle button click events).
o By implementing `ActionListener`, the class is required to provide the method `actionPerformed(ActionEvent e)`, which will be triggered when the button is clicked.
3. **Creating and Adding a Button**:
o A button (`Button button = new Button("Click Me");`) is created with the text "Click Me".
o The `add(button)` method adds the button to the applet's layout (the user will see this button).
4. **Registering the Event Listener**:
o `button.addActionListener(this);` registers the current class (`this`) as the listener for the button's action events. This means that whenever the button is clicked, the `actionPerformed()` method will be called.
5. **Handling the Event**:
o The `actionPerformed(ActionEvent e)` method is triggered when the button is clicked. It prints the message "Button Clicked!" to the console.

Key Concepts in the Example:

1. **Source (Button)**: The button is the source of the event. It generates an `ActionEvent` when it is clicked.
2. **Listener (EventApplet)**: The `EventApplet` class acts as the listener, which listens for the button's `ActionEvent` and handles it by implementing the `actionPerformed()` method.
3. **Event Registration**: The `addActionListener(this)` method connects the `ActionListener` (the `EventApplet` class) to the button, making it listen for button click events.
4. **Event Handling**: The `actionPerformed()` method is where the actual event handling takes place. When the event occurs (button click), this method is invoked to process the event.

Other Common Event Listener Interfaces:

Java provides various event listener interfaces to handle different types of events:

1. **ActionListener**: Used to handle actions (e.g., button clicks).
o `void actionPerformed(ActionEvent e);`
2. **MouseListener**: Used to handle mouse events (e.g., clicks, mouse movement).
o Methods: `mouseClicked()`, `mouseEntered()`, `mouseExited()`, `mousePressed()`, `mouseReleased()`.
3. **KeyListener**: Used to handle keyboard events (e.g., key presses).
o Methods: `keyPressed()`, `keyReleased()`, `keyTyped()`.
4. **WindowListener**: Used to handle window events (e.g., opening, closing, resizing).
o Methods: `windowOpened()`, `windowClosing()`, `windowClosed()`, etc.

Summary of Event Handling Steps:

1. **Create the Source**: Create the GUI component that will generate the event (e.g., a button).
2. **Implement a Listener**: Create a class or implement an interface that listens for the event. The listener must implement the necessary event-handling methods.
3. **Register the Listener**: Use the appropriate `addListener()` method (e.g., `addActionListener()` for a button) to register the listener with the source.
4. **Handle the Event**: Implement the listener's event-handling methods to respond when the event occurs.

Conclusion:

Event handling in Java is a crucial part of building interactive GUI applications, allowing the app to respond to user input. By using the event-delegation model, Java provides a flexible and modular approach to handling events where the event source delegates the event handling to listeners, which are responsible for managing events in a structured way.

6.6 Listener Interfaces in Java

Listener interfaces in Java are an integral part of event-driven programming. They are used to **capture events** that occur in GUI components, such as button clicks, mouse movements, or key presses. These interfaces define methods that must be implemented to handle specific events. The **Event-Delegation Model** is central to how listeners work: an event source (like a button or text field) generates an event, and an event listener (implemented by a class or anonymous class) reacts to that event.

Types of Listener Interfaces

Java provides many listener interfaces in the `java.awt.event` package and `javax.swing.event` package for handling various kinds of events. Below are some of the most commonly used listener interfaces:

1. **ActionListener:**
   - **Used for:** Capturing action events, typically generated by GUI components like buttons or menu items.
   - **Common event:** Button click, menu item selection.
   - **Methods:** `void actionPerformed(ActionEvent e)`
   - **Example:** A button click event.

```
button.addActionListener(new ActionListener() {
    public void actionPerformed(ActionEvent e) {
        System.out.println("Action Performed!");
    }
});
```

In this example:

   - `ActionListener` listens for action events like a button click.
   - `actionPerformed()` method is invoked when the button is clicked, printing "Action Performed!" to the console.

2. **MouseListener:**
   - **Used for:** Handling mouse events such as mouse clicks, mouse enter, mouse exit, etc.
   - **Common events:** Mouse click, mouse press, mouse release, mouse enter, mouse exit.
   - **Methods:**
     - `void mouseClicked(MouseEvent e)`
     - `void mousePressed(MouseEvent e)`
     - `void mouseReleased(MouseEvent e)`
     - `void mouseEntered(MouseEvent e)`
     - `void mouseExited(MouseEvent e)`
   - **Example:** Detecting a mouse click on a component.

```
someComponent.addMouseListener(new MouseListener() {
    public void mouseClicked(MouseEvent e) {
        System.out.println("Mouse Clicked!");
    }
    public void mousePressed(MouseEvent e) {}
    public void mouseReleased(MouseEvent e) {}
    public void mouseEntered(MouseEvent e) {}
    public void mouseExited(MouseEvent e) {}
});
```

In this example:

   - The `mouseClicked()` method is invoked when a mouse click occurs on the component.

3. **KeyListener:**
   - **Used for:** Capturing keyboard events.
   - **Common events:** Key presses, key releases, and key typing.
   - **Methods:**
     - `void keyPressed(KeyEvent e)`
     - `void keyReleased(KeyEvent e)`
     - `void keyTyped(KeyEvent e)`
   - **Example:** Detecting key presses.

```
someComponent.addKeyListener(new KeyListener() {
    public void keyPressed(KeyEvent e) {
        System.out.println("Key Pressed: " + e.getKeyChar());
    }
    public void keyReleased(KeyEvent e) {}
    public void keyTyped(KeyEvent e) {}
});
```

In this example:

o   `keyPressed()` is invoked when a key is pressed, and the key character is printed.

4. **WindowListener**:
o   **Used for**: Handling window events such as window opening, closing, resizing, etc.
o   **Common events**: Window opened, window closing, window closed, window iconified (minimized), etc.
o   **Methods**:
▪   `void windowOpened(WindowEvent e)`
▪   `void windowClosing(WindowEvent e)`
▪   `void windowClosed(WindowEvent e)`
▪   `void windowIconified(WindowEvent e)`
▪   `void windowDeiconified(WindowEvent e)`
▪   `void windowActivated(WindowEvent e)`
▪   `void windowDeactivated(WindowEvent e)`
o   **Example**: Handling the window closing event.

```
someWindow.addWindowListener(new WindowListener() {
    public void windowClosing(WindowEvent e) {
        System.out.println("Window is closing");
    }
    public void windowOpened(WindowEvent e) {}
    public void windowClosed(WindowEvent e) {}
    public void windowIconified(WindowEvent e) {}
    public void windowDeiconified(WindowEvent e) {}
    public void windowActivated(WindowEvent e) {}
    public void windowDeactivated(WindowEvent e) {}
});
```

In this example:

o   `windowClosing()` is invoked when the user tries to close the window.

5. **FocusListener**:
o   **Used for**: Handling focus events on components like text fields and buttons.
o   **Common events**: Gaining focus, losing focus.
o   **Methods**:
▪   `void focusGained(FocusEvent e)`
▪   `void focusLost(FocusEvent e)`
o   **Example**: Detecting when a text field gains or loses focus.

```
someTextField.addFocusListener(new FocusListener() {
    public void focusGained(FocusEvent e) {
        System.out.println("Text field gained focus");
    }
```

```
public void focusLost(FocusEvent e) {
    System.out.println("Text field lost focus");
}
});
```

In this example:

o `focusGained()` is invoked when the text field gains focus (user clicks inside the field).
o `focusLost()` is invoked when the text field loses focus.

Event Handling Process

1. **Register the Listener**: First, you associate the listener with a GUI component (e.g., button or text field). This is done using methods like `addActionListener()`, `addMouseListener()`, etc.
2. **Event Triggering**: When the user interacts with the component (e.g., clicks a button, types in a text field), the source component generates an event.
3. **Event Handling**: The listener, which has been registered for that event, processes the event by invoking the appropriate method (e.g., `actionPerformed()` for an `ActionListener` or `mouseClicked()` for a `MouseListener`).
4. **Perform Action**: Inside the event handling method, you can specify what action should be taken when the event occurs (e.g., printing a message, updating the UI, or performing calculations).

Using Anonymous Classes for Listeners

Instead of creating a separate class to implement a listener, you can use **anonymous classes**. This is a shorthand way of defining and instantiating a listener class in one step.

Example: Using an anonymous class for an `ActionListener`

```
button.addActionListener(new ActionListener() {
    public void actionPerformed(ActionEvent e) {
        System.out.println("Action Performed!");
    }
});
```

Here, an anonymous class implements the `ActionListener` interface and directly defines the `actionPerformed()` method. This is often used for simple event handling.

Summary of Common Listener Interfaces:

Listener Interface	Purpose	Common Methods
ActionListener	Handles action events (e.g., button clicks, menu items)	`actionPerformed(ActionEvent e)`

Listener Interface	Purpose	Common Methods
MouseListener	Handles mouse events (e.g., mouse click, mouse press)	`mouseClicked(MouseEvent e)`, `mousePressed(MouseEvent e)`, etc.
KeyListener	Handles keyboard events (e.g., key press, key release)	`keyPressed(KeyEvent e)`, `keyReleased(KeyEvent e)`, `keyTyped(KeyEvent e)`
WindowListener	Handles window events (e.g., opening, closing, resizing)	`windowClosing(WindowEvent e)`, `windowOpened(WindowEvent e)`, etc.
FocusListener	Handles focus events on components (e.g., gaining or losing focus)	`focusGained(FocusEvent e)`, `focusLost(FocusEvent e)`

Conclusion

Listener interfaces in Java are essential for implementing event-driven programming, allowing developers to capture and respond to user actions in GUI applications. By registering appropriate listeners, you can handle a wide range of events such as button clicks, mouse actions, key presses, and window state changes, making your applications interactive and responsive to user input.

6.7 Adapter and Inner Classes in Java

In Java, **Adapter Classes** and **Inner Classes** provide ways to simplify code, especially when dealing with event handling in GUI applications. These features are part of Java's object-oriented design principles, and they help make your event-driven programming easier and more organized.

1. Adapter Classes

Adapter classes in Java are a type of **abstract class** that provide empty implementations for all the methods in an interface. This allows you to implement only the methods you need to handle, without having to define the entire interface. Adapter classes are particularly useful in event handling when you don't need all the methods defined in an event listener interface.

Why Use Adapter Classes?

- **Simplification**: They eliminate the need to implement all methods of an event listener interface.
- **Convenience**: You only override the methods you're interested in.
- **Clean Code**: Reduces boilerplate code, making the code more readable and concise.

Example Using Adapter Class

Let's say you want to handle only the `mouseClicked` event, but the `MouseListener` interface has multiple methods, such as `mousePressed()`, `mouseReleased()`, `mouseEntered()`, `mouseExited()`. Instead of implementing all these methods, you can use `MouseAdapter`, which is an adapter class that implements the `MouseListener` interface and provides empty implementations for all of its methods.

```java
import java.awt.event.*;

public class MouseAdapterExample {
    public static void main(String[] args) {
        // Create a frame or component where mouse events can be handled.
        someComponent.addMouseListener(new MouseAdapter() {
            // Override only the method you're interested in
            public void mouseClicked(MouseEvent e) {
                System.out.println("Mouse Clicked");
            }
        });
    }
}
```

In this example:

- `MouseAdapter` is an abstract class that implements `MouseListener`.
- It provides empty implementations for all methods in `MouseListener`, so you only need to override `mouseClicked()`.
- This results in cleaner code when you need to handle specific events, without unnecessary code for events you're not interested in.

Common Adapter Classes

Java provides several adapter classes for different event listener interfaces. Some common ones include:

- `MouseAdapter` (for `MouseListener`)
- `KeyAdapter` (for `KeyListener`)
- `WindowAdapter` (for `WindowListener`)
- `ComponentAdapter` (for `ComponentListener`)
- `FocusAdapter` (for `FocusListener`)

These adapter classes simplify the event handling process by allowing you to implement only the methods you need.

2. Inner Classes

An **Inner Class** is a class that is defined within another class. Inner classes can be very useful in event-driven programming, where you want to define the event handling logic directly inside the class that generates the event. This reduces the need for creating separate, named classes for each event handler.

Why Use Inner Classes?

- **Encapsulation**: Inner classes can access the private members of the outer class, which can be useful in GUI programming when you need to manipulate the components of the outer class directly.
- **Organization**: Keeping the event handler within the outer class helps to keep related code together, making it easier to manage.
- **Reduced Boilerplate**: You don't need to define a separate class for every listener, which keeps the code compact and more maintainable.

Example Using an Inner Class

Here's an example of how an **inner class** can be used to handle an action event for a button click:

```java
import java.awt.*;
import java.awt.event.*;

public class ButtonExample {
    public static void main(String[] args) {
        // Create a frame and a button
        Frame frame = new Frame("Button Example");
        Button button = new Button("Click Me");

        // Add button and action listener using an inner class
        button.addActionListener(new ButtonHandler());

        // Set layout and add button to the frame
        frame.setLayout(new FlowLayout());
        frame.add(button);

        // Set frame size and make it visible
        frame.setSize(300, 200);
        frame.setVisible(true);
    }

    // Inner class that implements ActionListener
    class ButtonHandler implements ActionListener {
        public void actionPerformed(ActionEvent e) {
            System.out.println("Button Clicked!");
        }
    }
}
```

In this example:

- The `ButtonHandler` class is defined as an **inner class** within the `ButtonExample` class.
- The `ButtonHandler` class implements the `ActionListener` interface and overrides the `actionPerformed()` method to handle the button click event.
- This inner class is directly used to handle the event for the `Button` component, keeping the event handling code inside the same class as the rest of the GUI logic.

Benefits of Using Inner Classes:

1. **Access to Outer Class Members**: Inner classes have direct access to the members (including private variables) of their outer class. This is particularly useful in GUI programming when event handlers need to interact with components of the outer class.
2. **Less Code for Small Handlers**: If your event handler logic is relatively simple, using an inner class eliminates the need for defining a separate class.
3. **Encapsulation**: Inner classes can help you encapsulate event handling within the class where it is most relevant, improving the clarity of your code.

Anonymous Inner Classes

Sometimes, an inner class is used **directly at the point of instantiation**. This is called an **anonymous inner class**. It is commonly used for short, one-time event handling, making your code more concise.

Example of Anonymous Inner Class for ActionListener
```
button.addActionListener(new ActionListener() {
    public void actionPerformed(ActionEvent e) {
        System.out.println("Button Clicked!");
    }
});
```

In this example:

- An anonymous class is created and instantiated at the point of the event listener registration.
- The class implements the `ActionListener` interface and provides an implementation of the `actionPerformed()` method.
- This is a concise way to define event handling logic without needing to define a named inner class.

Comparison of Adapter Classes and Inner Classes

Feature	Adapter Classes	Inner Classes
Purpose	Simplify event handling by providing empty method implementations for listener interfaces	Used to handle events within the same class, providing more encapsulation
Flexibility	Useful for event listeners that don't need all methods implemented	Useful when you need a small, concise event handler inside a class
Usage	Extending adapter class and overriding required methods	Implementing interface or inheriting another class inside the class
Code Clarity	Reduces code clutter by not requiring implementation of unused methods	Keeps related event handling logic close to the event source class

Conclusion

- **Adapter Classes** provide an easy way to simplify event handling when you don't need to implement all methods of an event listener interface.
- **Inner Classes** help you keep event handling code within the same class that generates the event, which is useful for better encapsulation and easier management.
- Both **Adapter Classes** and **Inner Classes** are commonly used in Java GUI programming to create more maintainable, concise, and organized event-driven code.

6.8 Designing GUIs with AWT Controls

The **Abstract Window Toolkit (AWT)** is a set of application programming interfaces (APIs) used for creating graphical user interfaces (GUIs) in Java. AWT provides various components, also known as controls, which allow developers to design interactive applications. These components are the building blocks for creating windows, buttons, text fields, labels, checkboxes, etc.

AWT is part of the `java.awt` package and is built around the concept of event-driven programming, where user interactions with the GUI (e.g., mouse clicks, key presses) trigger events that the application can respond to.

Key AWT Components

Here's a detailed explanation of some basic AWT controls:

1. Button

A **Button** is a basic control that the user can click to trigger an event. Buttons are commonly used to perform actions such as submitting forms or triggering processes.

Usage:

- **Creating a Button:** You create a button using the `Button` class, and it is added to a container (e.g., a `Frame` or `Panel`).
- **Example Code:**

```java
import java.awt.*;

public class ButtonExample {
    public static void main(String[] args) {
        // Create a Frame
        Frame f = new Frame("Button Example");

        // Create a Button
        Button b = new Button("Click Me");

        // Add button to the Frame
        f.add(b);

        // Set layout and size
        f.setLayout(new FlowLayout());
        f.setSize(300, 200);
        f.setVisible(true);
    }
}
```

Explanation:

- `Button b = new Button("Click Me");` creates a new button with the label "Click Me".
- `f.add(b);` adds the button to the `Frame`.
- The button will be displayed in the window when the program runs.

Common Button Methods:

- `setLabel(String label)`: Changes the button's label.
- `addActionListener(ActionListener l)`: Registers an action listener to handle button clicks.

2. TextField

A **TextField** is a component used for single-line text input. It allows users to enter text, such as their name, email, etc.

Usage:

- **Creating a TextField:** You create a `TextField` object with a specified number of columns, which determines the width of the text field.
- **Example Code:**

```java
import java.awt.*;

public class TextFieldExample {
    public static void main(String[] args) {
        // Create a Frame
        Frame f = new Frame("TextField Example");

        // Create a TextField with 20 columns (width)
        TextField tf = new TextField(20);

        // Add text field to the Frame
        f.add(tf);

        // Set layout and size
        f.setLayout(new FlowLayout());
        f.setSize(300, 200);
        f.setVisible(true);
    }
}
```

Explanation:

- `TextField tf = new TextField(20);` creates a text field with a width of 20 columns.
- `f.add(tf);` adds the text field to the frame.
- Users can type text into the text field, and you can retrieve the input using `tf.getText()`.

Common TextField Methods:

- `setText(String text)`: Sets the initial text of the text field.
- `getText()`: Retrieves the text entered in the text field.
- `setEditable(boolean editable)`: Determines if the text field is editable.

3. Checkbox

A **Checkbox** allows users to select one or more options from a list of choices. It is typically used for boolean (yes/no) options.

Usage:

- **Creating a Checkbox:** A `Checkbox` can be created with an optional label, and you can specify whether it is selected by default.
- **Example Code:**

```
import java.awt.*;

public class CheckboxExample {
    public static void main(String[] args) {
        // Create a Frame
        Frame f = new Frame("Checkbox Example");

        // Create a Checkbox
        Checkbox cb = new Checkbox("Option");

        // Add checkbox to the Frame
        f.add(cb);

        // Set layout and size
        f.setLayout(new FlowLayout());
        f.setSize(300, 200);
        f.setVisible(true);
    }
}
```

Explanation:

- `Checkbox cb = new Checkbox("Option");` creates a checkbox with the label "Option".
- The checkbox is added to the frame, and by default, it is not selected.

Common Checkbox Methods:

- `setState(boolean state)`: Sets the checkbox state (selected or not).
- `getState()`: Returns the current state of the checkbox (true for selected, false for not selected).
- `addItemListener(ItemListener l)`: Registers an item listener to handle checkbox state changes.

AWT Layout Managers

AWT uses layout managers to control the placement of components inside containers (e.g., frames or panels). Common layout managers include:

- **FlowLayout**: Places components in a single row, and wraps them to the next line if necessary.
- **GridLayout**: Places components in a grid with a specified number of rows and columns.
- **BorderLayout**: Places components in five areas: North, South, East, West, and Center.

Example of Layout Manager:
```java
import java.awt.*;

public class LayoutExample {
    public static void main(String[] args) {
        Frame f = new Frame("Layout Example");

        // Set layout manager to FlowLayout
        f.setLayout(new FlowLayout());

        // Create components
        Button b1 = new Button("Button 1");
        Button b2 = new Button("Button 2");

        // Add components to the Frame
        f.add(b1);
        f.add(b2);

        // Set size and visibility
        f.setSize(300, 200);
        f.setVisible(true);
    }
}
```

Here, `FlowLayout` ensures that the components (buttons) are arranged in a row within the frame.

Other AWT Controls

Besides the basic components like buttons, text fields, and checkboxes, AWT offers various other controls such as:

- **Labels**: Display static text.
- **List**: Display a list of items.
- **TextArea**: For multi-line text input.
- **Choice**: A dropdown list that allows users to select one item.
- **Scrollbar**: Provides a scrollbar component for navigating through large content.

Conclusion

- **AWT Components**: Java's AWT package offers essential components such as buttons, text fields, checkboxes, labels, and more to create interactive GUIs.
- **Event Handling**: AWT controls are designed to trigger events (like button clicks or text input), allowing developers to define the desired behavior in response to these events.
- **Layout Managers**: AWT provides layout managers to control the arrangement of components within containers, ensuring a responsive and well-organized GUI design.

AWT is typically used for simple GUI applications in Java, but for more sophisticated user interfaces, **Swing** (a more advanced GUI toolkit in Java) is often preferred due to its enhanced capabilities and flexibility.

6.9 Swing Components of Java Foundation Classes

Swing is a part of the Java Foundation Classes (JFC) and provides a rich set of GUI components that are more flexible, lightweight, and pluggable compared to AWT components. Swing components are built entirely in Java, so they are platform-independent and provide a more modern look and feel compared to the older AWT components.

Swing is part of the `javax.swing` package, and it is widely used to build graphical user interfaces (GUIs) in Java applications. Swing components are also known as lightweight components because they don't rely on the underlying operating system's native windowing system, unlike AWT components.

Key Features of Swing:

- **Lightweight:** Swing components are written in pure Java, unlike AWT which relies on the native OS for rendering.
- **Pluggable Look and Feel:** Swing allows you to easily change the look and feel of an application. It supports various themes (Metal, Windows, Motif, etc.).
- **More Control:** Swing provides a higher level of customization, allowing developers to create complex UIs with advanced components.

Common Swing Components:

Below are some common Swing components:

1. JButton

A **JButton** is a button that triggers an event when clicked by the user. It is used for actions like submitting forms, opening windows, etc. The button text can be customized, and you can add icons and action listeners to the button.

Usage:

- **Creating a JButton:** You can create a `JButton` with a label, add it to a container (like a `JFrame`), and add an event listener to handle actions like clicks.

Example Code:
```java
import javax.swing.*;
import java.awt.event.*;
```

```
public class ButtonExample {
    public static void main(String[] args) {
        JFrame frame = new JFrame("JButton Example");
        JButton button = new JButton("Click Me");

        // ActionListener for the button
        button.addActionListener(new ActionListener() {
            public void actionPerformed(ActionEvent e) {
                System.out.println("Button clicked!");
            }
        });

        frame.add(button);
        frame.setSize(300, 200);
        frame.setVisible(true);
        frame.setDefaultCloseOperation(JFrame.EXIT_ON_CLOSE);
    }
}
```

Explanation:

- `JButton button = new JButton("Click Me");` creates a button with the label "Click Me".
- `addActionListener()` registers an event listener to handle the button click.
- The button will print "Button clicked!" when clicked.

Common JButton Methods:

- `setText(String text)`: Sets the text of the button.
- `addActionListener(ActionListener listener)`: Adds an event listener for the button's action events.

2. JTextField

A **JTextField** is a text input field that allows users to input a single line of text. It is commonly used for user inputs like names, search queries, and so on.

Usage:

- **Creating a JTextField:** You can specify the number of columns (the width) for the text field. You can also set a default text and retrieve the entered text.

Example Code:
```
import javax.swing.*;

public class TextFieldExample {
    public static void main(String[] args) {
        JFrame frame = new JFrame("JTextField Example");

        // Create a JTextField with 20 columns (width)
```

```
        JTextField textField = new JTextField(20);

        // Set default text
        textField.setText("Enter text here");

        frame.add(textField);
        frame.setSize(300, 200);
        frame.setVisible(true);
        frame.setDefaultCloseOperation(JFrame.EXIT_ON_CLOSE);
    }
}
```

Explanation:

- `JTextField textField = new JTextField(20);` creates a text field with 20 columns (width).
- `setText()` sets default text in the text field.

Common JTextField Methods:

- `getText()`: Retrieves the text entered in the text field.
- `setText(String text)`: Sets the text in the text field.
- `setEditable(boolean editable)`: Determines whether the text field is editable.

3. JTable

A **JTable** is used for displaying and editing tabular data in a grid format. It allows the display of multiple rows and columns and provides methods for manipulating the data programmatically.

Usage:

- **Creating a JTable:** You create a `JTable` by passing a two-dimensional array of data and a one-dimensional array of column names.

Example Code:

```
import javax.swing.*;

public class TableExample {
    public static void main(String[] args) {
        JFrame frame = new JFrame("JTable Example");

        // Data for the table
        String[][] data = {
            {"1", "Alice"},
            {"2", "Bob"}
        };
```

```
        // Column names
        String[] columns = {"ID", "Name"};

        // Create a JTable
        JTable table = new JTable(data, columns);

        // Add a scroll pane to the table (since JTable does not have a
scroll bar by default)
        JScrollPane scrollPane = new JScrollPane(table);
        frame.add(scrollPane);

        frame.setSize(300, 200);
        frame.setVisible(true);
        frame.setDefaultCloseOperation(JFrame.EXIT_ON_CLOSE);
    }
}
```

Explanation:

- `JTable table = new JTable(data, columns);` creates a table with the specified data and columns.
- `new JScrollPane(table);` adds a scroll bar to the table for better viewing when the table size exceeds the visible area.

Common JTable Methods:

- `getValueAt(int row, int column)`: Retrieves the value at the specified row and column.
- `setValueAt(Object value, int row, int column)`: Sets the value at the specified row and column.
- `getColumnName(int column)`: Retrieves the name of the column.

Other Important Swing Components:

- **JLabel:** Displays a short string or an image. It's often used to add text labels beside other components.
- **JComboBox:** A drop-down list of items from which the user can select one.
- **JCheckBox:** A checkbox that can be selected or deselected.
- **JRadioButton:** A radio button used in a group where only one option can be selected at a time.
- **JMenuBar, JMenu, JMenuItem:** For creating menus and menu items in the application.
- **JList:** Displays a list of items, allowing users to select one or more items.

Layout Managers in Swing:

Swing also provides various **layout managers** to arrange the components in the window. Common layout managers include:

- **FlowLayout:** Places components in a line, and wraps them if necessary.
- **BorderLayout:** Divides the window into five sections: North, South, East, West, and Center.
- **GridLayout:** Places components in a grid of rows and columns.
- **CardLayout:** Manages a collection of components that are displayed one at a time.

Conclusion:

Swing provides a wide range of components for building modern, interactive GUIs in Java. By using components like `JButton`, `JTextField`, and `JTable`, you can easily design and implement user interfaces that allow users to interact with your application. Swing is versatile, supports multiple look-and-feels, and is widely used for desktop applications in Java. The components discussed above are just a few examples, and Swing offers many more controls to cater to a variety of user interface requirements.

6.10 Layout Managers, Menus, Events, and Listeners

This section covers key concepts for designing user interfaces (UIs) in Java applications, particularly using the Abstract Window Toolkit (AWT) and Swing libraries. We'll delve into **Layout Managers**, **Menus**, and **Event Handling** with **Listeners** to create organized, interactive, and functional graphical user interfaces.

1. Layout Managers

In Java, **Layout Managers** are used to control the positioning and sizing of components (like buttons, text fields, labels, etc.) within a container (like a frame or panel). They help in automatically arranging the components in a consistent way based on the layout type, ensuring a flexible and adaptive UI.

Here are some of the most commonly used layout managers:

a. FlowLayout

- **Description:** The `FlowLayout` arranges components in a left-to-right flow, one after the other, similar to how text appears in a paragraph. If the container is resized, components are reflowed to new lines.
- **Usage:** Good for arranging components in a single row or column, or for small forms.

```
Example:
import java.awt.*;
import javax.swing.*;
```

```
public class FlowLayoutExample {
    public static void main(String[] args) {
        JFrame frame = new JFrame("FlowLayout Example");
        frame.setLayout(new FlowLayout());

        frame.add(new JButton("Button 1"));
        frame.add(new JButton("Button 2"));
        frame.add(new JButton("Button 3"));

        frame.setSize(300, 100);
        frame.setVisible(true);
        frame.setDefaultCloseOperation(JFrame.EXIT_ON_CLOSE);
    }
}
```

b. BorderLayout

- **Description:** The `BorderLayout` divides the container into five distinct areas: North, South, East, West, and Center. Each component added can be placed in one of these regions.
- **Usage:** Ideal for large applications with a central area and surrounding controls.

Example:
```
import java.awt.*;
import javax.swing.*;

public class BorderLayoutExample {
    public static void main(String[] args) {
        JFrame frame = new JFrame("BorderLayout Example");
        frame.setLayout(new BorderLayout());

        frame.add(new JButton("North"), BorderLayout.NORTH);
        frame.add(new JButton("South"), BorderLayout.SOUTH);
        frame.add(new JButton("East"), BorderLayout.EAST);
        frame.add(new JButton("West"), BorderLayout.WEST);
        frame.add(new JButton("Center"), BorderLayout.CENTER);

        frame.setSize(300, 200);
        frame.setVisible(true);
        frame.setDefaultCloseOperation(JFrame.EXIT_ON_CLOSE);
    }}
```

c. GridLayout

- **Description:** The `GridLayout` arranges components in a grid of rows and columns. Each component will occupy a single cell in the grid.
- **Usage:** Useful for creating forms or tables, where each component needs to occupy equal space.

Example:
```
import java.awt.*;
import javax.swing.*;

public class GridLayoutExample {
```

```
    public static void main(String[] args) {
        JFrame frame = new JFrame("GridLayout Example");
        frame.setLayout(new GridLayout(2, 2)); // 2 rows, 2 columns

        frame.add(new JButton("Button 1"));
        frame.add(new JButton("Button 2"));
        frame.add(new JButton("Button 3"));
        frame.add(new JButton("Button 4"));

        frame.setSize(300, 200);
        frame.setVisible(true);
        frame.setDefaultCloseOperation(JFrame.EXIT_ON_CLOSE);
    }
}
```

d. CardLayout

- **Description:** The `CardLayout` manager allows you to stack components on top of each other. Only one component is visible at a time. It's like a "stack" of cards, where you can flip between them.
- **Usage:** Used for creating applications with multiple views or forms, like wizards or tabbed panels.

Example:
```
import java.awt.*;
import javax.swing.*;

public class CardLayoutExample {
    public static void main(String[] args) {
        JFrame frame = new JFrame("CardLayout Example");
        CardLayout cardLayout = new CardLayout();
        frame.setLayout(cardLayout);

        JPanel card1 = new JPanel();
        card1.add(new JButton("Card 1"));
        JPanel card2 = new JPanel();
        card2.add(new JButton("Card 2"));

        frame.add(card1, "Card1");
        frame.add(card2, "Card2");

        frame.setSize(300, 200);
        frame.setVisible(true);
        frame.setDefaultCloseOperation(JFrame.EXIT_ON_CLOSE);

        cardLayout.show(frame.getContentPane(), "Card2"); // Show second
card
    }
}
```

2. Menus

Menus are used to provide options in a structured format to users. They typically appear as a bar at the top of the application window, often containing multiple items.

Menu Components:

- **MenuBar:** A container for menus.
- **Menu:** Represents a menu with multiple menu items.
- **MenuItem:** Represents a single item in a menu.
- **CheckBoxMenuItem:** A menu item that can either be checked or unchecked.
- **RadioButtonMenuItem:** A menu item that allows the user to select a single item from a group of options.

Example of Creating Menus:

```java
import java.awt.*;
import java.awt.event.*;

public class MenuExample extends Frame {
    public MenuExample() {
        // Create MenuBar and add to the frame
        MenuBar mb = new MenuBar();

        // Create a "File" menu
        Menu fileMenu = new Menu("File");
        fileMenu.add(new MenuItem("New"));
        fileMenu.add(new MenuItem("Open"));
        fileMenu.add(new MenuItem("Exit"));

        // Add File menu to MenuBar
        mb.add(fileMenu);
        setMenuBar(mb);

        setSize(300, 200);
        setVisible(true);
    }

    public static void main(String[] args) {
        new MenuExample();
    }
}
```

Explanation:

- `MenuBar mb = new MenuBar();` creates a menu bar.
- `Menu file = new Menu("File");` creates a menu named "File".
- `file.add(new MenuItem("New"));` adds items (e.g., "New", "Open") to the "File" menu.
- `setMenuBar(mb);` sets the menu bar to the frame.

3. Event Handling and Listeners

Event handling in Java is done using **listeners** and the **event-delegation model**. The model involves two main components:

1. **Event Source:** The object that generates the event (e.g., a button).

2. **Event Listener:** The object that processes the event (e.g., a class implementing `ActionListener` to handle button clicks).

Event handling in Java requires listeners, which are interfaces used to listen for different types of events like mouse clicks, key presses, window actions, etc.

Common Listeners:

- **ActionListener:** Handles action events like button clicks.
- **MouseListener:** Handles mouse events like clicks, movement, and pressing.
- **KeyListener:** Handles keyboard events like key presses.

```java
Example: ActionListener
import java.awt.*;
import java.awt.event.*;

public class EventHandlingExample extends Frame implements ActionListener
{
    Button button;

    public EventHandlingExample() {
        button = new Button("Click Me");
        button.addActionListener(this); // Adding ActionListener
        add(button);

        setSize(300, 200);
        setVisible(true);
    }

    public void actionPerformed(ActionEvent e) {
        System.out.println("Button Clicked!");
    }

    public static void main(String[] args) {
        new EventHandlingExample();
    }
}
```
Explanation:

- `button.addActionListener(this);` attaches the `ActionListener` to the button.
- `public void actionPerformed(ActionEvent e)` is the method that gets executed when the button is clicked, and it prints "Button Clicked!" to the console.

Conclusion

In Java, **Layout Managers** help organize and arrange components in a GUI, providing flexibility and responsiveness to different screen sizes. **Menus** allow developers to provide structured navigation and commands within the application, and **Event Handling** with

Listeners enables interaction between the user and the application. By understanding these key concepts, developers can design intuitive, responsive, and user-friendly interfaces in their Java applications.

6.11 Overview of Servlets

Servlets are powerful Java-based technologies used to build dynamic web applications. A **Servlet** is a server-side Java program that handles client requests and generates responses, typically used in web applications. Servlets are run within a **Servlet Container** (like Apache Tomcat or Jetty), which is responsible for managing the lifecycle of the servlet and handling requests from clients, often browsers.

Life Cycle of a Servlet

A Servlet's lifecycle is managed by the **Servlet Container**. The lifecycle includes the following phases:

1. **Initialization Phase (init() method)**
   o The servlet container calls the **init()** method of the servlet when it is first loaded into memory (typically when the servlet is first requested by a client or when the web server starts). This is where any initialization code for the servlet is executed, such as opening database connections or setting configuration values.
   o This method is called **once** during the lifetime of the servlet.

```
public void init() throws ServletException {
    // Initialization code, e.g., setting up resources
}
```

2. **Request Processing Phase (service() method)**
   o After initialization, the servlet container calls the **service()** method to process each client request. The **service()** method is called for every request and can respond to multiple types of HTTP methods (GET, POST, etc.).
   o The **doGet()**, **doPost()**, **doPut()**, etc., are used inside the `service()` method to handle specific HTTP requests.

```
public void service(HttpServletRequest req, HttpServletResponse res)
throws ServletException, IOException {
    // process request and generate response
}
```

3. **Destruction Phase (destroy() method)**
   o The **destroy()** method is called by the servlet container just before the servlet is destroyed, typically when the server shuts down or the servlet is being unloaded. This method can be used for cleanup tasks such as closing database connections or releasing resources.

o   This method is called **once** when the servlet is being removed from memory.

```
public void destroy() {
    // Cleanup code, such as closing resources
}
```

Example Servlet

Here's a simple servlet example that handles a **GET** request and generates a simple HTML response.

```
import javax.servlet.*;
import javax.servlet.http.*;
import java.io.*;

public class MyServlet extends HttpServlet {
    // doGet() method is called when an HTTP GET request is made
    public void doGet(HttpServletRequest req, HttpServletResponse res)
throws ServletException, IOException {
        // Set the content type of the response (HTML in this case)
        res.setContentType("text/html");

        // Get the output stream of the response to write data
        PrintWriter out = res.getWriter();

        // Output HTML content
        out.println("<html>");
        out.println("<head><title>My First Servlet</title></head>");
        out.println("<body>");
        out.println("<h1>Welcome to Servlets!</h1>");
        out.println("</body>");
        out.println("</html>");
    }
}
```

Explanation:

*   The doGet() method is overridden from the HttpServlet class. It is called when the client (e.g., a web browser) sends a **GET** request.
*   The method sets the response content type to text/html using the setContentType() method, indicating that the response will be HTML.
*   The **PrintWriter** object (out) is used to write HTML content back to the client.

Summary: Key Concepts

1. **Applets**:
o   Applets are small programs that run within a web browser. They are used to create interactive, client-side applications. They have their own lifecycle and can handle events, images, and animations.
2. **Event Handling**:

o   Event handling in Java is done using listeners, which are interfaces that respond to events (like clicks, key presses, or mouse movement). **Adapters** simplify event handling by providing default implementations, and **Inner Classes** allow for easy definition of listeners within the class.

3. **GUI Design**:
o   Java provides **AWT** and **Swing** libraries for creating Graphical User Interfaces (GUIs). Components such as **Buttons**, **TextFields**, and **Tables** are used to build interactive UIs. Layout managers like **FlowLayout**, **BorderLayout**, and **GridLayout** help organize components in a window.

4. **Servlets**:
o   Servlets are Java classes that run on a web server and are used to build dynamic web applications. They handle client requests and generate responses. The lifecycle of a servlet includes initialization, request processing, and destruction. Servlets are an essential part of server-side Java programming and form the backbone of many web applications.

50 MCQ ON THESE TOPICS

6.1 Introduction to Applets

1. What is an applet in Java?
    a) A standalone application
    b) A small program that runs within a web page
    c) A program used to manipulate databases
    d) A program that interacts with hardware
    Answer: b) A small program that runs within a web page

2. Which method is used to display an applet?
    a) display()
    b) init()
    c) start()
    d) paint()
    Answer: d) paint()

3. Which class is the superclass of all applets?
    a) Applet
    b) JFrame
    c) Component
    d) Canvas
    Answer: a) Applet

4. An applet is typically embedded in an HTML page using which tag?
    a) <applet>
    b) <object>
    c) <embed>
    d) <applet-code>
    Answer: a) <applet>

5. Which of these methods is automatically called when an applet is initialized?
    a) start()
    b) paint()
    c) init()

d) destroy()
Answer: c) init()

6.2 Writing Java Applets

6. What is the default size of an applet window?
   a) 300x300
   b) 500x500
   c) 300x100
   d) 400x400
   Answer: c) 300x100
7. What method in the applet class is invoked when the applet is started?
   a) start()
   b) init()
   c) run()
   d) load()
   Answer: a) start()
8. Which method is invoked to stop an applet?
   a) end()
   b) stop()
   c) destroy()
   d) exit()
   Answer: b) stop()
9. How can you load an image in an applet?
   a) loadImage()
   b) getImage()
   c) createImage()
   d) getResource()
   Answer: b) getImage()
10. What is the correct method signature for the `paint()` method in an applet?
    a) public void paint(Graphics g)
    b) public void paint(Graphics g, int x, int y)
    c) public void draw(Graphics g)
    d) public void render(Graphics g)
    Answer: a) public void paint(Graphics g)

6.3 Working with Graphics: Drawing Lines, Rectangles, and Ovals

11. Which method is used to draw a line in Java graphics?
    a) drawLine()
    b) draw()
    c) line()

d) drawShape()
Answer: a) drawLine()
12. Which method is used to draw a rectangle?
    a) drawRect()
    b) drawRectangle()
    c) rectangle()
    d) drawBox()
    Answer: a) drawRect()
13. How do you draw an oval in Java graphics?
    a) drawOval()
    b) drawCircle()
    c) oval()
    d) drawEllipse()
    Answer: a) drawOval()
14. Which method is used to fill a rectangle with color?
    a) fillRect()
    b) fillRectangle()
    c) rectangleFill()
    d) paintRect()
    Answer: a) fillRect()
15. Which method allows you to set the color of the graphics object in Java?
    a) setColor()
    b) color()
    c) setGraphColor()
    d) changeColor()
    Answer: a) setColor()

6.4 Incorporating Images and Sounds

16. What class is used to load an image in an applet?
    a) Image
    b) Audio
    c) AppletImage
    d) Media
    Answer: a) Image
17. How can you play an audio file in an applet?
    a) playAudio()
    b) audioPlay()
    c) play()
    d) AudioClip
    Answer: d) AudioClip
18. Which method is used to play a sound in an applet?
    a) playSound()
    b) sound.play()

c) audioClip.play()

d) play()

Answer: c) audioClip.play()

19. What is the class used to load and display an image?

a) ImageIcon

b) ImageLoader

c) ImageDisplay

d) IconImage

Answer: a) ImageIcon

20. To display an image in an applet, which method would you use?

a) drawImage()

b) displayImage()

c) showImage()

d) renderImage()

Answer: a) drawImage()

6.5 Event Handling Mechanisms

21. In Java, event handling is based on which model?

a) Push model

b) Pull model

c) Observer model

d) MVC model

Answer: c) Observer model

22. Which is the root interface for event listeners in Java?

a) EventListener

b) ActionListener

c) MouseListener

d) WindowListener

Answer: a) EventListener

23. Which method is called when an action is performed in event handling?

a) actionPerformed()

b) eventPerformed()

c) handleEvent()

d) processEvent()

Answer: a) actionPerformed()

24. What class is used to handle mouse events in Java?

a) MouseEvent

b) MouseListener

c) MouseHandler

d) MouseAction

Answer: b) MouseListener

25. What is the purpose of the `WindowListener` interface?

a) To handle keyboard events

b) To handle window state changes
c) To handle mouse events
d) To handle action events
Answer: b) To handle window state changes

6.6 Listener Interfaces

26. Which of the following is not a part of the `ActionListener` interface?
    a) actionPerformed()
    b) eventOccurred()
    c) addActionListener()
    d) removeActionListener()
    Answer: b) eventOccurred()
27. What method of `KeyListener` is used to handle key press events?
    a) keyPressed()
    b) keyTyped()
    c) keyReleased()
    d) keyDown()
    Answer: a) keyPressed()
28. Which listener interface is used for handling mouse events?
    a) MouseListener
    b) MouseMotionListener
    c) MouseAdapter
    d) All of the above
    Answer: d) All of the above
29. Which method of `MouseListener` is used to handle mouse click events?
    a) mousePressed()
    b) mouseClicked()
    c) mouseReleased()
    d) mouseMoved()
    Answer: b) mouseClicked()
30. Which interface is used to handle window events in Java?
    a) WindowListener
    b) WindowEvent
    c) WindowAdapter
    d) Both a and c
    Answer: d) Both a and c

6.7 Adapter and Inner Classes

31. What is the purpose of an adapter class in Java?
    a) To define abstract methods

b) To provide default implementations of event listener methods

c) To manage inner classes

d) To handle multi-threading

Answer: b) To provide default implementations of event listener methods

32. Which of the following classes is an adapter class?

a) MouseAdapter

b) ActionListener

c) KeyListener

d) WindowListener

Answer: a) MouseAdapter

33. How do inner classes benefit event handling in Java?

a) They can access the outer class's members

b) They are faster than regular classes

c) They are used to handle graphical interfaces

d) None of the above

Answer: a) They can access the outer class's members

34. Which class can be used as an inner class for handling mouse events?

a) MouseAdapter

b) MouseListener

c) MouseEvent

d) MouseHandler

Answer: a) MouseAdapter

35. Which method is used to add an event listener to a GUI component?

a) addListener()

b) attachListener()

c) addEventListener()

d) addActionListener()

Answer: d) addActionListener()

6.8 Designing GUIs with AWT Controls

36. Which of the following is not an AWT component?

a) Button

b) TextField

c) Label

d) JPanel

Answer: d) JPanel

37. Which method is used to create a button in AWT?

a) new Button()

b) new JButton()

c) createButton()

d) addButton()

Answer: a) new Button()

38. How do you set the text of a label in AWT?
    a) label.setText()
    b) label.set()
    c) label.setLabelText()
    d) label.text()
    Answer: a) label.setText()
39. What method is used to add a component to a container in AWT?
    a) add()
    b) insert()
    c) append()
    d) attach()
    Answer: a) add()
40. Which AWT component is used to create a text input field?
    a) TextField
    b) TextArea
    c) Button
    d) Label
    Answer: a) TextField

6.9 Swing Components of Java Foundation Classes

41. Which of the following is not a Swing component?
    a) JButton
    b) JLabel
    c) JTextField
    d) Button
    Answer: d) Button
42. Which method is used to set the text of a Swing button?
    a) setText()
    b) setLabel()
    c) changeText()
    d) buttonText()
    Answer: a) setText()
43. What is the default layout manager for Swing containers?
    a) FlowLayout
    b) GridLayout
    c) BorderLayout
    d) GridBagLayout
    Answer: a) FlowLayout
44. Which method is used to create a JLabel in Swing?
    a) JLabel()
    b) createLabel()
    c) new JLabel()

d) addLabel()
Answer: c) new JLabel()

45. Which of the following is a correct way to create a Swing JFrame?
    a) new JFrame()
    b) createJFrame()
    c) JFrameWindow()
    d) openFrame()
    Answer: a) new JFrame()

6.10 Layout Managers, Menus, Events, and Listeners

46. Which layout manager arranges components in rows and columns?
    a) FlowLayout
    b) GridLayout
    c) BorderLayout
    d) CardLayout
    Answer: b) GridLayout

47. What class is used to create menus in Java?
    a) Menu
    b) JMenu
    c) MenuBar
    d) JMenuItem
    Answer: b) JMenu

48. Which method is used to create a menu item in Java?
    a) new MenuItem()
    b) new JMenuItem()
    c) createMenuItem()
    d) addMenuItem()
    Answer: b) new JMenuItem()

49. How do you handle events in Swing?
    a) By using listeners
    b) By using event handlers
    c) By using action handlers
    d) By using events directly
    Answer: a) By using listeners

50. Which layout manager is used to organize components into regions like north, south, east, and west?
    a) GridLayout
    b) FlowLayout
    c) BorderLayout
    d) CardLayout
    Answer: c) BorderLayout